D1430478

Inerrancy and the Spiritual Formation of Younger Evangelicals

Inerrancy and the Spiritual Formation of Younger Evangelicals

CARLOS R. BOVELL

Wipf & Stock
PUBLISHERS
Eugene, Oregon

INERRANCY AND THE SPIRITUAL FORMATION
OF YOUNGER EVANGELICALS

ISBN 10: 1-59752-861-7
ISBN 13: 978-1-59752-861-0

Chapter four contains a slightly modified form of "Eucharist Then, Scripture Now: How Evangelicals can Learn from an Old Controversy." *Evangelical Review of Theology* 30 (2006): 322–338. Used by permission.

Scripture quotations marked NASB are taken from the *New American Standard Bible.* Copyright © 1960, 1962, 1963, 1968, 1971, 1972, 1973, 1975, 1977, 1995 by The Lockman Foundation. Used by permission. (www.Lockman.org)

Scripture quotations marked REB are taken from the Revised English Bible. Copyright © Oxford University Press and Cambridge University Press 1989.

Unless marked otherwise, Scripture references are taken from the King James Version of the Bible.

Manufactured in the U.S.A.

Contents

Preface

"Biblical authority—as manifest in the discursive practice of framing one's speech in relation to the Bible—is one of the foundational assumptions of evangelical communities, one of the practices in which community members, in order to *be* community members, participate."

—Brian Malley[1]

"The Bible alone could not carry all the freight of born-again Protestantism because many mainline Protestants also believed in the Bible alone. Therefore, the Bible inerrant became evangelicalism's creed."

—Daryl G. Hart[2]

"While it was relatively easy for the rank and file to believe in inerrancy, it was nearly impossible for most of them to prove it. It was enough to know that there were trusted teachers who could."

—Timothy P. Weber[3]

"The entire experience of opening the windows just a little bit and letting the fresh breezes of honest doubt blow through the musty dogma of biblical inerrancy had proved to be profoundly unsettling."

—Rudolph Nelson[4]

MANY YOUNGER evangelicals[5] bombarded by the vicissitudes of being spiritually-developing, existentially-sensitive Christians in the

---

[1] *How the Bible Works: An Anthropological Study of Evangelical Biblicism.* (New York: Altamira Press, 2004), 140, italics in original.

[2] *Deconstructing Evangelicalism: Conservative Protestantism in the Age of Billy Graham.* (Grand Rapids: Baker, 2004), 149.

[3] "The Two-Edged Sword: The Fundamentalist Use of the Bible" in *The Bible in America: Essays in Cultural History.* (ed. N. O. Hatch and M. A. Noll; New York: Oxford University Press, 1982), 117.

[4] *The Making and Unmaking of an Evangelical Mind: The Case of Edward Carnell.* (New York: Cambridge University Press, 1987), 189.

[5] Robert E. Webber's phrase for an evangelical roughly thirty years or younger. See the introductory chapter below.

twenty-first century are no longer holding out for inerrancy. Still, a good number of evangelical leaders and teachers formatively pressure their students toward inerrancy, implicitly or otherwise, in such a way that it has become "a psychological necessity of membership in the fundamentalist [read conservative evangelical] organizations that one should be convinced that everyone outside is completely 'liberal' in theology, or at least that he has no stable defences against the adoption of a totally liberal position."[6] The tragedy is that many evangelical leaders and teachers themselves have doubts about inerrancy but are sociologically—ecclesiastically and institutionally—condemned to silence. To take an extreme case, when the brother of a famous twentieth century Christian apologist was asked about the apologist's breakdown, he immediately explained that "his brother's breakdown resulted from building a whole career on something he did not really believe."[7] It does not take long for a younger evangelical to come to the realization that many of her evangelical leaders and teachers are much like Carnell, knowing deep down that critics are right but unable to publicly admit it.

Younger evangelicals are almost singularly dependent upon their leaders and teachers for their formative understanding of the Bible. Many are brought up on inerrancy by their families, in churches and elsewhere. Malley calls the evangelical understanding of biblical authority a "sacred postulate" and claims that "[t]his identification captures the fact that interviewees not only didn't understand it but also were relatively unconcerned about not understanding it—it is regarded as unquestionable, a fundamental postulate within the community, and so there is no practical need for them to have a well-developed theory of biblical authority."[8] Weber's quotation above pertains with much more force to younger evangelicals. Although they really are not sure how inerrancy is proven, younger evangelicals take solace in the fact that their leaders and teachers do. Nelson provides a perfect example: admitting he had never even read any of Carnell's apologetic works, he rationalized, "Knowing he had those credentials, who needed actually to *read* his books?"[9]

The popular argument developed by Weber's "rank and file" believers seems to go something like this:

[6] James Barr, *Fundamentalism*. 2nd ed. (London: SCM Press Ltd., 1981), 165. British writers tend to refer to evangelicals as fundamentalists.

[7] Rudolph Nelson, *The Making and Unmaking of an Evangelical Mind*, 212.

[8] *How the Bible Works*, 139.

[9] *The Making and Unmaking of an Evangelical Mind*, 5, italics his.

Suppose someone says some item of divine revelation is incoherent or leads to a contradiction. Either we have misinterpreted the divine revelation and need to backtrack and rework the interpretation, or there is something wrong with the argument that led us to posit incoherence or a contradiction . . . [I]f divine inspiration secures the inerrancy of scripture, then any argument that appears to show error in scripture must be false, or the argument merely shows that we have misunderstood the scripture.[10]

Younger evangelicals, however, are increasingly flirting with a third option: *perhaps inerrancy itself has been misunderstood.* After all, they do not have the financial, ecclesiastical and institutional stakes of their professors and pastors. However, they still suffer many of the same existential and communal risks as their leaders. I have written this book to help urge evangelical leaders and teachers to more actively support the fledgling disbelievers among them in their search for ways out of wholesale liberalism or even total unbelief. Leaders and teachers play an important role in the spiritual development of their students. In fact, many times it becomes their spiritual responsibility to engage candidly with those who are struggling.

Younger evangelicals are wondering whether the dogmatic argument for inerrancy is forced. Some have even surmised that the maximal-conservative argument is not only a major liberal concession but possibly also a disingenuous way to save evangelical face.[11] Barr has been forthright enough to suggest that conservatives owe critics an apology. Unfortunately, they probably owe their students one, too. But, alas, in the grown-up and public world of conservative evangelicalism, where searching out the mysteries of the faith must almost always be done to the constituents' satisfaction, all offended parties will simplify have to exercise the privilege of forgiving their debtors.[12]

The "recognitions" that follow are presented for the benefit of evangelical teachers and leaders who insist upon teaching their students that the Bible is the word of God written and, as such, contains no errors in

[10] William J. Abraham, *Crossing the Threshold of Divine Revelation.* (Grand Rapids: Eerdmans, 2006), 142. Abraham does not capitalize "scripture".

[11] Barr's terms: "dogmatic" refers to the argument that since Christ believed such and such so should everyone who professes belief in him and "maximal-conservative" to the argument promoting watered-down authorship claims such as the Pentateuch may not be entirely Mosaic, but it is essentially Mosaic; the Psalter may not be entirely Davidic, but it is essentially Davidic, etc. See *Fundamentalism*, 72–89.

[12] Compare Preston Jones, "More Scandals of the Evangelical Mind" *First Things* 84 (June/July 1998): 16–18. Source: http://www.firstthings.com/ftissues/ft9806/opinion/jones.html.

the originals. As a rule, Christian philosophers and theologians occupy themselves with big-picture, theoretical questions while biblical scholars concern themselves with detailed biblical and extra-biblical data. As one who has involved himself with both, I decry a painful inability to synthesize these two realms of inquiry with spiritual and intellectual integrity. Accordingly, the present work looks to illustrate lines of critical thinking that a "younger evangelical" might experience during the course of spiritual maturation.

Acknowledgments

A NUMBER OF evangelical teachers and leaders have contributed in one way or another to the completion of this manuscript. Yet there is a select handful of professors that has enthusiastically received my thoughts and remarks regarding the relationship between inerrancy and the spiritual development of younger evangelicals. To these I would like to express my gratitude even if most chose not in the end to explicitly associate themselves with this book.

I would also like to thank the Reverend Harald Peeders for his constant encouragement; the staff at Wipf and Stock for making this book possible; Jamie, Elena and Mateo for their patience; and Jen for her love.

Introduction

FOR ALL the hype over the interface between postmodernism and evangelicalism and over the advent of "post-evangelicalism,"[1] there remains a sizable constituency within evangelicalism that continues to affirm that the Bible is the Word of God and is therefore inerrant in its autographs. Within this broad slice of conservative evangelicalism I have observed a sort of disconnect among evangelical teachers and leaders between a desire to be doctrinally faithful and a desire to responsibly look after the spiritual formation of the youth under their care.[2] Too often, evangelicals presume that by striving after the former they automatically achieve the latter; however, in some cases, this could not be further from the truth. Although it would not be fair to assume that all conservative evangelicals fit this mold, certain strands of conservative evangelical theology and philosophy contain insidious doctrines that hamper and, in some cases, stunt the spiritual formation of younger evangelicals. The term, "younger evangelicals," was recently used by Robert E. Webber to describe primarily those evangelicals born after 1975. The present work focuses upon contemporary tensions associated with biblical inerrancy that Webber could only mention in passing.[3] For some younger evangelicals the tension has proven existentially unbearable and the absence of an alternative, accept-

---

[1] The market is currently flooded with books on postmodernity and Christianity. Three of the more balanced works are Roger Lundin, *The Culture of Interpretation: Christian Faith and the Postmodern World.* (Grand Rapids: Eerdmans, 1993); Anthony C. Thiselton, *Interpreting God and the Postmodern Self: On Meaning, Manipulation, and Promise.* (Grand Rapids: Eerdmans, 1995); and William J. Wainwright, ed., *God, Philosophy, and Academic Culture: A Discussion between Scholars in the AAR and the APA.* (Atlanta: Scholars Press, 1996). Bruce Ellis Benson, *Graven Ideologies: Nietzsche, Derrida, and Marion on Modern Idolatry.* (Downers Grove, IL: InterVarsity Press, 2002) views postmodernity very positively; Brian Ingraffia, *Postmodern Theory and Biblical Theology: Vanquishing God's Shadow.* (New York: Cambridge University Press, 1995) absolutely negatively.

[2] "Evangelicals" in this work refers to those Christian believers of whatever denomination (or non-denomination) who affirm the views of Scripture associated with the Evangelical Theological Society, the Evangelical Philosophical Society, and other like-minded affiliations.

[3] *The Younger Evangelicals: Facing the Challenges of the New World.* (Grand Rapids: Baker, 2002).

ably orthodox position on biblical authority has unnecessarily exacerbated the pains of spiritual development.[4] In response, evangelical leaders might consider providing an alternate doctrinal refuge.

Over twenty years ago Raymond Brown had these words to say of the state of Roman Catholic theological training: ". . . [A]nd only now are we encountering a generation of Catholic theologians who were nurtured in their first studies on a critical approach to the Bible, rather than appropriating it late in life and having to unlearn some of their early formation."[5] As Brown pointed out then, to critically engage what it means for the Bible to be the word of God only *after early spiritual formation is over* can result in a loss of faith. Having attended, however briefly, at least three evangelical schools over the last ten years, I can attest to how penetrating Brown's insight really is. In fact, my own experience suggests that this critical engagement with Scripture should begin in high school youth groups and other teenaged religious forums in order to help curtail future loss of faith.

Countless ecclesiastical, parachurch, and professional organizations such as the Evangelical Theological Society and the Evangelical Philosophical Society (ETS/EPS) continue to teach up-and-coming evangelical leaders that the Bible alone is the Word of God and, for this reason, is and will always be "inerrant" in the originals. What is not generally shared is that many leaders and teachers who belong to these and other like-minded organizations insist upon this high view of the Bible *while they are still in the process of investigating and reflecting upon what the Bible really is and how it came to be.* D. A. Carson has made mention in different contexts of "reflective" and "more thoughtful" Christians who "have always" been nuanced in their beliefs about the Bible and "not very well informed believers" who "understand so little about the humanness of the Bible."[6] Well, this book is written for evangelical leaders and teachers, reflective or not, who are concerned about the spiritual formation of their students

---

[4] In some circles, inerrancy has unhappily been identified as the only doctrine necessary for describing what is minimally required to consider oneself an evangelical Christian. See, for example, D. G. Hart, *Deconstructing Evangelicalism: Conservative Protestantism in the Age of Billy Graham.* (Grand Rapids: Baker, 2004), 131–151.

[5] Raymond E. Brown, *The Critical Meaning of the Bible: How a Modern Reading of the Bible Challenges Christians, the Church, and the Churches.* (Mahwah, NJ: Paulist Press, 1981), 2.

[6] See, for example, D. A. Carson, *The Gagging of God: Christianity Confronts Pluralism.* (Grand Rapids: Zondervan, 1996), 167, 365, for the former and his "Three Books on the Bible: A Critical Review" in *Reformation 21: The Online Magazine of the Alliance of Confessing Evangelicals.* Source: http://www.reformation21.org/Past_Issues/May_2006/Shelf_Life/Shelf_Life/181/vobId__2926/pm__434/ for the latter.

and how they are affected by failures in their attempts to make sense of an ETS/EPS-like statement in the context of historical and psychological factors that not only comprise our human experience but so fundamentally contributed to Scripture's own composition and compilation.

Younger evangelicals quickly figure out that although the investigation into what the Bible really is is perpetually underway, the verdict is inexplicably always already out that it is without "errors." To wit, the implicit message is: no matter what we should find by way of scholarly research, the Bible will always be the Word of God, which means, if it is to mean anything at all, without error in the originals. In addition, younger evangelicals are implicitly and explicitly taught that inerrancy is the watershed doctrine of historic, orthodox Christianity. Yet few evangelicals in positions of leadership (scholarly writers, professors, youth leaders, etc.) who inculcate an ETS/EPS doctrine of Scripture have acknowledged the potential and actual damage they are spiritually inflicting upon younger evangelicals by insisting on the paramount import of this particular dogma of Scripture.

In the face of a broader evangelical predilection for certainty and a faith that was given once and for all, younger evangelicals are never given the opportunity to critically ask, "What is Scripture?" Evangelicals are trained to have an innate sense that the formal battle for the Bible is never over and to explicitly watch for unbelief in other writings that they read. Amazingly, the smoldering legacy of an older era has not necessarily yielded a clarification of the issues. If "How can we wed our traditions with modernity?" is the question that non-Christian religions are still asking, "How can we wed the Bible with modernity?" is still the question that evangelicals of all stripes, young and old, are asking scholarly and churchly leaders.[7] The information network of conservative evangelicalism is such that evangelical church and para-church leaders turn to evangelical theologians and philosophers for answers and the answers that these leaders give are presently couched in terms of the development of a biblical "worldview."

A worldview, or a pre-reflective story with its set of presuppositions, always shapes the way that the world is interpreted by humans. Contemporary evangelical wisdom holds that instead of interpreting the

---

[7] "Modernity" in this instance refers to the intellectual and industrial effects of the Enlightenment. For example, how is an African woman who believed that a witchdoctor's curse had been cast on her that prevented her from becoming pregnant to respond when it dawns on her that a relatively routine technological procedure allowed her to conceive soon after it was performed? Or how is a Christian parent to respond when she realizes that pills and not prayer are what is keeping her child from extreme emotional episodes?

Bible in terms of modernity, a believer is to strive to interpret modernity (or "postmodernity" for that matter[8]) in terms of the biblical story. In other words, a believer should try to set the biblical system of beliefs (or, others would say, story) against modernity's system of beliefs (or story), but this patented evangelical response tends to preclude an adequate appreciation for the specific examples and situations that give rise to the critical examination of Scripture in the first place. From the vantage of historical-criticism, for example, neglected contributions of biblical studies come to mind. Interestingly enough, non-evangelical biblical scholars have reached the limits of historical investigation and have begun to subsume historical criticism into larger theological and philosophical investigations—so much so that scholarly circles, evangelical and otherwise, are presently witnessing a backlash against historical criticism, arguing for the return of theological hermeneutics and the like. Among critical scholars, there is the post-critical turn; in conservative circles of "not very well informed believers," however, it does not seem that the careful observations of historical and biblical scholars were ever really appreciated at all but rather perpetually gainsaid by policing evangelical philosophers and evangelical systematic theologians.

Conservative evangelicals have taken solace in the fact that critical scholarship is itself informed by a worldview. Perhaps, it is time to question whether the place of worldviews in evangelical circles has become too privileged. Perhaps, a pattern has been psychologically and spiritually set such that it is no longer possible for conservative leaders to see the trees on account of the forest. My argument in this book is that there is a paradigmatic need for a counterbalance: more care should be taken in allowing specific critical problems their due consideration by younger evangelicals. One way to accomplish this is to insist that historical and biblical scholarship should more openly and critically inform evangelical philosophy and theology. My present concern is that the conversation between the disciplines has gone in the other direction for too long; the spiritual formation of many younger evangelicals is unnecessarily being put at risk.

---

[8] John Caputo explains that "[p]ostmodernity is a continuation of modernity by another means, a kind of hyperbolic modernity or hypermodernity, a way of being ungrateful, a way of moving on with modernity." See John Caputo, "Metanoetics: Elements of a Postmodern Christian Philosophy" in *The Question of Christian Philosophy Today*. (ed. F. J. Ambrosio; New York: Fordham University Press, 1999), 189–223. See also Lee Hardy, "Postmodernism as a Kind of Modernism" in *Postmodern Philosophy and Christian Thought*. (ed. M. Westphal; Bloomington and Indianapolis: Indiana University Press, 1999), 28–43.

Perhaps, a fundamental complaint regarding the spiritual formation of younger evangelicals can be tersely summarized by (of all people!) Aristotle:

> [W]e see the experienced compassing their objects more effectually than those who profess a theory without the experience . . . [E]xperience, indeed, is a knowledge of singulars, whereas art, of universals . . . If, therefore, anyone without the experience is furnished with principle, and is acquainted with the universal, but is ignorant of the singular that is involved therein, he will frequently fall into error . . .[9]

Theology and philosophy are geared toward generalizing and universalizing theories whereas historical and biblical scholarship tends to examine individual cases. A predilection for theory and system on the part of many evangelical leaders, it seems, is driving evangelical youths to "frequently fall into error," as Aristotle puts it. What's more, inerrancy, time and again, has proven an unhelpful purview from which to attempt to systematically account for individual critical cases. The result is often to habitually turn a blind eye toward many of the critical cases in question.[10]

What a profound existential toll to take on a young believer! Surely this will immediately affect spiritual development and that in successively negative ways. I suggest that in an attempt to keep evangelical youths on a positive spiritually formative trajectory, evangelical leaders should bear in mind that theology and philosophy should not produce theories or systems that ignore or neglect the critical data. Countervailing data will eventually be found out or even personally experienced by our young people and it will then be too late to recover the dialogue with them. Nothing less than the spiritual welfare of the next generation of evangelicals is at stake.

It is commonly held today that the very collection of data is inherently theory-laden and one can readily accede this. Nevertheless, when an evangelical theory that purports to describe the divine nature of the Bible grounds Christian existence (not only doctrines) to a high view of Scripture in such a way that Scripture has to constantly find the strength to hold a young person's "being-in-the-world" together, the theory endangers evangelical youths to the extent that they are not given resources ver-

[9] Aristotle, *The Metaphysics*, Book I, 981a. (trans. J. H. McMahon; Amherst, NY: Prometheus, 1991). Might one simplistically describe the problem as preferring Plato over Aristotle?

[10] Compare John J. Brogan's objection in "Can I Have Your Autographs? Uses and Abuses of Textual Criticism in Formulating an Evangelical Doctrine of Scripture" in *Evangelicals and Scripture: Tradition, Authority and Hermeneutics.* (ed. V. Bacote, L. C. Miguelez, and D. L. Okholm; Downers Grove, IL: InterVarsity, 2004), 93–111, 108.

satile enough for handling the intellectual and existential vicissitudes that are part and parcel of being a younger evangelical in the modern world.

The young person I have in mind is any believer between whatever ages correspond to those phases of life that extend from the later high school years to the (sometimes extended) periods that cover undergraduate, graduate and, perhaps, early doctoral study. In other words, that long stretch of time during which a person is formatively and gradually working out a firmer sense of who he or she is as a person and what his or her place is in the world. I suppose the terminal point could arbitrarily be set at about thirty years of age, the time at which an individual typically has a more or less enduring sense of identity to which he or she cleaves throughout the course of his or her life.

In what follows, I proffer some of the critical discoveries that have caused me during these very years to realize how badly I myself had fallen into error by accepting the dogma of inerrancy before encountering any of the critical details. On account of swallowing evangelical systematizing tendencies "feathers and all" I found myself unable to deal with the fruits of my own historical-critical studies (to say nothing of the work of other scholars in these and other areas). As a help to evangelical leaders and to other younger evangelicals, I present six academic investigations that collectively caused me to recognize that it simply is not helpful to Christian thinking to affirm something like the ETS/EPS dogma of inerrancy.

These critical recognitions are not presented in chronological order and they are not intended as a comprehensive account. I simply aim to muster a handful of individual cases wherein my own construal of inerrancy, received as it was from my tutors of the faith, failed to prove serviceable for understanding what God is doing (and has done) among his people. As the power of these cases grew over time, in a recognizably Kuhnian fashion, a sense of unease impressed upon me until finally a cumulative case obtained and the inerrancy paradigm came crashing down. I surmise that my initial adoption of the inerrancy paradigm has had severely deleterious effects upon my personal spiritual formation.

My notion of spiritual formation involves that continual growth in faith that propels "baby Christians" from being infants to becoming more developed spiritual and intellectual beings. I have in mind especially that time when one is undergoing that formative intellectual moment that spans a Christian's educational pursuits. It is during these times that inerrancy faces its darkest hours. Being challenged from every quarter, open to friendly and unfriendly fire, how devastating to watch the holy book go down in flames without event! The Word of God, "errors" and all, burns to a lifeless heap of ashes before one's very eyes. If that were not bad enough, the faith, in its entirety, is often presented in such a way that without an inerrant Scripture, there is no faith at all. And without faith—especially now that it has been tasted (Heb 6.4–6)—there are very few places of refuge for a younger evangelical in this condition.

But these younger evangelicals should be spared! I, personally, found myself woefully ill-prepared for engagement with critical scholarship during my biblical and theological training—and that at conservative schools. All but a spiritual degenerate I became as I bungled each encounter with biblical criticism. Retrospectively, I candidly reckon that the experience could not be wholly explained by some unacknowledged, unconfessed sin(s) on my part; much rather it was the inerrant view of Scripture that caused those intensely painful days of spiritual confusion.[11] The real motivation behind this book is that it took me ten years of searching simply to recognize this; two years and counting to consider what to do next. There is no reason for anyone or anyone's students to endure those same ten years, or longer, in existential purgatory. In fact, it is precisely so that others who are in (or will soon find themselves in) similar circumstances might be spared that extended sense of existential angst that I offer the present treatise.

In what follows I seek to illustrate why the dogma of inerrancy is unhelpful to younger evangelicals and why evangelical leaders should either discontinue its dissemination or begin supplementing it with acceptable, alternate theories. I realize that the paradigm of inerrancy is one that reigns sociologically and psychologically in both conspicuous and latent ways in evangelicalism-at-large. Nevertheless, conservative evangelicalism, in particular, would be (especially in the long run) immeasurably helped by its decline or, at the very least, its supplementation. Adapting Noll's observations, made some fifteen years ago for the purposes of expressing the younger evangelical's contemporary plight: evangelical scholarship's failure to "[make] plain the ramifications of narrow academic questions for larger matters of belief" has proven "especially damaging [for younger evangelicals] because their community combines high expectations in regard to the

---

[11] Whereas Kevin Vanhoozer attributes a "hermeneutics of procrastination" to untoward spiritual conditions in one's heart, I decry the contributions of the stultifying burdens placed upon the heart by inerrancy in the first place. See Kevin Vanhoozer, "Lost in Interpretation? Truth, Scripture, and Hermeneutics" in *Whatever Happened to Truth?* (ed. A. Köstenberger; Wheaton, IL: Crossway Books, 2005), 93–129.

Bible's divine character with relatively little appreciation for the study of the Bible's human phenomena."[12]

Among conservatives there persists the widespread perception of the Bible as the errorless Word of God. Admittedly, there is great spiritual comfort to be taken in a Bible that is inerrant, yet I have experienced firsthand that if and when this comfort is shaken, it feels as if the faith is irretrievably lost. This sense of lost-ness is so great that evangelical leaders and teachers should be taken to task for not better preparing younger evangelicals for its contingency as part of their spiritual responsibilities. Noll once warned that "[e]vangelical scholars . . . need to take more pains, not less, in showing the relation of their research to larger issues of belief."[13] Fifteen years and hundreds of thousands of pages later, very little progress has been made in this area. If the requisite skills for "the ordering of research within larger intellectual contexts"[14] have not yet been acquired by evangelical leaders and teachers, then for the sake of the spiritual welfare of the younger generation of believers, inerrancy views of Scripture should not be inculcated to them as a foundational issue or, at the very least, presented as but one of several acceptably orthodox views. Perhaps, other views of Scripture are not affected by the six recognitions that follow, but the Evangelical Theological and Philosophical Societies' dogma of an inerrant, original Bible will too often fail younger evangelicals when they are in need of it most.[15] Evangelical leaders and teachers should begin taking more responsibility for the possibility that if and when a younger evangelical disavows inerrancy he or she may see no choice but to lose faith entirely.[16]

I do not suppose that my experience can be wholly blamed upon the acceptance of methodological naturalism or any comparable, non-

---

[12] Mark A. Noll, *Between Faith and Criticism: Evangelicals, Scholarship, and the Bible in America.* 2nd ed. (Grand Rapids: Baker, 1991), 170.

[13] Noll, *Between Faith and Criticism,* 170.

[14] Noll, *Between Faith and Criticism,* 170.

[15] Compare John Webster's suggested pattern of a simultaneous unworkability and necessity in *Holy Scripture: A Dogmatic Sketch.* (New York: Cambridge University Press, 2003), 11.

[16] I was appalled to learn that some evangelical apologists of a previous generation publicly argued that the only sensible alternative to Christian belief is suicide. (See Nelson, *The Making and Unmaking of an Evangelical Mind,* 211–214.) Inerrantists should take more seriously the analogous psychological effects of all-or-nothing rhetoric on younger evangelicals. If they deliberately contrive inerrancy apologetic so that its disbelief is equated or directly associated with outright apostasy, perhaps the present work can help redirect attention to more pastoral considerations.

Christian worldview.[17] I have heard remarks to this effect on many occasions. My response to the worldview strategy is given in Recognition 1: "Evangelical Worldview Philosophy Is 'Corrupting' Youths." This opening section is an attempt to loosen the hold that worldview philosophy seems to have on evangelical leaders, teachers, and students. It is based on a paper that was presented at the 2004 Civitas Conference, "After Worldview: An Interdisciplinary Conference" at Cornerstone University, Grand Rapids, Michigan. I am very grateful for the positive feedback that I received from several evangelicals who appreciated the suggestion that evangelicalism may be suffering from worldview addiction. Since evangelical apologetic efforts tend to begin immediately with worldview considerations, I thought it best to open this work with a reflection on the limits of worldview philosophy. For sometime now it has been said that what one pre-understands will influence one's reading of Scripture, but cannot the act of reading the Bible itself and trying to discover what it in fact is—especially in light of what scholarship has found regarding the Bible, its history and its cultural milieu—*cause* the already ETS/EPS pre-understanding of a younger evangelical to change to an un-ETS/EPS understanding? Although the debate has been ongoing for the better of one hundred years, evangelical leaders and teachers have still not prepared themselves (or much less admitted to themselves that it can and does happen among their students) for this pastoral contingency.

Recognition 2 is a philosophical deliberation on the prevalent expression of the inerrancy doctrine of Scripture and its effects on how younger evangelicals envisage that evangelical scholarship should be done. In this chapter, I specifically exegete the EPS doctrinal affirmation. I argue that intrinsic to this evangelical understanding of "the Bible" lurks an ambiguity, an ambiguity that leads to equivocation in EPS-type formulations of Scriptural authority. The ambiguity is then exploded in light of Second Temple hermeneutical practices. I conclude that evangelical teachers and leaders should provide alternate images of evangelical believing criticism.

---

[17] Or modernism for that matter. Carl Raschke's juxtaposition of inerrancy and postmodernism, for example, misses the mark as far as I can see. His alternate construal of scriptural truth as a progressive, sacred "troth" that begins with Abraham can be rejected as sheer fantasy once one becomes convinced that Abraham never existed, that the exodus never took place, that Moses had very little to do with composing the Pentateuch, etc. More importantly, no inerrantist worth his salt will agree to framing discussions about biblical authority in terms of *either* inerrancy *or* authenticity for the two are seen as concomitants. See Carl Raschke, *The Next Reformation: Why Evangelicals Must Embrace Postmodernity*. (Grand Rapids: Baker, 2004).

The main argument of this chapter was presented as a talk given at the 2005 Civitas Conference: "After Evangelicalism" at Cornerstone University. After the talk, two professors from different evangelical institutions commented to me that they could not imagine raising these potentially critical questions about inerrancy—*or publicly taking any steps whatever to critically examine the doctrine.* Considering that evangelical churches and institutions hold to inerrancy tooth and nail or at least something very close to it[18] and that there would very likely be some negative repercussions for evangelical leaders and teachers in their respective universities/seminaries/organizations for raising questions in the first place, how were they to even broach the subject? Perhaps the broader pragmatic argument of this book can help encourage more candid discussion. An earlier version of the second chapter was published online as "Scriptural Authority and Believing Criticism: The Seriousness of the Evangelical Predicament," *The Journal of Philosophy and Scripture* 3.1 (2005): http://www.philosophyandscripture.org/Issue3-1/Bovell/Bovell.html.

Following the second recognition, I digress from the main argument in order to provide an illustration of the hopelessly paradoxical position in which critical believing scholarship finds itself. The case in point is the contemporary application of I Tim 2.11–15. The issue of women's ordination is a paradigmatic instance of how conservative evangelicals can so deeply disagree over what Scripture teaches, suggesting to younger evangelicals (among other things to be sure) that inerrancy may not be as sufficient a norm for faith and practice as previously imagined.

The third Recognition investigates the similarities between a fully divine and fully human Savior and a fully divine and fully human Scriptures. After a brief engagement with Norman Geisler's syllogistic argument for inerrancy, I suggest that the tension between the divine and human is not always fairly presented in such analogies and that evangelical interpretations of divine standards for the Bible and Christ are categorically disparate, rendering the comparison between them impertinent to younger evangelicals. I attempt to draw an analogy between Christ's sinlessness and Scripture's errorlessness and conclude that the analogy is not only not necessary, but only vaguely helpful.

Chapter four presents the fourth Recognition and was previously published in slightly modified form as "Eucharist Then, Scripture Now: How Evangelicals can Learn from an Old Controversy" in *Evangelical*

---

[18] Compare Harriet A. Harris, *Fundamentalism and Evangelicals.* (New York: Oxford University Press, 1998).

Review of Theology 30 (2006): 322–338.[19] Recognition 4 works to allow
for a clearer perspective on the evangelical preoccupation with Scripture.
In my own classroom experience, I have noticed how it is usually much
easier to acknowledge tacit motivations that egg disputants on in historical
controversies, especially those that are seemingly unrelated to one's own
theological agenda. For example, if a conservative evangelical student were
to study, say, a heated dispute over the meaning of a Catholic sacrament,
chances are that a young evangelical would approach the issue in a more
objective manner. In order to shed light on some of the implicit factors
that contribute to the anxiety over the trustworthiness of the Bible, I set
out to draw a comparison between contemporary controversies amongst
evangelicals regarding the Bible and sixteenth century disputes over the
Eucharist. The parallels between the existential, ecclesial and social factors
that contributed to Luther's position on the Eucharist, in particular, and
those that influence present day evangelicals can help bring to the fore
some of the historically situated-ness of evangelical doctrines of Scripture.
Though it is very common to give lip service to the historicity of doctrinal
constructions, comparing one of Luther's controversies with present day
battles for the Bible can help show how there is more to formulating doctrine and living the Christian life than simply defending what one happens
to think that the Bible teaches.

Nevertheless, even in the face of these recognitions I was for some
time able to continue trusting in inerrancy. Irrespective of the difficulties
experienced in articulating a doctrine of Scripture, I was convinced that
on account of the concept and phenomenon of a biblical canon, evangelicals always had a safe place of retreat where they could go back to the
drawing board as it were. The last two Recognitions purpose to demonstrate that neither Scripture nor "Tradition" (nor any other aspect of the
faith) can be said to have "ultimate authority" for the believer. The nature
of the case is more adequately apprehended by understanding that each
aspect of authority creates and sustains the other. Or as a recent statement
by Catholics and Evangelicals puts it: "We affirm together the coinherence
of Scripture and tradition."[20] To absolutize one particular of the formative
and constitutive factors that eventuated in the biblical canon, as rhetori-
cally effective and psychologically reassuring as it may be, is not practi-

[19] I am grateful to the editor for permission to incorporate the article into the present work.

[20] "Your Word Is Truth: A Statement by Evangelicals and Catholics Together" in *Your Word is Truth: A Project of Evangelicals and Catholics Together*. (ed. C. Colson and R. J. Neuhaus; Grand Rapids: Eerdmans, 2002), 1–8, 5.

cally or historically commensurate with what seems to actually have taken place during the formation of the Bible. God's people are always creatively developing concepts and contexts with which to facilitate a faithful and meaningful interaction between the divine and a given cultural milieu.

A final chapter draws the Recognitions together in a brief, but candid, discussion that reiterates that dogmas of inerrancy should only be promulgated if those bits and pieces of historical and biblical data that do not necessarily cohere with the inerrancy dogma are also considered with integrity and not explained away. If evangelical teachers continue with a pietistic optimism with respect to the strength of the inerrancy doctrine for the demands of the 21st century, considerable portions of the upcoming generation of evangelicals will not be able to stand against the cultural tides. Who can tell what their reactions will be to the recognition that the actual nature of the Bible does not agree with what they were initially told by their trusted leaders, their original defenders of the faith?

This book is only secondarily written with younger evangelicals in mind, though I certainly hope that they will take the time to wrestle with the material presented here. (I have appended an Afterword for any who venture to do so.) The book is primarily intended for evangelical teachers and leaders, whoever they may be, who are interested in learning more of the tensions that younger evangelicals can experience when burdened with an inerrancy dogma of the ETS/EPS type. The book need not be read from cover to cover. Philosophers, for example, might take some interest in Recognitions One and Two; theologians in Recognitions One, Three, and Four; historians in Recognitions Four, Five, and Six; and biblical scholars in Recognitions Two (along with the discursus), Five, and Six. It goes without saying, though, that readers are encouraged to read the entire book. One advantage to reading the whole is that it brings to light the interdisciplinary nature of the recognitions and reveals in one volume how the inerrancy dogma fares from different vantages. The details that accrue in multiple disciplines are not so easily reconciled.

I make no pretense of providing knockdown arguments for the positions taken below. What follows can only nudge readers to respond in appropriate ways. After all, entire books could easily be written for each of the chapters below. Hence, only the contours of possible trajectories of younger evangelical thought are presented here: some in more detailed fashion (chapters 5 and 6); others with broader strokes (chapters 1 and 3). Nevertheless, it is sincerely hoped that some will pause to consider the possibility that inerrancy can be antithetical to the spiritual formation of younger evangelicals and that, unless new evangelical dogmas of Scripture are also presented as acceptably orthodox, there will be little peace for younger evangelicals who wish to remain faithful "people of the book." For what Francis Collins says of intelligent design applies with much more force to the dogma of inerrancy: "The disproof of an unnecessary theory like ID can shake the faith of those who are asked to equate their belief in God with their belief in the theory."[21]

[21] Francis S. Collins, "Faith and the Human Genome" *Perspectives on Science and Christian Faith* 55 (2003): 142–153, 151–152.

Recognition One

Evangelical Worldview Philosophy Is "Corrupting" Our Youths

A HIGH VIEW of Scripture is what has traditionally identified evangelicals.[1] It is often asserted that non-evangelical doctrines of Scripture are to be attributed to non-Christian worldviews. Evangelical teachers are, therefore, instructing younger evangelicals to "do battle" at the worldview level since non-evangelical estimations of Scripture are invariably linked to non-Christian suppositions.

Of interest to us is how trend-prone evangelical Christian youth teachers and leaders can be. From WWJD to the Prayer of Jabez, evangelicalism-at-large seems to be especially susceptible to vogues. Since evangelicalism is at heart a grassroots movement, it, perhaps, should not surprise that when a particular idea gains in its ascendancy, it is very difficult to keep it in check. Perhaps for this reason, even evangelical academics have set their (and God's) stamps of approval on the current pedagogical trend involving worldview philosophy.[2] For example, Chuck Colson has so strongly affirmed the new vogue that he professes, "I am convinced that meshing prison ministry with worldview teaching is God's providential plan for Prison Fellowship."[3]

---

[1] Please recall that "evangelicals" in this work refers to those evangelicals of whatever denomination (or non-denomination) who align themselves according to their views of Scripture with the Evangelical Theological Society, the Evangelical Philosophical Society and other like-minded affiliations.

[2] As Gregory A. Clark calls it in "The Nature of Conversion: How the Rhetoric of Worldview Philosophy Can Betray Evangelicals" in *The Nature of Confession: Evangelicals and Postliberals in Conversation*. (ed. T. R. Phillips and D. L. Okholm; Downers Grove, IL: InterVarsity, 1996), 201–218. Though worldview emphases in non-evangelical philosophy have for the most part run their course, evangelical worldview philosophy, though initially posited about a century ago, has only recently taken root within evangelicalism-at-large.

[3] Chuck Colson, "Prison Ministry and Worldview: A Match Made in Heaven" *Jubilee Extra* (June 2004): 7.

Worldviews are presented to young believers as coherent paradigms founded upon Christian beliefs and traditions that ready one for confrontation with alternate and competing paradigms. The philosophy seems to have the advantage of unifying life's manifold experience into an integrated whole. Even so, evangelical teachers may find themselves guilty of "corrupting" their youths[4] and setting them up for a spiritual fall.

Salient features of worldview philosophy (at least as employed by its most influential proponents) typically include: an insistence upon coherence, strategic approaches to effect the nullification of the plurality of "non-Christian" worldviews, and a concomitant validation of the elusive and much coveted "Christian" worldview. In this chapter, I suggest that evangelicals have set their youth up for a serious fall by over-welcoming worldview philosophy into their circles. Though worldview philosophy may prove serviceable to younger evangelicals in eliciting a much needed, critical self-awareness, the worldview mentality should be disseminated more discriminately—making clear to youth groups and college fellowships, for example, that worldview philosophy is *a historically and culturally convenient tool* that may prove helpful in developing, with varying success, a greater sense of critical awareness. To the consternation of many evangelical leaders and teachers, the worldview vogue may prove particularly insidious to younger evangelicals when they discover or are made aware of its inherent methodological limitations.

The limitations arise naturally on account of the dimension of religion that allows for mystery and paradox. Christianity, as a religion, will produce worldviews that are inevitably 1) inconsistent to varying degrees; 2) inherently plural; 3) "synthesis-frustraters." Insistence upon the single import of worldview philosophy may be ironically unsettling younger evangelicals under the pretenses of more firmly grounding their beliefs. Evangelical leaders should more openly acknowledge worldview philosophy's conceptual limitations when promulgating it to its young people in order not to unnecessarily further ostracize them in the course of their spiritual formation.

I. Coherence

"To think intelligently today is to think worldviewishly" reads Os Guinness' endorsement of the third edition of Sire's *The Universe Next*

---

[4] That is, giving them bad advice or leading them astray. See Plato's *The Apology of Socrates.*

Door.[5] Definitions of worldviews vary, but there seems to be a general agreement on what a Christian worldview is supposed to do. According to Sire, ". . . [T]o discover one's own worldview . . . is a significant step toward self-awareness, self-knowledge, and self-understanding."[6] Colson writes that "[d]eveloping the proper worldview is essential, both for properly ordering our lives and for influencing the world around us."[7] Moreland and Craig have suggested that an important function of philosophy is to "help someone form a rationally justified, true worldview, that is, an ordered set of propositions that one believes, especially propositions about life's most important questions."[8] Within another tradition, a worldview has been said to be "the comprehensive framework of one's basic beliefs about things."[9] Although the author just quoted and others within his tradition would insist that *all* areas of human living should be informed and affected by their Christian worldview, the most common assertion regarding worldviews is that *everybody* has a worldview whether they know it or not. A major task in worldview philosophy, consequently, is to promote the judgment that *the* Christian worldview is the most coherent one constructible.[10]

It has been my experience, however, that on account of the mysteries of the faith Christian worldviews must admit a measure of non-coherence. There are several topics pertaining to the Christian faith that possess more than a fair share of mystery and are generally not satisfactorily explicable to the inquiring mind. Among the most famous are the Trinitarian doctrine of God; the Chalcedonian definition of Christ; the nature of the inspiration of the Scriptures; issues dealing with the compilation of the

---

[5] James W. Sire, *The Universe Next Door: A Basic Worldview Catalog.* 3rd ed. (Downers Grove, IL: InterVarsity, 1997), back cover.

[6] Sire, *Universe*, 16.

[7] Chuck Colson, "Prison Ministry and Worldview: A Match Made in Heaven" *Jubilee Extra* (June 2004): 7.

[8] J. P. Moreland and William Lane Craig, *Philosophical Foundations for a Christian Worldview.* (Downers Grove: InterVarsity, 2003), 13.

[9] Albert M. Wolters, *Creation Regained: Biblical Basics for a Reformational Worldview.* (Grand Rapids: Eerdmans, 1985), 2.

[10] Note the rhetorical appeal in the idea of *the* Christian worldview, for example, in the apologetic work, *To Everyone an Answer: A Case for the Christian Worldview* (ed. F. J. Beckwith, W. L. Craig and J. P. Moreland; Downers Grove, IL: InterVarsity, 2004). Much better is Moreland and Craig's *Philosophical Foundations for a Christian Worldview.* An observation that cannot be pursued here is that it is often assumed that a biblical worldview (or *the* biblical worldview) and a Christian worldview (or *the* Christian worldview) are identical. Not only can it be a tenuous road that connects the former to the latter, it is sometimes an unbelievably arduous task to establish the former in the first place. I set out to illustrate in upcoming chapters that biblical studies is not so easily domesticated.

Scriptures; the death and resurrection of Jesus Christ; the creation of the universe; the existence and domain of angels and demons; the existence and locations of heaven and hell; the origin of evil; the coincidence of key divine characteristics with human free will; and so on.[11]

The inherent mystery that attends these topics thins, if even marginally, the strands upon which Christian worldview philosophy is comprised. Such a marginal dwindling is enough, I hold, to undermine the worldview methodology to such a degree that its need for supplementation is intrinsic.

As an example, consider for a moment the coincidence of the traditional "attributes" of God and human free will. Every position that one takes is fraught with mystery. I have not read every available treatise on God's relation to time or on his means of obtaining knowledge (or lack thereof), but I am aware of the main options and have done a bit of research on the history of the doctrine of inherited sin, for example. I have also seriously wrestled with Sir Anthony Kenny's *God of the Philosophers* and how the arguments presented there have moved the estimable philosopher to agnosticism.[12] The family of controversies that surround these questions has made it apparent to me that there will always come a point, when pressed, that one has to cry, "Mystery!" Whether it be by proclaiming, for example, that God's providence "extendeth itself even to the first fall . . . yet so as the sinfulness thereof proceedeth only from the creature and not from God"[13] and crying, "Mystery!" when asked how God managed to do this; or by believing, ". . . on the part of God's will and desire the grace is universal, but as regards the condition it is particular"[14] and crying, "Mystery!" when asked how such a thing could be; mystery abides. Whether one speaks with a Calvinist, an Amyraldian, an Arminian, a determinist, a compatibilist, a libertarian, whomever, all one needs to do is stress the opposite point (be it sovereignty or free will in these cases) hard enough and the other person will need to cry, "Mystery!", at some point.[15]

---

[11] How to relate the divine and human, as we shall see in chapters three and four, is a basic dilemma that perpetually plagues evangelical views of Scripture.

[12] Anthony Kenny, *The God of the Philosophers*. (New York: Oxford University Press, 1979).

[13] See chapter V of the Westminster Confession (1646) in *Creeds of the Churches: A reader in Christian Doctrine from the Bible to the Present*. (ed. John H. Leith; Louisville: John Knox, 1982), 200.

[14] As did Amyrald. Quote is from Philip Schaff's exposition, *Creeds of Christendom*, 1.481.

[15] Ben Witherington III has found occasions to fault Calvinism, Dispensationalism and

This inevitable cry for mystery raises little qualms for devout religionists[16]—in fact, many would object if it were somehow eliminated—but I believe it conceals something intrinsic to the Christian faith that is seldom spoken of among believers. In a famous essay, Quine has helpfully distinguished between three types of paradox:

> A veridical paradox packs a surprise, but the surprise quickly dissipates itself as we ponder the proof. A falsidical paradox packs a surprise, but it is seen as a false alarm when we solve the underlying fallacy. An antinomy, however, packs a surprise that can be accommodated by nothing less than a repudiation of part of our conceptual heritage.[17]

Countless Christian thinkers have exercised their spirits and intellects in exploring these topics and have assured the Church that the antinomies of the faith are indeed antinomies and not falsidical paradoxes. Even so, I do not think it too much to apply Quine's observations concerning one of the antinomies he touches upon in his memorable essay to these efforts collectively: "Each resort [at resolution] is desperate; each is a departure from natural and established usage. Such is the way of antinomies."[18] Hasker has recently attempted to articulate certain of the antinomies that beset divine providence, but I think that Kenny's presentation is the most concise: "If God is to have infallible knowledge of future human actions, then determinism must be true. If God is to escape responsibility for human wickedness, then determinism must be false."[19] On account of such an intractable predicament, Christians cannot but concede Quine's wry comment, "One man's antinomy is another man's falsidical paradox."[20] Or,

---

Wesleyanism for not being able to satisfactorily account for the diversity of biblical data in *The Problem with Evangelical Theology: Testing the Exegetical Foundations of Calvinism, Dispensationalism, and Wesleyanism.* (Waco, TX: Baylor University Press, 2005). Compare Trevor Hart, "Systematic—In What Sense?" in *Out of Egypt: Biblical Theology and Biblical Interpretation.* Scripture and Hermeneutics 5. (ed. C. Bartholomew, M. Healy, K. Möller, and R. Parry; Grand Rapids: Zondervan, 2004), 341–351.

[16] William Dembski, for instance, actually counsels readers to cry, "Perplexity!" when faced with an irresolvable error in Scripture. See his essay, "The Problem of Error in Scripture" in *Unapologetic Apologetics: Meeting the Challenges of Theological Studies.* (ed. W. A. Dembski and J. W. Richards; Downers Grove, IL: InterVarsity, 2001), 79–94, 93–94.

[17] W. V. Quine, *The Ways of Paradox and Other Essays.* Rev. ed. (Cambridge, MA: Harvard University Press, 1976), 9.

[18] Quine, *Ways of Paradox and Other Essays,* 9.

[19] William Hasker, "The Antinomies of Divine Providence" *Philosophi Christi* 4.2 (2002): 361–375; Kenny, *The God of the Philosophers,* 121.

[20] Quine, *Ways of Paradox and Other Essays,* 9.

in more existentially relevant terms, the believer's mystery understandably becomes the unbeliever's absurdity.

Perhaps for this reason, many Christians insist, in good faith, upon the category of antinomy for their mysteries but practically concede falsidical paradoxes in order to get on with daily living. They do so by pragmatically incorporating competing worldviews to answer dialectically motivated needs that are consequential of the Christian antinomies.[21] In other words, a fair measure of inconsistency is intuitively admitted and accepted, perhaps, if I may boldly add, to the effect that believers have intuited at some basic level that the Christian faith does not have the resources with which to answer its own questions.[22] I have not the space to elaborate here, but even if something along these lines is granted, the way for plurality has been irrevocably opened.

II. Plurality

Ancient proverbs flourished to the effect that mature persons should be both "wise" and "simple" at the same time. Rom 16.19 preserves one form: "But yet I would have you wise unto that which is good, and simple concerning evil." Compare the Midrash of the Song of Songs: "God saith of the Israelites: Towards me they are as sincere as doves, but towards the Gentiles they are as serpents."[23] The most familiar expression of the saying is, of course, found in Matt 10.16: "Be ye therefore wise as serpents and simple as doves." Note the difference amongst the three but especially that feature which sets Jesus' words apart from the others. The former two establish that one can be "simple" with respect to one thing and "wise" with respect to another. The Jesus saying insinuates that it is possible and desirable to be both simple and wise with respect to the same thing simultaneously. I suggest that this can serve as an illustration of the indicative plurality that believers are to assume as they engage the world.

---

[21] See S. Reiss, "The Sixteen Strivings for God" *Zygon* 39.2 (2004): 303–320.

[22] Perhaps in an analogous way to that in which "[a]rithmetic is not sufficient to prove its own consistency." (J. N. Crossey, et. al., "Gödel's Incompleteness Theorems" in *What is Mathematical Logic?* [ed. J. N. Crossley, et. al.; New York: Oxford University Press, 1972; repr. New York: Dover, 1990], 45–58, 57.) Compare John Webster's diagnosis in *Holy Scripture: A Dogmatic Sketch.* (New York: Cambridge University Press, 2003), 11. The conclusion that Christianity is unable to solve its own problems reaches at least as far back as Nietzsche.

[23] Cited in W. D. Davies and Dale C. Allison, Jr., *A Critical and Exegetical Commentary on The Gospel According to Saint Matthew.* (Edinburgh: T & T Clark, 1991), 181.

Virtually every Matthean commentary harmonizes the serpent and dove perspectives under some grand schema. Let us, however, resist that temptation by positing semantic approximates for the two. Let us, for the sake of the present discussion, allow "wise as a serpent" to mean "critical as a skeptic" and let us say that "simple as a dove" means "naïve as a trusting believer." This way whether one takes the metaphors to touch upon political outlooks, military and non-military stances, or some other range of activity or relationship we can still emphasize the diametric involved.

Not a few scholars have commented upon the stress that is caused by the dual responsibility of both maintaining a critical mind and preserving a sympathetic naivety when they study Scripture, construct theology, interact with others, etc. Crosby, for example, inquires of similar tensions when, in a review of a recent work, he asks:

> And how do openness and *conviction* relate to one another? Would not the openness tend to make theology a mere ethnography or detached, neutral description of different religious traditions, including one's own? And would not the conviction lead in the direction of a kind of grit-your-teeth persistence in upholding the particularities of one's own tradition in the face of all challenges or influences from other ones?[24]

Familiar to all is a situation wherein a writer is grating toward "outsiders" and gratulatory to "insiders," but remarkable and scarce is the person who is truly both to both.

It is not uncommon for seminarians and college students to remark on how academic training has jeopardized their church experiences. How do I now engage a sermon with childlike expectation with these newly acquired critical tools? Or, in our terms, how do I remain a dove now that the serpent has awoken within me? Pertinent here may be the fact that early Christian tradition identified Jesus' generic "serpent" with the serpent of Gen 3.[25] Neither is it insignificant that the dove became a widespread symbol associated with the Holy Spirit. At the very least, we can say

---

[24] Donald A. Crosby, "The Character of Pragmatic Historicist Theology: Review of Sheila Greeve Davaney, 'Pragmatic Historicism: A Theology for the Twenty-First Century' (Albany: SUNY, 2000)." *Journal of Religion and Society* 4 (2002). Source: http://moses. creighton.edu/JRS/2002/2002-a2.html, italics in original. For Davaney's response, see "The Character of a Pragmatic Historicist Theology: A Response to Reviews of Sheila Greeve Davaney, 'Pragmatic Historicism: A Theology for the Twenty-First Century'." Source: http://moses.creghton.edu/JRS/2002/2002-a3.html.

[25] Because the same words for "wise" and "serpent" appear both in Matt 16.10 and Gen 3.1 (LXX)?

that two opposing moods are indicated here: criticism versus trust or some comparable opposition. On the hermeneutical spiral there is no turning back.[26]

Seminarians' and other students' experiences are not confined to church. We can see how similar things are happening in Christian academia where ideas (and those who come up with them) are often judged and classified with respect to dove or serpent alignment. For example, one may be deemed un-Christian by others for doubting the existence of Adam and Eve. If he explains that the opening chapters of Genesis seem to have been deliberately created with hopes of supplying post-exilic Israel with a much needed Exile-looking cosmology,[27] he would likely be chided for operating within an un-Christian worldview. "Presuppositions dictate outcomes" is the platitude. His view of the world in its totality must have gone askew since worldviews—or at least this is what everyone is supposed to believe—are by their very nature so closely knit that one change affects the whole system. As I reflect upon such charges, I rather surmise that life experiences (including religious ones) are sometimes filtered through multiple worldviews at once. What would be wrong with a young person discounting the Eden story while insisting that Christ has risen from the dead?[28]

A last example can be taken from "the contradictions in the theology of Jeremy Taylor" that Allison has detected.[29] In the case of Jeremy Taylor, a well-known 17th century Anglican bishop, competing emphases can be discerned between his public writings and his private prayers. His public discourses taught that a Christian's good life is that which predicated his being accepted by God for baptismal efficacy, for worthy Eucharist participation, etc., but his private correspondences revealed that he believed that sin prevented such a life and that God's love toward humans persisted in spite of such a failure. Taylor's legacy is judged today to be a pastorally unfavorable one, but his two doctrinal faces represent what I think can be

---

[26] Naugle, for his part, suggests that we should seek to harmonize this plurality. See David K. Naugle, *Worldview: The History of a Concept.* (Grand Rapids: Eerdmans, 2002), 320.

[27] See, for example, Carlos R. Bovell, "Gen 3.21: The History of Israel in a Nutshell?" *ExpTim* 115 (2004): 398–403.

[28] Regarding the creation story: the strife that the creation-evolution debate has caused evangelical youth is well known. One evangelical church boasted that its youth group studied nothing but creationism for the nine months during which its young people were in school in order to counter the public schools' effects on its members!

[29] C. Fitzsimons Allison, *The Rise of Moralism: The Proclamation of the Gospel from Hooker to Baxter.* (Seabury, 1966; repr., Vancouver: Regent, 2004), ch. 4.

called multiple worldviews, each emphasizing its respective vantage in turn. Without opening the proverbial can of doctrinal worms too widely, what I am trying to drive home is the reality that the semi-Calvinistic maxim bespeaks: "Preach as if Calvinism is true, but evangelize as if Arminianism is true." Just as mathematicians are Platonists on weekdays and formalists on weekends[30] and scientists conceive of light as waves or particles depending upon the circumstance, so do Christians exercise worldview flexibility. In other words, believers naturally shift into different worldviews depending upon for what a particular occasion calls.[31] In these and other ways, the Christian faith may naturally lend itself to multiple worldviews in order that the faithful may responsibly and practically reckon with their mystery-filled beliefs and their relation to day-to-day living.

III. Synthesis

Every commentary I can remember harmonizes the dove and serpent perspectives. I naturally am led to try the same, but as I attempt to do so, I also keep in mind that Western Christianity is sometimes in danger of over-rationalizing the faith or, at the very least, inordinately given to unifying tendencies. If, in the examples above, I am immediately moved to ask, "but are these really examples of conflicting worldviews (if they are *world*views at all)?" perhaps, it is indicative of an unconscious over-synthesizing drive. I would say, nevertheless, that they *are* conflicting *world*views that happen to both be Christian (and I would clarify that that was precisely the point that I wanted to make in the last section).[32] In any event, such questions, however answered, presumably are themselves posed and

---

[30] Reuben Hersh, *What is Mathematics, Really?* (New York: Oxford University Press, 1997), 39.

[31] See Lawrence Beyer, "Keeping Self-Deception in Perspective" in *Self-Deception and Paradoxes of Rationality.* (ed. Jean-Pierre Dupuy; Stanford, CA: CSLI Publications, 1998), 87–111. Years ago, Blamires had noticed that there would be times when Christians must become temporary non-Christians in order to join in contemporary discourse because, if not, she would be "the only Christian present" and therefore engage only in a "private monologue". See Harry Blamires, *The Christian Mind: How Should a Christian Think?* (Ann Arbor, MI: Servant, 1962). I think a reason that Christians find themselves shifting between worldviews lies in the paradoxical doctrines that comprise the core of Christian beliefs.

[32] From another perspective, Kraft states that what Schaeffer, Sire and others call "worldviews" are not really worldviews. Charles H. Kraft writes that different cultural contexts will produce different Christian worldviews. See his *Anthropology for Christian Witness.* (Mary Knoll, NY: Orbis, 1996), 67–68.

addressed within worldviews and I am wont to say that this further exacerbates worldview philosophy's affinity for synthesis.

Is it a problem that the notion of worldview depends upon a certain worldview? According to Naugle and others, this is not necessarily a problem since it is inevitable of all thinking.[33] But perhaps this should be given further thought because when Christians talk about worldviews, the concept in question seems deliberately, and perhaps somewhat tendentiously, posed in Christian terms.[34] The lists of seven (or four or however many) questions according to which worldviews are contrived are all ones to which Christians believe that their faith can provide an answer and are ones that are important to Christians. For example, I have not found "Was there ever life on Mars?" or "In how many galaxies does there exist a rationally and morally conscious species?" to be among the key questions to ask. Evangelical worldview definitions revolve around how, on a presuppositional level, one understands the fundamental aspects of reality. It is interesting to note that such a definition heavily overlaps with proposed definitions of "religion" and "metaphysics."

Yandell defines "religion" as "a conceptual system that provides an interpretation of the world and the place of human beings in it, bases an account of how life should be lived given that interpretation, and expresses this interpretation and lifestyle in a set of rituals, institutions, and practices."[35] Smith and Oaklander define "metaphysics" as that discipline

---

[33] This understanding appears repeatedly in Naugle's *Worldview: The History of a Concept.*

[34] The assumption, for example, that everyone has a worldview and that it is inherently religious is not gratuitous. Richard Taylor, to use an analogous situation, denies that everyone has a metaphysics. (I compare worldview with metaphysics below.) To automatically assume that everybody must have a "worldview" and to insist further that this worldview is inherently religious unnecessarily flattens the playing field. Consider Chet Raymo's remarks, for example: "There's a 'God-shaped hole in many people's lives,' says physicist and Anglican priest John Polkinghorne. He's right, at least about there being a hole in our lives. To call the hole 'God-shaped' begs the question . . ." (*Skeptics and True Believers: The Exhilarating Connection Between Science and Religion.* [New York: MJF, 1998], 1, quoting John Polkinghorne, *The Faith of a Physicist.* [Princeton, NJ: Princeton, 1994], 5, 14.) See also C. G. Prado, "Haunted by Plato and Torquemada" in *Walking the Tightrope of Faith: Philosophical Conversations About Reason and Religion.* (ed. H. Hart, R. A. Kuipers and K. Nielsen; Atlanta: Rodopi, 1994), 128–132.

[35] Keith E. Yandell, *Philosophy of Religion: A Contemporary Introduction.* (New York: Routledge, 1999), 16 (italics in original). This has been called the "functional" definition. Clouser, for his part, wants to do away with references to the like of rituals. If his wish is granted, the resemblance to metaphysics is strengthened. See Roy A. Clouser, *The Myth of Religious Neutrality: An Essay on the Hidden Role of Religious Belief in Theories.* (Notre Dame: Notre Dame, 1991), 1–34.

that answers "(1) What is the basic nature of reality and what are the basic kinds of items that make up reality? (2) Why does the universe exist?"[36] Now there is definitely an overlap between these two definitions and it has been notoriously difficult to satisfactorily define either of these two words, but by defining "worldview" in such a way that it so closely resembles "religion" and "metaphysics," it seems to me that Christian worldview teachers are assuming that *the* Christian worldview is so comprehensive and so grand that it can accommodate, anticipate and synthesize every other person's deepest questions.

For example, how does one initiate a conversation that aims to emphasize worldviews? Well, one tack that might be taken—and this is the tack that is promulgated in countless churches and amongst Christian college students especially—is to bring every conversation, in however meandering a way, back to "first principles." Peck and Strohmer are typical when they instruct, "One enlightening way is to begin with a part. Ask basic questions of an issue or subject, and repeatedly ask them until there is no way of answering further."[37] Or in other words keep asking questions about "more ultimate issues" until, in essence, they have to cry, "Mystery!" James Sire explains that he teaches students to tactfully keep asking "Why?" until the answers stop coming.[38] This will take you back to what holds things together for a particular person—what Peck and Strohmer call "god" (or "God," if they prove to be "biblical" Christians). Take the lead of secular writers:

1. What is the nature of our world? How is it structured . . . ?

2. Why is our world the way it is, and not different . . . ?

3. Why do we feel the way we feel in this world, and how do we assess global reality, and the role of our species in it?[39]

and run with them back to an "Ultimate" and discern, Is this God or is this an idol? That, in a nutshell, is what will distinguish *the* Christian worldview from non-Christian ones. But could this not be construed as a

[36] Quentin Smith and L. Nathan Oaklander, *Time, Change and Freedom: An Introduction to Metaphysics.* (New York: Routledge, 1995), 2.

[37] John Peck and Charles Strohmer, *Uncommon Sense: God's Wisdom for Our Complex and Changing World.* (Sevierville, TN: Wise Press, 2000), 280.

[38] James Sire, *Naming the Elephant: Worldview as a Concept.* (Downers Grove, IL: InterVarsity, 2004).

[39] D. Aerts, L. Apostel, et al. *Worldviews: From Fragmentation to Integration.* (Brussels: VUB, 1994), 25.

"language-game" with the word "why" whose existence or non-existence is not in need of explanation?[40] In other words, it is no big deal if not everybody plays this game.

Either way, Christians seem to be engaged here in a variety of "damage control." I have heard that C. S. Lewis had an especially keen eye for recognizing what he understood to be "loaded questions", but this is precisely what worldview philosophy aims to do: load the questions.[41] Recall the overlap in the definitions of "worldview," "religion," and "metaphysics." At first it was hard for me to appreciate how evangelicals really do stack the deck in favor of an instinctual drive for synthesis. From within the parameters of evangelicalism itself, it is no easy task to perceive, much less appreciate, those things that seem so natural to us but strange to others, yet consider the observations made by Mandair in a recent essay on the philosophy of religion: "[T]he point at which the philosophy of religion originated as a discipline was motivated as much by an intellectual development of religion as by cultural politics and political necessity—the 'need' to save 'us,' the West, from the impending dangers of encounter, contact and contamination by alien ideas from the East."[42] I interpret Mandair minimally to be saying here that sometimes what first appears to be a decided *intellectual* turn toward rational and critical reasoning can also be understood as a defensive, protective *ideological* strategy when viewed from another angle. Although I do not consider myself a postmodern by any stretch of the imagination, I have come to appreciate for myself that worldview philosophy is not an innocent, harmless tool that merely facilitates critical Christian self-analysis and strategic cultural engagement. Worldview philosophy also has a rarely acknowledged ideological underside; a built-in, self-reinforcing feature that makes a believer especially ripe for self-perpetuating, worldview addiction, as it were.

---

[40] What is an explanation anyway? For suggestions, see Paul Teller, "On Why Questions" *Nous* 8 (1974): 371–380; and in another vain, these and related articles in *Synthese* 120.1 (1999): Rebecca Schweder, "Causal Explanation and Explanatory Selection," 115–124; Matti Sintonen, "Why Questions, and Why Just Why-Questions?" 125–135; and Max Urchs, "Complementary Explanations," 137–149.

[41] After all, worldview philosophy has not been developed by Christians for purposes of dialogue but for debate. For suggestions on the distinctions between the two, see Leonard Swidler, "Dialogue Decalogue: Ground Rules for Interreligious Dialogue," *JES* 20 (1983): 1–4, available online at http://www.usao.edu/~facshaferi/DIALOG00.HTML.

[42] Arvind-Pal S. Mandair, "What if *Religio* Remained Untranslatable?" in *Difference in Philosophy of Religion*. (ed. Philip Goodchild; Burlington, VT: Ashgate, 2003), 87–100, 88. Compare with the issues raised in Gregory R. Peterson, "Think Pieces: Religion as Orienting Worldview" *Zygon* 36 (2001): 5–19.

For instance, the probing, question-asking worldview philosophy was initially adapted by evangelicals as a systemic response to real or perceived systemic attack and as such requires that Christians sustain a heavy systematic emphasis whether or not the cultural or intellectual context calls for it. In other words, the potentially helpful conceptual tool of "worldview" morphs all too easily into a dialogical muscling kit in the hands of evangelizing Christians, lending itself to an exaggerated, if not false, sense of accomplished synthesis. Heightened are its dangers when used in response to a culture that, at the moment, is far more fragmented than solid.

To see what I mean about loading the questions, imagine briefly if worldview philosophy were unleashed in such a way that it set Christian against Christian, youth against youth. This is typically what has happened in the denominational struggles that seem to define evangelical churches. The only way to check denominational fragmentation and keep the insuperable denominational differences from the eyes of students is to load the questions in such a way that the denominational problem no longer surfaces. In more than one way, the synthesis provided by worldview philosophy is overstated—at least to the degree that it must allow for a plethora of understandings under the rubric of "evangelical Christianity."

Add to these the varieties contained within the "liberal" churches, the Roman Catholic churches, the Orthodox churches and Seventh-Day Adventists and so on and it is not hard to see that what was thought to be *the* Christian worldview as evangelicals understand it is really but a variant within a matrix of Christian worldviews whose continuity is not always readily apparent. Furthermore, how often is what one evangelical denomination holds to be a biblical worldview denied as unbiblical by another? Deciding who is Christian and who is not has never been an easy matter,[43] but surely worldview philosophy unduly contributes to an exaggerated sense of solidarity (by way of its heavy emphasis on synthesis) that is simply not reflective of the current, or historical, ecclesial state of affairs.

IV. Concluding Remarks

I have endeavored in this chapter to suggest, albeit in a rather sweeping manner, that evangelical worldview philosophy can "corrupt" youths when accepted as a God-send. Religious worldviews are by their very nature not as consistent as often touted, more inherently plural than typically

---

[43] See, for example, Wolfgang Wischmeyer, "A Christian? What's That? On the Difficulty of Managing Christian Diversity in Late Antiquity" in *Studia Patristica* XXXIV. (ed. M. F. Wiles and E. J. Yarnold; Leuven: Peeters, 2001), 270–281.

acknowledged, and overly wistful with respect to synthesis. But vogues, by their nature, will hardly do as historically contingent and culturally convenient tools for self-criticism that can and should be supplemented. Unless their leaders and teachers tell them otherwise, younger evangelicals will have to realize for themselves that (in Donogan's words) "no matter how tempting it may be to identify an entity asserted as part of religious revelation with an entity asserted by philosophy (or science), their identity should always be regarded as disputable philosophical doctrine, and not as part of the deposit of faith."[44] In short, worldview philosophy can and should be supplemented, allowing younger evangelicals a broader horizon for their evangelical theorizing and greater latitude in intellectual discourse generally.

Younger evangelicals should not be dismayed if there ever comes a time or an occasion during which they happen to espouse a "worldview" that raises questions that are precluded by more accepted paradigms for conceiving Scripture. It is merely part of the course of wrestling with the mysteries of the faith and stretching oneself to conceive how they might impinge upon everyday living. Religious worldviews will have fuzzy bounds on account of their religious nature and a common way for evangelicals to work through them is by shoring up their faith in Scripture by introducing equivocal connotations to the word "Bible."[45] To help us better see this, let us expound upon the case of the believing biblical scholar which was considered only cursorily in the present chapter.

---

[44] Alan Donogan, "Philosophy and the Possibility of Religious Orthodoxy" in *Reflections on Philosophy and Religion.* (ed. A. N. Perovich, New York: Oxford University Press, 1999), 3–13, 6.

[45] Another reason may be that, by their very nature, theology and philosophy are inherently inimical to the Christian faith. See, for example, Donald Wiebe, *The Irony of Theology and the Nature of Religious Thought.* (Buffalo: McGill-Queen's University Press, 1991).

Recognition Two

Equivocation Should Be Pointed Out to the Young Evangelical

ACADEMIC STUDY of literature that one considers sacred can be a tricky business. A believing student must continuously find ways to concurrently openly receive and "objectively" critique the literature in question. Acute difficulties abound especially for younger evangelicals[1] who base their beliefs primarily on the Bible because their beliefs are such that they must simultaneously approach what they perceive as an authoritative Scripture with both faith and suspicion. For all the diversity that has begun to increasingly characterize evangelicalism, an amazingly popular expression of faith amongst young American Christians remains: "The Bible alone, and the Bible in its entirety, is the Word of God written and therefore inerrant in the originals."[2] A statement like this sociologically and theologically aims to communicate the import of a doctrine of Scripture that emphasizes its divine origin and consequent authority. However, in spite (or perhaps because) of the vogue of acknowledging one's historical moment and attendant, though often latent, presuppositions, evangelical teachers should be reminded that it appears a virtual impossibility to be both a believer and a critical scholar at the same time—a sort of believing critic, if you will. Evangelical teachers should endeavor to disabuse younger evangelicals of the icon of an evangelical believing scholar who holds to an EPS-type of inerrant Bible or, at the very least, acknowledge acceptable alternative images of believing scholarship. This conclusion is

---

[1] For readers who skipped the introduction, "evangelicals" in this work refers to those Christian believers of whatever denomination (or non-denomination) who affirm the views of Scripture associated with the Evangelical Theological Society, the Evangelical Philosophical Society and other like-minded affiliations.

[2] These words articulate the defining affirmation of the Evangelical Philosophical Society (EPS), an organization that publishes a journal that, according to the editor, "has the highest circulation of any philosophy of religion journal on the planet." See Craig J. Hazen, "Editor's Introduction," *Philosophia Christi* 4: (2002), 299. A second and last sentence of the EPS doctrinal affirmation reads: "God is a Trinity: Father, Son and Holy Spirit, each an uncreated person, one in essence, equal in power and glory."

warranted by the intractability of at least two problems, one that will be illustrated by the discussion in this chapter.[3]

First is the tendency for conservative Christian scholars to wittingly or unwittingly allow one characteristic of Scripture (authority) to dominate their intellectual queries, not least those that investigate the phenomenon of Scripture itself. It seems that too often the parameters within which such scholarship is conducted can become predictably restrictive in order to preclude results that are incompatible with conservative Christian affirmations.[4] Dispositions are noticeably defensive even in works where an insistence upon Scripture's ultimate authority is never mentioned and remains unsaid. Mark Noll describes the underlying conviction well: "If research is not the servant of infallibility, it will become its destroyer."[5]

To their credit, one conservative seminary I attended attempted to methodologically compensate for these limitations by pre-supposing the inerrancy of Scripture; however, on account of newly expanded parameters—and this is the second problem—conclusions from critical scholars were regularly accepted that were, at least in my view, in considerable tension with the above affirmation. These biblical scholars, then, found themselves battling for their Bibles with their right hands while they accepted critical conclusions that undermined these very convictions with their left.

The results of critical scholarship have by no means affected only conservative Christian scholars; they have forced believing scholars of every tradition (not only within Christianity) to respond in their own ways.[6] This chapter reconsiders the prospects of the enterprise of a believ-

---

[3] For another discussion regarding failures to integrate Christian philosophy/theology with biblical studies, see Carlos R. Bovell, "Historical 'Retrojection' and the Prospect of a Pan-Biblical Theology" *ExpTim* 155 (2004): 397–401.

[4] For complaints that this is happening in evangelical textual criticism, see John J. Brogan, "Can I Have Your Autographs? Uses and Abuses of Textual Criticism in Formulating an Evangelical Doctrine of Scripture" and, less explicitly, J. Daniel Hays, "Jeremiah, the Septuagint, the Dead Sea Scrolls and Inerrancy: Just What Exactly Do We Mean by the 'Original Autographs'" in *Evangelicals and Scripture: Tradition, Authority and Hermeneutics.* (ed. V. Bacote, L. C. Miguelez, and D. L. Okholm; Downers Grove, IL: InterVarsity, 2004), 93–111 and 133–149.

[5] Mark A. Noll, *Between Faith and Criticism: Evangelicals, Scholarship, and the Bible in America.* 2nd ed. (Grand Rapids: Baker, 1991), 157.

[6] From a Jewish perspective, David Weiss Halivni, *Revelation Restored: Divine Writ and Critical Responses.* (Boulder, CO: Westview, 1997) and, even more candidly, *The Book and the Sword.* (Boulder, CO: Westview, 1996). From a Muslim perspective, Shabbir Akhtar, "Critical Qu'ranic Scholarship and Theological Puzzles" in *Holy Scriptures in Judaism, Christianity and Islam.* (ed. H. M. Vroom and J. D. Gort; Atlanta: Rodopi), 1997, 122–127.

ing criticism by collectively considering a handful of findings within biblical scholarship and highlighting a tension that can easily affront believing Christian scholars. The chapter is intended as a representative example of the lurking incompatibilities that beset academic study within the context of religious allegiance, especially with respect to religionists who view themselves as people of the book.

I. What Does "Bible" Mean?

The above EPS affirmation, to expound upon a personal example, claims that the Bible is the Word of God and inerrant *in the originals*, meaning, presumably, the autographs. The claim implies that even though a complicated prehistory and a convoluted subsequent history can be admitted for several (if not all) of the writings contained in Scripture, there can only be one particular phase, even if it is beyond historical recovery, during which God inspired the holy writings. Consequently, it was only during that phase that the divine authority was imbued. It is held that obviously subsequent handlings of the text cannot be considered authoritative in the same way that this elusive and vague autograph phase of production is. After all, there might be errors or corruptions in these. In the same way, there is no infallible, divine authority in any of the traditions that pre-exist the autograph, even if it turns out that that pre-existing material was in large measure (or even singly) responsible for the specific content of that autograph. That both pre- and post-histories of the Bible can shed much light on the Bible is freely admitted (though not by all), but these are never as authoritative as the autograph itself. The divine authority resides in the autograph plain and simple, end of story.

Can this understanding of authority be maintained, given what we know of the early production and use of Scripture?[7] Could it ever have been practically meaningful for any believer living at any time throughout history to affirm such a thing? The latter question may prove anachronistic, but it has become increasingly difficult for me to see how such an emphasis on autographs can be insisted upon without accepting a version of divine dictation (and the majority of conservatives do not). Still, even if *that* is conceded, I have begun to wonder how the degree to which the interpretive traditions of a non-inspired, non-authoritative Second

---

[7] See, for example, for historical concerns: Harry Y. Gamble, *The New Testament Canon: Its Making and Meaning.* (Eugene, OR: Wipf and Stock; repr. Fortress, 1985); Lee M. McDonald, *The Formation of the Christian Biblical Canon.* Rev. and Enl. (Peabody, MA: Hendrickson, 1995); and for literary concerns: James E. Brenneman, *Canons in Conflict: Negotiating Texts in True and False Prophecy.* (New York: Oxford University Press, 1997).

Temple Judaism, for example, permeate the New Testament writings does not speak against any theory of inspiration and authority that allows for a measure of divine "perfection" to affect the autographs only. I have not concerned myself with the question of the identity of an inspired text in light of subsequent textual transmission, preservation, translation and availability;[8] I have rather begun to inquire after the relative status of late Second Temple and early Christian traditions in light of how intrinsic these are to the Scriptures' own identity. In fact, without its profound infusion of prevailing traditions, the New Testament writings lose a great deal of the coherence that it apparently evinced to its earliest readers. We can even go so far as to say that the New Testament that we read today is *not* the New Testament of the first Christians insofar as the New Testament that we handle has been of historical and cultural necessity stripped of its Second Temple context. The conservative hermeneutical truism that stipulates a Bible without a context is no Bible at all has come to plague me to the effect that a Bible without an infallible context simply cannot be infallible.

"Aha!" A naysayer might interject, "You have simply confused 'text' and 'interpretation'!" I, too, had hoped that in a naïve way I had made some such category mistake (and maybe I have), but I have tried to take care in articulating the matter more clearly: Is it the mere words that make the page of a printed or copied Bible part of *the* Bible? After all, strings of words that appear on a sheet (in whatever language or translation) that happen to match those that are read (in whatever language or translation) in the opening chapters of Genesis, for example, do not in themselves constitute "the Fall," do they? If Genesis 3 were omitted, Christians would likely feel that their Bibles were not intact, but can the same be said if one took out "the Fall"? Obviously (is it?), the Fall is a derived concept, a full-blown interpretation that goes above and beyond the strings of words that appear on a page. Still isn't it curious that if a chapter heading that read "The Fall" were removed and replaced with, say, "The Maturation" or "The Prank," many conservative Christians would feel as if they were not reading the Bible at all?

The evangelical conception of "Bible" works on at least two different levels: one where the actual text is in mind, the very words that comprise a verse (B_1), and one where an interpretation is in mind, where the rubber actually hits the road and academic reflection begins (B_2). This means that

---

[8] A still-burgeoning field of study, see Eugene Ulrich, "The Bible in the Making: The Scriptures Found at Qumran" in P. W. Flint, ed. *The Bible at Qumran: Text, Shape, and Interpretation.* (Grand Rapids: Eerdmans, 2001), 51–66.

if I were to say, "The Bible alone, and the Bible in its entirety, is the Word of God written and therefore inerrant in the originals" (hereafter, *) there would be a need to elaborate and indicate to which Bible I am referring, whether B_1 or B_2. It appears to me that equivocation is inevitable whenever * is affirmed.

Logical instincts compel to avoid equivocation and one might do so by maintaining B_1 throughout *: "Only the very words in this book, and all of these very words, are the Word of God written and therefore these very words are inerrant as they appeared in the originals." Let us call this (or something like this) $*_1$. Here, I might understand that the very words in the elusive autographs were God's very words and that God never slipped up in his spelling or had a prophet or apostle write the incorrect word. I might also be affirming that the grammar and syntax of every biblical clause was immaculate (how about punctuation?). However, I do not see the point in making a big deal of this (unless I were interested in claiming that my God is a God who can guarantee proper spelling and grammar). Obviously, this is not the reason why conservatives affirm *. Any attempt to get at that reason would call upon B_2.

"Interpretation of this book alone, and the interpretation of all its parts, is the Word of God written and therefore inerrant in the originals" ($*_2$). This seems more like—but is not quite exactly—what I would think that I were saying if I said *. However, notice how the phrase "interpretation of this book" is now the stand-in for "Bible" in the original *. In other words, I understand *both* something like B_1 *and* something like B_2 to be implied by the word "Bible" in *. Without B_1 I would not have B_2, but without B_2 I have no use for B_1, especially with respect to authority (which is what the whole "written" and "inerrant" business is supposed to achieve). So I would be forced to equivocate when affirming * or, at the very least, *insist that both B_1 and B_2 are somehow implied, if not conflated, in the one word "Bible."* Only usage and intention can determine which aspect is primarily in view in a given occurrence.

Now with respect to B_2, many conservatives are given to connecting interpretation in one way or another to some type of authorial intent. I will not make a particular issue out of that here. The books of the Bible did not just drop out of heaven, after all; they were composed, edited, etc. within various literary, cultural and historical matrices by living, breathing human beings who existed during distinct historical eras in determinate geographic locales (even if they cannot be determined). Perhaps, texts proper (B_1) can arguably be identified and distinguished without reference to such contexts (though I doubt it), but the possibility of discourse (B_2) is absolutely abandoned when contexts are thus disregarded (as if that could be done). By continuing to rely upon authorial intent, it seems to me that many conservatives are recognizing that B_2 inherently implies a further delineation such as B_{2a} and B_{2b}, where B_{2a} is the author's interpretation of what he has written and B_{2b} is a hearer/reader's interpretation of what is written. The objective in much of conservative Christian hermeneutics is to have B_{2a} and B_{2b} coincide as closely as possible. That leaves us with $*_3$: "The authors' own interpretations of their writings (contained in this book alone as far as conservatives are concerned), and their interpretations in all their parts, are the Word of God written and therefore inerrant in the originals." It is this and other similarly implicit claims that prove so problematic for the maintenance of a full-fledged believing criticism.

A truncated version of $*_3$ (which I'll call $T*_3$) reads as follows: "The authors' own interpretations of their writings (contained in the Bible alone as far as we are concerned) . . . is inerrant in the originals." One problem that appears immediately is that what these authors (i.e., the biblical writers) so frequently do in their writings and the interpretations that they depend upon in their writings have proven unmanageable insofar as I have tried to find a way to integrate them into a statement like $T*_3$. The problem nags on at least two fronts: There is an academic restraint that obtains from the use of the terms like "inerrant/infallible" and a related critical selectivity, which results from the insistence upon a notion like "the original." Let me try to explain.

II. The Bible is Extrabiblical

The degree to which the B_2-dimension of the New Testament depends upon its literary, cultural and historical matrices should be considered disproportionate, in my opinion, to the degree to which conservatives and others can approach the Scriptures—particularly in its autograph phase—as an ultimate source of authority. Theoretically, I could imagine holding another opinion if it were the case that the New Testament depended solely upon what Christians traditionally call the Old Testament and that the New Testament was grounded in this Old Testament in such a way that it did not rely upon pre-existing extra-biblical interpretive traditions. Perhaps, then some case could be made for an authoritatively inspired autograph.[9] But the reality of the matter is quite the contrary. For the sake of

---

[9] I think that only pushes the problem back to the Old Testament; however, nearly every recent conservative defense of Scripture has somehow based itself upon Jesus Christ. In other words, beginning with the OT has not been seen as a feasible option.

space I will only briefly mention the conclusions of two studies by biblical scholars.

In a study of the book of James, Peter H. Davids observes that

> the author of James needs the reader to supply the traditional em-bellishments of the biblical account to fully understand the passage . . . The freedom with which James combines the canonical with the extra-canonical means that he apparently had no firm boundary in his mind between the two . . . his apparent biblical references are not so entirely biblical at all.[10]

I find it impossible to believe (if Davids is right—I suppose a conservative could always contest this) that James had thought that only the autograph was vested with divine authority when he seems to have in a number of places (in order to make his points) mined traditional embellishments more than he did the B_{2a}'s of the autographs that (should have?) comprised his authoritative Old Testament. In other words, in various sections of his letter, James (even if he did so theoretically) does not *practically* distinguish between a primary, authoritative autograph and a secondary, interpretive tradition. On pains of oversimplification, for James there was not only a B_1 and a B_{2a} (was there a B_{2a} at all?), but something more like a B_3, which I will categorize by example.

The mention of Job, for instance, in the epistle of James implies that the author was working with a B_3. B_3 will be for us a renegade B_{2b} that was given such a life of its own by a religious community that it effectively eclipsed its B_{2a} source. It, in fact, becomes B_{2a} for all intents and purposes, giving rise to a case where extra-biblical tradition takes the place of the author's own interpretation of the biblical material by way of embellishment, elaboration and/or supplementation. One can find examples of this in the book of Jude, the Pauline corpus and other places.

In the book of Jude, the author employs "midrash on midrash,"[11] quoting and alluding to extra-biblical material just as often as he does biblical material. Of course, in the case of Jude, Ellis (as do countless other

[10] Peter H. Davids, "Tradition and Citation in the Epistle of James" in *Scripture, Tradition, and Interpretation: Essays Presented to Everett F. Harrison by His Students and Colleagues in Honor of His Seventy-fifth Birthday.* (ed. W. Ward Gasque and William Sanford Lasor; Eerdmans, 1978), 113–126. He covers a number of passages, including James' references to Job and Elijah. Compare Davids, "The Use of the Pseudepigrapha in the Catholic Epistles," in *The Pseudepigrapha and Early Biblical Interpretation.* JSPSup 14. (ed. J. A. Charlesworth and C. Evans; Sheffield: Sheffield Academic Press, 1993), 228–245.

[11] E. Earle Ellis, *Prophecy and Hermeneutic in Early Christianity.* (Grand Rapids: Baker, 1993), 156 n.

conservative scholars) proffers a cautious caveat, insisting upon Jude's (and by implication this is believed to hold for all NT writers) conscious distinction between canonical and non-canonical writings.[12] But if one is convinced, on the basis of Davids' and others' arguments, that Ellis' caveat is not easily maintained, can he still affirm *? In other words, how does * fare when lore, tradition, custom and canon were practically (and sometimes theoretically) indistinguishable for some of the NT writers? There definitely seems a tension here wherein a believing scholar must decide, at least on some level, what she will allow to have the final say, faith or criticism, Scripture or scholarship?

A most interesting example is the "movable well" tradition that Paul seems to have unconsciously accepted in 1 Cor 10.4.[13] If we grant that none of the writings that contain a variation of the movable well tradition were ever considered "canonical," it is hard for me to doubt that the oral or written tradition itself was seen as sure (i.e., this is what "really" happened), authoritatively filling in perceived exegetical gaps of the OT.[14] Whether there was an oral or written exegetical tradition, as it were, to which it would have been perfectly legitimate for Paul to appeal, conservatives would not find a "movable well" tradition in any text that they (or any Christian as far as I know) would acknowledge as Scripture (and, therefore, as authoritative). So instead of appealing to a B_2 to make his point, Paul, here and elsewhere, appeals to a B_3 *as if it were a B_2*.

Of course, conservatives are free to disagree with the conclusions that are being drawn with respect to James and Paul, but *if* a conservative be-

---

[12] On the failure of canonical/extracanonical dichotomies, compare John Barton, *Holy Writings, Sacred Texts: The Canon in Early Christianity*. (Louisville, KY: Westminster/John Knox), 1997.

[13] Though Ellis (*Prophecy*, 209–212) proposes (following Driver) that "the adoption of such a puerile fable would be 'totally out of harmony' with the character of Paul's mind" and (against Driver) that "Paul and the Targum [of Onkelos] are related more directly to a particular interpretation of the passages of the prophets [Ps 77.20; 104.41; Is 48.21, etc.] than to each other", Enns surmises that "Paul's matter-of-fact reference to 'the rock that followed them' seems dependent on a tradition of a 'moveable well' (*Bib. Ant.* 10:7; 11:15; 20:8; *t. Sukk.* 3.11; *Tg. Onq.* To Num 21:16–20)." See Peter Enns, "Biblical Interpretation, Jewish" in *Dictionary of New Testament Background*. (ed. Craig A. Evans and Stanley E. Porter; Downers Grove, IL: InterVarsity, 2000), 159–165, 164.) If these two biblical scholars appear at first glance to be saying the same thing, it should be noted how Ellis is trying to trace Paul's interpretation in I Cor 10.4 more directly to the Old Testament whereas Enns surmises that Paul's reference to a popular interpretive tradition was an unconscious supplanting of the biblical story with Second Temple lore. See also Enns, "The Moveable Well in 1 Corinthians 10:4: An Extrabiblical Tradition in an Apostolic Text," *Bulletin for Biblical Research* 6 (1996): 23–38.

[14] See Enns, "Movable Well."

liever were to accept them, would not his scholarship force him to disaf-firm *? Perhaps, he might consider following Richard Swinburne, who, in his book, *Revelation: From Metaphor to Analogy*, proposes that modern readers of Scripture must weed out cultural presuppositions before deciding upon the truth or falsity of a statement compared therein.[15] Roughly, Swinburne suggests that readers must convert B_3's into B_2's when engaging Scripture academically. He writes:

> In order to separate statement from presupposition, we must ask, whatever the speaker's actual beliefs, what were the common beliefs of the culture which they could reasonably presuppose that the speaker shared with them; and whatever the actual purpose of his utterance, can any such presupposed beliefs be siphoned off, leaving what the culture would naturally suppose to be the main message intact? If they can, we must then judge the truth-value of the utterance by criteria to which the falsity of the presuppositions is irrelevant.[16]

Paul most certainly believed in "the well . . . that had provided Israel with water during the march through the desert."[17] In fact, the whole culture understood something along the lines that God had provided Israel with a rock or a well (traditions differ) that followed them in their travels in order that they might have water for their journey. According to Swinburne, "the statement is whatever the speaker, by public criteria, is seeking to add to the existing beliefs of the hearers."[18] Paul writes in 1 Cor 10.4 that the Israelites "were drinking from a spiritual rock that followed them; and that rock was Christ." (NASB) Irrespective of how one might understand Paul here, [19] what Paul is adding to pre-existing beliefs is, minimally, that "that rock was Christ".

If we were to follow Swinburne, the fact that Paul, along with his hearers/readers, assumed the movable well tradition is entirely irrelevant to the "something new" that Paul is asserting. In conservative terms, the *authoritative* Word of God resides primarily in Paul's teaching that "that rock

---

[15] *Revelation: From Metaphor to Analogy*. (New York: Oxford University Press, 1992), 28–38.

[16] Swinburne, *Revelation*, 31.

[17] *The Legends of the Jews: Moses in the Wilderness*. (ed. Louis Ginzberg; Baltimore: Johns Hopkins, 1939), 308. Of course, nothing can be said regarding any association of the well with Miriam as recorded here. For more on the well traditions with respect to Paul, see the aforementioned works by Enns and Ellis along with the works cited therein.

[18] Swinburne, *Revelation*, 32.

[19] For a survey of various proposals, see Anthony C. Thiselton, *The First Epistle to the Corinthians*. NIGTC. (Grand Rapids: Eerdmans, 2000), 719–730.

was Christ" and not in the presuppositions behind the assertion. Some would go on to argue that since the presuppositions are not themselves iterated in Scripture, they cannot be construed as the Word of God. It seems to be the case, though, that without the pre-existing beliefs, Paul's identification of the rock with Christ is meaningless. What rock is Paul talking about? The rock that *moved*, the one that *followed* them. *That* rock was Christ. It does not seem to me that a reader can simply disregard the cultural presuppositions in this case. I know of no conservative who believes that there was a rock (or a well—the tradition developed over time) that followed the Israelites around for forty years in order to give them water (how many are even aware of the tradition?). Quite the contrary, many biblical scholars (not only conservative) have argued singly against the possibility that Paul could have so naively accepted the popular tradition at face value. Such a thought is somewhat of an embarrassment to a believing conservative scholar, but if she resists the instinctual search for alternative explanations or is convinced that they are unsatisfactory, what she seems to have is a situation where she, as a conservative scholar, can admit that she has succeeded in roughly approximating a B_{2a} but has found that it is intrinsically linked to a B_3 in such a way that it is not possible to extricate the one from the other or the other from the one in a meaningful way. The B_{2a} wholly depends upon a B_3.

What does all this mean for a "believing scholarship," at least from a conservative perspective? My conclusion has been that on account of the practices of some of the NT writers, * must be considerably revised to something analogous to $T*_4$: "The prevalent interpretation of the author's interpretation of their own writings is inerrant in the originals." And with this, any hope of meaningfully affirming something in line with the aims of the original * comes crashing down. There arise at least three problems that we shall adumbrate below.

1. The idea that the Bible alone is the Word of God is confused on account of the fact that the canon itself does not seem to understand itself this way: How can a B_{2a} alone be the Word of God when it so intimately depends on a B_3 for its intelligibility? How can a non-Word of God become the Word of God only as it is appropriated in the Bible? Isn't there a bit of fudging going on here on the part of conservatives (quite a bit of B_{2b}-ing and B_3-ing under the guise of B_{2a})?[20]

---

[20] Note here the relative paucity of conservative attention given to the problem of the NT's heavy reliance upon Greek versions of the OT, for example (Moises Silva being a

2. It follows, then, that the emphasis on "written" needs to be re-thought on account of the distinctions that must be made between B_1, B_{2a}, B_{2b} and B_3:

    a. Though different versions of B_1's are extant, B_{2b}'s and B_3's often circulate orally and are those that become authoritative;

    b. (Related to (1)) The "written" Word of God must now include at least *some* non-canonical materials;

3. In the end, the insistence upon "originals" is unwanted: the historical development of B_{2b}'s and B_3's necessitates that there be an allowance for the divine inspiration of successive revisions and interpretations (or uses).

III. The Bible is Always Already Interpreted

Conservative philosophers and theologians should, in light of these and other considerations, at least begin to acknowledge (or at the very least be made more aware) that it may be the case that with nothing but considerable difficulty can a biblical scholar continue to claim anything like "the Bible alone, and the Bible in its entirety, is the Word of God written and therefore inerrant in the originals." The existence of a discrete autograph seems impertinent and it may be the case that conservatives have well-intentionally, yet stubbornly, committed themselves to a pious chimera. Scripture always exists as an "interpreted Bible" if not a "rewritten Bible": the Christian Bible repeatedly usurps, builds upon and even coincides with varying streams of tradition, lore, and cultural stock.[21] Given the B_3-ness of the unrecoverable autograph phase of production, conservative scholars should buffer their claims about the authority of their Scriptures, at least as they are contemporarily articulated in conservative scholarly circles. By extension, non-conservative (or even non-Christian, by analogy) claims of authority might also be in need of similar attenuation. Religion's indelible dependence upon, and explicit inclusion of, contemporary culture, tradition and interpretation should preclude religious scholars from confessing statements comparable to * as she conducts her scholarship. Otherwise,

notable exception). I touch upon this in chapter five below.

[21] For example, Craig A. Evans writes, "In a sense, exegesis precedes Scripture, for the latter is largely the product of the former." See Evans, "Luke and the Rewritten Bible: Aspects of Lukan Hagiography" in *The Pseudepigrapha and Early Biblical Interpretation*. JSPSup14. (ed. J. H. Charlesworth and C. A. Evans; Sheffield: Sheffield Academic Press, 1993), 170–201, 170. It was from his essay that I first learned of the phrase "rewritten Bible" and the like.

there is a great danger that either historic distinctions between canonical and non-canonical will become arbitrary or scholars will turn blind eyes toward what might be called, "tradition history." Either way, one will almost always have to give way; be it religion or its academic study, faith or criticism.

In some quarters evangelical philosophers have begun helpfully appropriating speech act theory in an attempt to illuminate evangelical doctrines of Scripture. It would seem that the foregoing discussion points to where an application of speech act theory fails to address the problems of inerrancy that occupy this book. Clark, when commending speech act theory to his readers, explains:

> The illocutionary force of these nondescriptive utterances depends on contextual realities described by true propositions and understood by believers as part of background knowledge. *For this reason, even though evangelical theology should go beyond inerrancy in describing a doctrine of Scripture, it cannot abandon a commitment to the truthfulness of the Bible without ceasing to be evangelical.*[22]

The present chapter expressly proposes to show how constitutionally crucial "contextual realities" are to the inherent meaning of biblical writings in the first place and that these contextual realities are folkloric, cultural deposits. An appeal to speech-act theory at this point might reveal an under-appreciation of the complexities involved since the Scriptures are intrinsically constituted by an unwieldy, composite tradition that spans a number of centuries. Not only is it ultimately unhelpful for the case of inerrancy to view biblical writings as individual autographs *per se* (which was what was argued above[23]), but one of the main blessings of speech act theory is precisely how it allows interpreters of Scripture *to leave the human writer's false beliefs behind.*[24]

IV. Conclusion

By privileging Scripture's use in Second Temple Interpretation, I set out above to draw attention to other facets of Scripture—namely, the *inter-*

---

[22] David Clark, "Beyond Inerrancy: Speech Acts and an Evangelical View of Scripture" in *For Faith and Clarity: Philosophical Contributions to Christian Theology.* (ed. J. K. Beilby; Grand Rapids: Baker, 2006), 113–131, 123, italics mine.

[23] See also chapter five below.

[24] Compare Nicholas Wolterstorff, "The Promise of Speech-act Theory for Biblical Interpretation" in *After Pentecost: Language and Biblical Interpretation.* Scripture and Hermeneutics 2. (ed. C. Bartholomew, C. Greene, and K. Möller; Grand Rapids: Zondervan, 2001), 73–90, 85.

pretive traditions that have made their way into Scripture—that tend to be obscured when authority of "the Bible" is given disproportionate consideration. Perhaps by doing this, believing scholars can ponder ways to begin toward the establishment and practice (of at least one kind) of non-defensive, un-equivocating believing-criticism. A first obvious step is to actively ensure that the implicit message received by younger evangelicals is *not* that a believing scholar of the EPS variety is the *only type* of believing scholar to aspire to.[25] One obvious way to do this would be to abandon the EPS expression of the nature of Scripture for a more workable alternative. Even if it were a personal possibility for leaders to privately do so, many will find that it is an institutional impossibility to publicly do so. Evangelical leaders and teachers, then, must, at the very least, ensure that social and spiritual provision is given *to those under their care* for the personal (and public) possibility that inerrancy will fail to be meaningful to them as a description of the Bible's authority.

In the next chapter, I provide a contemporary example of the no-win situation in which young evangelical hopefuls tend to find themselves. Younger evangelicals have become very sensitive to the crucial roles that hermeneutics and uncritical assimilation of social constructions play for Christian conceptions and interpretations of biblical revelation. Such a realization is not merely another manifestation of latent (and not so latent) postmodern influences but also the disconcerting result of observing firsthand how evangelicals cannot agree amongst themselves on a host of basic issues. Although inerrancy was called upon to be the shibboleth that distinguished "faithful" orthodox believers from liberal unbelievers, many younger evangelicals have witnessed for themselves how inerrancy is no help at all for deciding whether women should be ordained, for example. In this chapter we shall attempt to reconstruct both sides of the women's argument, focusing more or less on the traditionalist position (which the author happens to affirm), and note how a younger evangelical might justifiably conclude that irrespective of which conclusion one takes up, inerrancy proves itself almost wholly irrelevant to the discussion.

---

[25] Mark Noll, for example, describes various types of evangelical scholars active in the academia of the 1990s in *Between Faith and Criticism: Evangelicals, Scholarship, and the Bible in America.* 2nd ed. (Grand Rapids: Baker, 1991). For British developments, see Nigel M. De S. Cameron, "Scripture and Criticism: Evangelicals, Orthodoxy and the Continuing Problem of Conservatism" in *A Pathway into the Holy Scripture.* (ed. P. E. Satterthwaite and D. F. Wright; Grand Rapids: Eerdmans, 1994), 237–256.

Discursus

Wrestling with 1 Tim 2.11–15, A Case in Point

THOUGH EVANGELICAL theological argumentation is still blackened by an inherited predilection for objectivity and proof-texts, it is not to be supposed that the NT authors were fazed by either of these two concerns. By contrast, they unabashedly read their own situations into their texts and made a very full use of their Scriptures (and other sources) when interpreting and citing texts in support of a specific conclusion.[1] In fact, the scientific impetus of evangelical hermeneutics seems inordinately strict when compared with extant examples of ancient exegesis. For this reason, evangelical hermeneutical practices pose problems with regard to the authority of Scripture in a more urgent way than did those of early Judaism or the early church. That varieties of Second Temple "non-scientific" hermeneutics have found their way into the NT has not yet been taken seriously with respect to the way it ramifies biblical authority.[2]

What follows is an investigation of the exegetical argument of 1 Tim 2.11–15. The motivation is that evangelical readers might begin to (1) realize just how scientific their own interpretive expectations have become, (2) reexamine the nature of the authority of Scripture in light of ancient interpretive practices, and (3) reconsider what issues are at stake in the women's debate. The thesis offered here is that irrespective of what position an evangelical takes in the women's debate, the authority of Scripture is compromised. The first section begins with a brief survey of contempo-

---

[1] See, for example, Dale C. Allison, Jr. *Scriptural Allusions in the New Testament: Light from the Dead Sea Scrolls.* Dead Sea Scrolls Library and Christian Origins Library 5. (North Richland Hills, TX: Bibal Press, 2000); E. Earle Ellis, *Prophecy and Hermeneutic in Early Christianity.* (Grand Rapids: Baker, 1995).

[2] Although see now, Peter Enns, "Apostolic Hermeneutics and an Evangelical Doctrine of Scripture: Moving Beyond the Modernist Impasse," *WTJ* 65 (2003): 263–287. Compare Dan G. McCartney, "The New Testament's Use of the Old Testament" in *Inerrancy and Hermeneutic: A Tradition, A Challenge, A Debate.* (ed. H. Conn; Grand Rapids: Baker, 1988), 101–116. The topic is a sticky one for inerrantists. Perhaps evangelicals are satisfied with the proposal found in Richard Longenecker, *Biblical Exegesis in the Apostolic Period.* 2nd ed. (Grand Rapids: Eerdmans, 1999).

rary approaches to the issue of women's ordination and argues that egalitarian positions relinquish evangelical claims to an authoritative Bible. The remainder and bulk of this discursus assumes for the sake of argument that, at least on the face of it, Paul's argument is based upon Scripture and that he is appealing to Scripture in order to make a theological point.[3] A suggestion is made that, in order to appreciate Paul's exegetical argument, evangelical readers need to suspend their scientific demands of inner-biblical exegesis. Pains are then taken to imitate the hermeneutical mindset of a first century exegete, offering an imaginative, but representative, example of the types of things that Paul could have been thinking in 1 Tim 2.9–15. During the course of this section of the book, two main points are made: (1) Paul's exegetical argument depends upon non-scientific text associations and (2) Paul was arguing theologically for a perpetual patriarchy amongst God's people on account of his understanding of gender traits. Complementarians are then asked to explain how Scripture can be considered authoritative today in light of the "non-scientificality" of inner-biblical exegesis and especially the particular example of Second Temple theological argumentation given in 1 Tim 2.9–15.

I. Egalitarian Evangelicals and the Authority of Scripture

Egalitarians, for our purposes, are those who are for the ordination of women. Many evangelical egalitarians have rightly argued that the socio-cultural dimension of Paul's injunctions against women in 1 Tim 2 and elsewhere cannot be denied. Two predominant egalitarian arguments are that Paul intended his restriction to affect only one specific Christian community or that Paul was forced to prohibit women on account of various cultural factors that are no longer operative. Craig Keener provides an example of the first when he writes:

> It would be surprising if an issue that would exclude at least half the body of Christ from a ministry of teaching would be addressed in one text, unless that text really addressed only a specific historical situation rather than setting forth a universal prohibition.[4]

Brian J. Dodd is typical of those who proffer the second:

---

[3] Pauline authorship is assumed throughout. "The author" can easily be substituted by those who disagree.

[4] *Paul, Women and, Wives.* (Peabody, MA: Hendrickson, 1992), 101.

... it may be that Paul's later restrictions on women's behavior were necessary because of the implications his converts were drawing from his very progressive views on such things [gender roles]. When Paul saw how far they were taking his teaching and the effects it was having on those he was seeking to convert, he may have pulled in the reins . . .[5]

Scholars have taken diverse approaches and have begun to ask very complex questions by connecting the issue of women in ministry to prevailing sociological patterns. In response to a declaration issued by the Roman Catholic Church some scholars have deliberated as follows:

Only within some heretical sects of the early centuries, principally Gnostic ones, do we find attempts to have the priestly ministry exercised by women . . .

How are we to interpret the constant and universal practice of the church? Does the negative fact thus indicate a norm, or is it to be explained by historical and by social and cultural circumstances? In the present case, is an explanation to be found in the position of women in ancient and mediaeval society and in a certain idea of male superiority stemming from that society's culture?[6]

A different approach would be to take a step back methodologically and to begin asking pragmatic questions like, What would prompt a person to question the universality of the prohibition in the first place? One obvious answer is that the prohibition seems nonsensical or worse, unconscionable, given the reader's own cultural context. Such tremendous tension inevitably exerts considerable pressure upon the reader's pre-understanding in light of what a particular text apparently teaches. This conflict between the reader's sensibilities and a text's time-conditioned hortatory message has engendered at least two hermeneutical responses. The first is to challenge the cultural understanding of the biblical writers; the second is to neutralize the content of a text in such a way that its apparent message ceases to be its actual message.

For example, evangelicals have experienced ceaseless controversy concerning the lack of agreement between the current scientific consensus and the Genesis creation account. Evangelicals who disagree with the historically popular, literal, 144-hour interpretation have tended to re-examine

---

[5] *The Problem with Paul.* (Downers Grove, IL: InterVarsity, 1996), 26.

[6] J. Gordon Melton commenting on the "Declaration of the Sacred Congregation the Question of the Admission of Women to the Ministerial Priesthood (1976)," in *The Churches Speak On: Women's Ordination.* (ed. J. Gordon Melton; Detroit: Gale Research, Inc., 1991), 12–13.

the opening chapters of Genesis in order to determine whether there are any viable alternatives to the literal approach. Each alternate reading "neutralizes" the text, quelling its hitherto apparent force and discovering a different meaning altogether. By contrast, others have admitted that the Genesis account is a stubborn one that does not submit to fresh re-readings. In this case, an evangelical may elect to analyze the cultural assumptions that are implicit within a given text. He might then proceed to filter out an abiding "word from God" that survives the contingent historical and cultural vicissitudes that occasioned its inscripturation. He might argue that because the creation account is time-conditioned, its true meaning is rooted "behind" the given text in a way that is practically independent of and/or virtually unaffected by the cultural milieu during which the text itself was written. Those evangelicals who do not accept the literal view typically explore one (or both) of these two options.[7]

A third approach, however, is to critically examine the cultural assumptions *of the contemporary reader*.[8] It is now common knowledge that a contemporary reader possesses a historical consciousness that can either grant her tremendous access to the text or effectively bar her from it. Scholars have argued for both positive and negative consequences of a historical awareness, but the moral seems to be that the historic process can work both positively and negatively and indeed may work both at the same time.

For example, Mardi Keyes believes that the gospel was intended as good news for women, but that unfortunately *the church* has become bad news for many women.[9] She contends that Scripture is always contrary to sinful cultural practices and assumptions and that the blame for ongoing social injustices based on gender lies in the patriarchal system of the church. She asserts that the "clear" New Testament evidence should not be silenced by others that are riddled by problems.[10] She continues:

> You may be surprised that what I am saying does not match the practice of much of the church throughout history or even today. Too often Christians have fallen captive to human traditions that conflict with the radical New Testament message.

---

[7] To juxtapose the gender question and the creation question does not mean to imply that the tact taken in one debate must be that taken in the other.

[8] A fourth approach would be to neutralize any extrabiblical data that provided reasons for disagreement. This is the tact of many young-earth creationists.

[9] *Feminism and the Bible*. (Downers Grove, IL: InterVarsity, 1995), 28.

[10] Keyes, *Feminism*, 13, speaking of 1 Cor 14.33–35 and 1 Tim 2.12.

Judging from her writings, what may partially motivate Keyes is the perception that Christianity has grown out of touch with contemporary mores and that one inexcusable cause for this is the church's historic decision to restrict ordination to men. Her strategy is to divide the church from the Scriptures and argue that the church "fell captive" to its historic moment, whereas the Scriptures, however, have always taught the truth (i.e., Keyes' egalitarian position). In other words, the church's practice has become an unnecessary obstacle to a contemporary hearing of the gospel, but it is not the case that the Scriptures have ever endorsed the church's practice. It is obvious to us now—or so the argument goes—that it was a thoroughgoing patriarchy that supported the practice, while Scripture, of course, embraced no such arrangement.

To her credit, Keyes has rightly recognized that each generation of Christians will most likely consider only those interpretations that are culturally plausible and that unbelievers will only consider those religious options that are culturally plausible. Hence, Christians need to be aware of cultural factors. Unfortunately for Keyes, however, by allowing her historical consciousness to accomplish the separation of generations of believers from the true meaning of the biblical text, she has at once undermined her own cultural right to the meaning of biblical texts. What I mean is that Keyes' clear texts may very well have been our predecessors' obscure texts and their plain ones, Keyes' obscure ones.[11] These conjectures can only be offered as hypotheses here, but still, this is no small dilemma to ponder, for it seems to imply that the Bible will mean different things to different people at different times. In other words, Keyes' argument would be helped along if she proposed that *at present* it seems that the Bible supports such and such a stance and not that it has *always* taught such and such a teaching (or that it always will).

It is no secret that today's cultural ethos is such that it cannot provisionally entertain Paul's prohibition, much less seriously accept it as presently binding. In fact, with so many scholars and clergy obsessed with the correction of male oppression (especially white male oppression), 1 Tim 2 as a durable injunction is utterly unthinkable, indeed, a major embarrassment or even deeply offensive.[12] This contemporary disposition rings so truly that many evangelical thinkers are seeking to ground the disposition itself in Scripture. Thus, it behooves faithful Christians (so the argument

[11] Evangelicals must learn to be more sophisticated when applying this old Reformation principle since one person's clear text is another's abstruse one.

[12] Yet it becomes anachronistic to relentlessly turn our noses at bygone eras for not being as progressive as we.

goes) who are committed to Scripture's authority to account for Paul's teaching in some way that does not offend and yet at the same time does not detract from Scripture's divine authority. The former is understood to be the crucial lifting of an unnecessary obstacle; the latter is taken to be a rudiment of orthodoxy. The perplexing dilemma that many evangelicals precariously bear follows naturally: how can one steal the sanction of Scripture from Paul's prohibition against women without robbing the sacred writings of their divine punch? Resolution can take interesting turns when the invalidity of Paul's prohibition is pre-understood as an unnecessary obstacle. The most consistent way to achieve these desired results is to revisit what is meant by the authority of Scripture. Countless Christians have been more than willing to do this, some with more caution than others.

The sundry arguments that posit 1 Tim 2.12 was situational and limited in scope converge, for the most part, on one consideration: Paul was as successful as he was in missionary endeavors because he did not allow any other obstacle to belief other than the cross. Richard Hays, for example, in *The Moral Vision of the New Testament*, is so disturbed by 1 Tim 2.12 that he disallows Pauline authorship for that particular verse.[13] He is critical of Paul for those portions that he has written when he writes:

> Paul wrestles constantly with the hermeneutical task of relating the gospel freshly to the situation in his target churches; 1 Timothy assumes that the norms must be merely guarded and passed along. Indeed, there is a positive impatience with theological argumentation: Those who disagree with the officially sanctioned "sound teaching" are said to manifest "a morbid craving for controversy and for disputes about words" (1 Tim. 6:4). It is difficult to imagine Paul dismissively avoiding theological controversy in this manner. Do we see here the evidence of a bad case of apostolic burnout?[14]

In other words, Paul does not seem to be as nuanced here as he should have been. His game was clearly off.[15] An otherwise admirable saint should not be emulated for his work here. An instinctive evangelical rejoinder might very well carry the following sentiment: "Well, drastic situations call for drastic measures—if a Pauline text offends you, cut it off; perhaps,

---

[13] (San Francisco: HarperCollins, 1996), 67.

[14] Hays, *Moral Vision*, 71.

[15] Compare Luke Timothy Johnson, *The First and Second Letters to Timothy*. Anchor Bible 35A. (New York: Doubleday, 2001), 206–208.

it is better to enter the twenty-first century without 1 Timothy then to be politically cast away with an intact Bible!" We should note again, though, that it is contemporary extrabiblical knowledge and sensibilities that are prompting changes in interpretation. This is only natural; perhaps, conservative evangelicals should be more sympathetic.[16]

Hays is, after all, wrestling with the same dissonance that (egalitarian) evangelicals are. He expresses particular concern with 1 Tim 2.11–15 because "the peculiarity of the passage has given rise to various imaginative exegetical attempts at damage control, but the overall sense of the text is finally inescapable: women (or perhaps wives) are to be silent and submissive and to bear children."[17] If Hays is right here, his conclusion is unavoidable for those who reject the possible contemporary applicability of 1 Tim 2.12 in one way or another: 1 Tim 2.12 is not a legitimate part of the canon.[18] Though the majority of evangelicals would never openly stand for so flagrant a dismissal, they are actually in the same boat as Hays. In fact, his conclusion seems to follow necessarily for evangelicals because, on account of the evangelical methodological insistence, existing tensions are magnified between what the text actually says, *the authority with which it says it*, and the reader's expectation of what the text should say and how it should say it. This is an especially grave predicament to a constituency that is committed to scientific hermeneutics. In other words, egalitarian evangelicals must secretly cast their ballots with Hays (with whose conclusion they do not agree) precisely because they agree that the text is not authoritative here even though it is an otherwise authoritative text. The paradoxical situation is such that these evangelicals must both aver their allegiance to the text and surreptitiously endeavor to undermine it for the sake of their commitments to an authoritative Bible and an egalitarian

---

[16] Analagously, the same also holds true for debates that surround the creation account (or for any hermeneutical debate for that matter) and this is not necessarily a bad thing. Yet it is hard for me not to deem disingenuous those who say that it was primarily their reading of Scripture that sparked their interest in non-six twenty-four hour day interpretations, for example.

[17] Hays, *Moral Vision*, 67–68.

[18] Whether it be by claiming that Paul for whatever reason was not himself when he was writing the letter (because he was "nervous" [Johnson, *Timothy*, 206]) or by arguing that when we read "women" in v 12 we should remember "women currently in Ephesus" (see S. H. Gritz, *Paul, Women Teachers, and the Mother Goddess at Ephesus: A Study of 1 Tim 2:9–15 in Light of the Religious and Cultural Milieu of the First Century*. (New York: University Press of America, 1991), the conclusions effectively remove this section of 1 Tim from its place in the canon and treat it as if it were really located somewhere in Leviticus, if anywhere at all. Unfortunately, the problem cannot be dismissed so easily: the portions of Leviticus that are no longer binding are so for *theological* reasons not solely cultural or situational ones.

interpretation. They have somehow retreated from the text in such a way that they are evangelical and non-evangelical at the same time. Surely, this poses a serious problem with regard to an allegedly authoritative Bible.

II. Complementarian Evangelicals and the Authority of Scripture

Complementarian evangelicals are those who agree that the 1 Tim prohibition somehow binds the church today. We shall now explore Paul's exegetical arguments for his prohibition. The plan is to point out how Paul's argument depends on non-scientific exegesis and then ask how scientific evangelicals who would not otherwise accept his line of argumentation can nevertheless profess the validity of his conclusion.

By coupling the beginning of 1 Tim 2.11 with the end of v 12, the verses evince the following structure: "Let a woman learn in silence . . . she is to keep silent" (γυνη εν ησυχια . . . ειναι εν ησυχια). A sequence of contrasts is presented: silence/teaching; submission/authority; women/men and the prohibition begins and ends with "in silence."[19] The former in each of the three pairs correspond as do the latter in each pair. The structure of the text reinforces the surface meaning: men can teach and have authority; women should be silent and submit.

What the text says is more than evident to complementarians; however, these evangelicals are encouraged to take Paul's exegesis of the Eden narrative more seriously and less naively. In fact, given Paul's record with controversy, it would appear that that is precisely what he anticipated that his hearers/readers would do.[20] The two arguments that he employs are based upon his own reading of the Genesis creation narrative according to complementarians. They are (1) "Adam was formed first, then Eve" and

---

[19] Other scholars have also identified an inclusio here. See, for example, *Nelson's New Illustrated Bible Commentary* (ed. E. Radmacher, R. B. Allen, H. W. House; Nashville: Thomas Nelson, 1999), 1598.

[20] For as much as Paul talks about not depending upon human wisdom, he relies heavily upon rhetoric to persuade his readers (2 Cor 11; Phlm, etc.). See Duane Wilson, ed. *Persuasive Artistry: Studies in New Testament Rhetoric in Honor of George A. Kennedy.* JSNTS 50. (Sheffield: Sheffield Academic Press, 1991). For the early expectation and probability of a wide distribution of the NT writings, see Harry Gamble, *Books and Readers in the Early Church: A History of Early Christian Texts.* (New Haven: Yale University Press, 1995), 95–101 and Michael B. Thompson, "The Holy Internet: Communication Between Churches in the First Christian Generation" in *The Gospels for All Christians: Rethinking the Gospel Audiences.* (ed. Richard Bauckham; Grand Rapids: Eerdmans, 1998), 49–70.

(2) "Adam was not deceived, but the woman was deceived and became the transgressor."

The first argument is a good example of the "prominence" value of New Testament times. Chris Seeman writes, "Prominence implies an ordering of priority on the basis of time, space, or rank . . . This sequencing of priority-evaluation is often indicated in the Bible by the categories 'first' and 'last'."[21] It is important to note that a very high degree of authority inheres in this appeal to the order of creation, for it is an order that no human can or could have altered. [22] The fact that Adam was created first was beyond anyone's control, and in light of the Scriptural story, it was not merely a matter of contingency. It has traditionally been inferred that since God had created man first that man has been given the priority or prominence. The question that complementarians must answer is, In what way or capacity has man been given priority? Most complementarians do not see women as irrelevant or inferior. They typically tend to mean that compared to the woman, man has a primary "something." Given the context of 1 Tim 2, Adam is understood to represent Christian men and Eve Christian women in today's churches. Since the value of prominence itself has also been subject to seething criticism, we shall briefly try to defend its appropriation on behalf of complementarians.[23]

Others have surmised that general outlines for gender roles are taught in the creation account.[24] For our purposes, we shall highlight several fea-

---

[21] "Prominence," in *Handbook of Biblical Social Values.* (ed. J. J. Pilch and B. J. Malina; Peabody, MA: Hendrickson, 1998), 167.

[22] Compare Matt 19.4–6 where Jesus appeals to creation in order to counter an argument from Torah. That 1 Cor 11.2–16 also invokes an argument from creation is sometimes thought to demonstrate Paul's exegetical flippancy. In defense of the complementarians, we can proffer that 1 Cor 11.2–16 is still binding when considered as a dispute over authority, but when presented as a dispute over shawls the details do not pertain. For the rabbinic backdrop of the 1 Cor passage, see Mary Rose D'Angelo, "The Garden: Once and Not Again: Traditional Interpretation of Genesis 1:26–17 in 1 Corinthians 11:7–12" in *Genesis 1–3 in the History of Exegesis: Intrigue in the Garden* (ed. Gregory Allen Robbins; Lewiston, NY: Edwin Mellon Press, 1988), 1–42.

[23] Stanley J. Grenz, for example, comments that if the order of creation were truly significant, woman would actually be the pinnacle of creation since she was created last. (*Women in the Church: A Biblical Theology of Women in Ministry.* [Downers Grove, IL: InterVarsity, 1995], 161.) But consider Gen 1.16: "God made the two great lights—the greater light to rule the day and the lesser light to rule the night—and the stars." In Gen 37.5–11, Joseph, his father and his brothers all understand the relation of the sun, the moon and the stars to be that of the father, mother and children, a classic patriarchic interpretation.

[24] For example, Michael F. Stitzinger, "Genesis 1–3 and the Male/Female Role

tures of the narrative to determine whether it is reasonable to conclude that man indeed plays a primary role. The most important feature already appears in our text: YHWH created Adam first and Eve second. Further developments in the narrative also suggest man's primary role in the creation story. For example, when the serpent set out to deceive, he targeted the woman and not the man, yet it is clear in the story that the man was his ultimate target. If the man was the serpent's ultimate target, then the man is at least in some sense primary. In addition, the facts that YHWH gave the commandment about the Tree to the man (the woman had not even been created yet); that YHWH brought the woman to the man to see what he would call her, just as YHWH had done with the other creatures; that the man actually did name the woman; that he called her "woman"; that Adam and Eve are often referred to as "the man and his wife";[25] that Adam's name doubles as a personal name and the name of the race; that the woman was considered to be man's helper;[26] that Adam again names the woman "Eve"; that YHWH comes looking for Adam (and not Eve) in the garden, all (especially when taken cumulatively) seem to support the idea that man is primary in the creation story. The question remains, though, primary with respect to what? Therefore, rather than engage in a confutation of each of the above narrative observations, we shall concede the plausibility of the prominence argument and return to this question (or at least one similar to it) upon examining Paul's other argument: "Adam was not deceived, but the woman was deceived and became a transgressor."

What is Paul implying when he writes that the woman was deceived but Adam was not? How did Eve's deception render her unfit for teaching and how does what happened to Eve relate to every other woman's ability to teach? Complementarians cannot keep silent here, though they will need to tread carefully as they offer their explanations. They would be wise not to perpetuate the myth that women are more easily deceived than men, especially considering past abuses and today's cultural climate.[27]

Relationship," *Grace Theological Journal* 2 (1981): 23–44.

[25] Incidentally, the only time we read "her husband" is when she gives the fruit to him. Eve takes center stage for the first time and the man is for one verse defined in relation to her.

[26] Writers often point out that other biblical texts call YHWH the helper of Israel, but this does not negate the implications of Eve being called Adam's "helper." See David J. A. Clines, *What Does Eve Do To Help? and Other Readerly Questions for the Old Testament.* JSOTSup 94. (Sheffield: Sheffield Academic Press, 1990).

[27] A common explanation up through a few generations ago—for example, Barnes wrote: "It is undoubtedly implied here that man in general has a power of resisting certain kinds of temptation superior to that possessed by woman, and hence that the headship properly belongs to him." By contrast, Susan Foh probably errs in the other direction when she

But do they have any other options? In addition, even if that was what Paul was thinking, exactly how does Paul come to such a conclusion from his reading of the Eden narrative?[28] One can imagine at least three main sources for Paul's conclusion: his culture, his personal experience, and his knowledge of Scripture and tradition. It would seem that complementarians must insist that the prohibition is supported by Paul's reading of Scripture since the other sources are so contingent and restricted that they cannot possibly bind the church throughout the ages. Though Paul's reading is indubitably a cultural reading, complementarians must contend that it is not *merely* a cultural reading, but also a theological one. Hence, we shall, on behalf of a hypothetical complementarian, attempt to contrive an interpretation of the Eden narrative that offers the Pauline argument of 1 Tim 2.14 as evidence against women teachers without wholly succumbing to first (or twenty-first) century cultural pre-understandings. We should, however, be prepared to employ first (and not twenty-first) century hermeneutical methods.

III. Midrashic Interpretation vs. Evangelical Hermeneutics

Complementarians seem to implicitly argue that Paul's exegetical proof is a legitimate one. We should note, though, that 1 Tim 2.14 is an instance of something like what Gerald Bray has called "scribal (or Pharisaic) interpretation." One approach within Pharisaic interpretation that appears in our text involves "reading Scripture as a legal document, in which examples of behaviour could be taken out of context and made to apply in ways which went well beyond anything the text actually said."[29] In other words, with respect to the present text, Eve's deception is being used as a "legal" precedent for Paul's prohibition. Such exegetical whimsy would most certainly not be accepted from a present-day expositor. The question is, must complementarians substitute Paul's obsolete line of reasoning with a modern one? Or asked another way, how can a post-Enlightenment thinker really take Paul seriously here? What are the obligations for complementarians to those who disagree with them with regard to accounting for Paul's an-

---

claims that "verse 14 is simply a statement of past fact." See Foh, *Women and the Word of God: A Response to Biblical Feminism.* (Philipsburg, NJ: Presbyterian and Reformed, 1979), 127.

[28] See Keener, *Paul, Women and Wives,* 116–117.

[29] *Biblical Interpretation: Past and Present.* (Downers Grove, IL: InterVarsity, 1996), 57.

tiquated argument style?[30] What does the fact that Paul actually employs such argumentation ramify with respect to the authority of Scripture?

These questions do not apply to egalitarians since they not only deny Paul's argument, they deny his conclusion also. On the other hand, since complementarians accept Paul's conclusion, they either have to explain how they can disregard an invalid argument while adhering to its conclusion or validate the ancient exegetical strategy to the satisfaction of contemporaries. The best option for the complementarian may be to circumvent these difficult questions altogether by offering an interpretation that explains the Eden narrative in a way that does not rely upon the interpretive method delineated above. We shall offer such an attempt after which we shall posit a conclusion.

In an attempt to consciously avoid the conclusion that women are more gullible than men, we shall take the tact that 1 Tim 2.14 argues the same point as 2.13. In other words, that Eve was deceived and Adam was not is directly related to the fact that she was created second and he first. Succinctly stated, though the woman was deceived and became the transgressor, Adam was held accountable. To begin, we note that when Gen 3.22 explains YHWH's concern—"the man has become like one of us, knowing good and evil; and now, he might reach out his hand and take also from the tree of life, and eat, and live forever"—the woman is not mentioned. Gen 3.24 relates how YHWH "drove out" the man, but again the woman is not mentioned. Presumably, the woman did not *not* "become like one of us" nor did she remain behind in the garden. Thus one might infer that the man is the one to whom the main responsibility had been given. It seems quite fair to say that as far as the creation account is concerned, the man is accountable to YHWH in a way that the woman is not. But all this has already been touched upon in Paul's prominence argument from the order of creation where man was said to be primary with respect to *something* in a way that the woman was secondary. We shall consider the prominence argument in more detail in order to determine whether it can somehow be related to the deception argument.

An emphasis is placed on the fact that the woman transgressed because she was deceived. The commandment had not been given directly to the woman so readers might infer that she did not apprehend the commandment as well as Adam did. Perhaps, her addition to the commandment suggests this. It is curious, though, that the woman is not once ad-

---

[30] Douglas Spanner, for example, senses his responsibility when he offers supplementary argumentation for the implementation of Paul's prohibition. See Spanner, "Men, Women and God" *Churchman* 108 (1994): 101–118.

monished by YHWH for eating the fruit or even for being deceived: it was for giving fruit to the man that she is only implicitly rebuked by the narrator.[31] Another oddity is that YHWH gives no reason for his judgment against Eve. It is as if her actions were incidental in spite of the fact that they proved so crucial. This leaves a gaping lacuna in the narrative that virtually every subsequent tradition naturally attempts to fill. For example, *Jubilees* adds to its retelling of the biblical account that YHWH "was angry with the woman also because she had listened to the voice of the serpent and eaten." (3.23) *Life of Adam and Eve*, for its part, records Eve herself relating these very events: "Turning to me, the LORD said to me, 'Since you have listened to the serpent and ignored my commandment, you shall suffer birth pangs . . .'" (*Apocalypse* 25.1) The writer of the *Greek Apocalypse of Ezra* portrays Ezra as being upset with God over Eve: "If you had not given him Eve, the serpent would never have deceived her." The Scriptures, though, are silent with regard to YHWH being angry that Eve had "listened to the voice of the serpent" or even that she had eaten.[32] The length of the ׳ כ clause in Gen 3.17, especially in light of its absence in v 16, also supports the idea that the man was responsible to God in a way that the woman was not. Hence, Adam was the prominent figure in Eden on account of his being created first, on account of being given the commandment directly and on account of God's holding him responsible. In sum, we have attempted to present a case where 1 Tim 2.13–14 offers two arguments that make the same point: God has elected men for certain things in a way in which he has not elected women. Men are responsible to God in a way that women are not.

In our exposition, we too have taken Adam and Eve to be archetypes for all humans in our interpretation. *If* an interpretation like the one offered here is representative of those that a complementarian would offer, it employs the same interpretive generalization that marks Paul's exegesis. Still, we have not managed to explicitly address what role deception plays in the archetypical analogy. Why wasn't God (as) angry at Eve? Because she was deceived? Partly. More precisely, and (unhappily) unavoidably, *because it was expected that she would be deceived*. Commenting on the narrator's presentation of Eve's decision and action, Von Rad wrote:

---

[31] In Eve's case, as in the serpent's, the wrong committed is determined by the response given by the previous character in Gen 3.8–14. In other words, Eve's wrong was that the man could say, "The woman whom you gave to be with me, she gave me fruit from the tree, and I ate." That she gave him fruit is the wrong committed. That he ate it is the man's.

[32] Quotations from *The Old Testament Pseudipigrapha*. 2 vols. (ed. James Charlesworth; New York: Doubleday, 1983, 1985).

> The narrator expresses no shock; he does not expect his reader to become indignant either. On the contrary, the unthinkable and terrible is described as simply and unsensationally as possible, completely without the hubbub of the extraordinary or of a dramatic break, so that it is represented from man's standpoint almost as something self-evident, inwardly consistent![33]

"Of course she was deceived!" was the thought that ran through hearers'/readers' minds. Likewise, Cassuto wrote, "It is the way of the world for the man to be easily swayed by the woman."[34] Adam and Eve are everyman, everywoman, but in what ways? We offer the following archetypes, which are, unfortunately, for all intents and purposes, stereotypes. The man was made to guard and till the garden. The woman was made to "help" the man reproduce.[35] Initially, there were no plants or herbs because YHWH had not brought rain and *because there was no man to till the ground.* YHWH and men are understood to be they who tend to the land at least for the purposes of the creation narrative. YHWH increases the difficulty with which men and women will carry out their respective assignments in the future. That Paul may very well have thought along these lines is supported by his own reiteration of what he (and the Eden narrator) saw to be the woman's God-given task in 1 Tim 2.15. YHWH and the men are they who run the church.

It may well have been the case that Paul was further influenced by an old rabbinic interpretation of Gen 2.22 that understood that Eve had been "built" (and not "formed") because YHWH was specifically "constructing" her that she would be able to bear children.[36] He also almost certainly interpreted the female gender in terms of the popular taxonomy of women of the time, based upon the Hebrew Scriptures, that went as follows: (1) Minor daughter; (2) Wife; (3) Widow (without an heir); (4) Daughter (no longer a minor); (5) Divorced woman; and (6) Widow with an heir.[37] The first three were dependent upon the father, husband and husband's brother respectively. The latter three were considered independent. Note how women were categorized with respect to the men with whom they

---

[33] *Genesis.* (Philadelphia: Westminster Press, 1961), 87.

[34] Umberto Cassuto, *A Commentary on the Book of Genesis: From Adam to Noah.* (Jerusalem: Magnes Press, 1998), 148.

[35] Compare Clines, *What Does Eve Do To Help?*

[36] Leila Leah Bronner, *From Eve to Esther: Rabbinic Reconstructions of Biblical Women.* (Louisville, KY: Westminster John Knox, 1994) 28–30.

[37] Judith Romney Wegner, *Chattel or Person? The Status of Women in the Mishnah.* (New York: Oxford University Press, 1988), 12–14.

were most closely related according to their age. The most common category was the second and the woman's influence under the authority of her husband seems to have been culturally understood in something like the following way:

A. There is this case, involving a certain pious man, who was married to a pious woman, but the couple did not produce children. They said, "What good do we do for the Holy One, blessed be he [if we do not produce children, so increasing God's image]?"

B. They went and divorced one another. The man went and married a wicked woman, and she made him wicked.

C. The woman went and married a wicked man, and she made him righteous.

D. This proves that everything depends on the woman.[38]

A man's character was understood to depend in large measure on that of his wife. Vern Poythress' observation that Christ's church, the household of God, is repeatedly described as a type of great family is helpful here.[39] The dynamics that are observed within the family are those that obtain in the church.[40] In the prototypical and archetypal case, "Adam was not deceived"—he listened to the voice of his wife. "Eve was deceived and became a transgressor." In these two verses is an argument from a (stereotypical) family dynamic: A man is the head of a household, but a woman can easily do him in, or in biblical terms: "A good wife is the crown of her husband, but she who brings shame is like rottenness in his bones" (Prov 12.4). Eden, the world, and the family all evince the prominence of the man and the influence that a woman can have on a man. In other words, women can (easily) get men to do things that no one else can. The first type of influence that comes to mind is sexual in nature. A woman can entice a man more easily than she knows (hence the warnings in Prov 7 and elsewhere.) For this reason, the sensual allure of a woman in the eyes of a man was often used in the OT for other uncannily strong impulses that led men to do the wrong thing: follow false teachings, listen to false proph-

---

[38] *Gen. Rab.* 17.7.2, taken from Jacob Neusner, *Christian Faith and the Bible of Judaism: The Judaic Encounter with Scripture.* (Grand Rapids: Eerdmans, 1987), 67.

[39] "The Church as Family: Why Male Leadership in the Family Requires Male Leadership in the Church" in *Recovering Biblical Manhood and Womanhood: A Response to Evangelical Feminism.* (Wheaton, IL: Crossway, 1991), 233–247.

[40] Note the requirements for church leadership given in 1 Tim 3.

ecy and worship false idols.[41] Without denying that the ancients could distinguish between a metaphor's literal and figurative meanings, the two were often apprehended as a composite whole and were sometimes not effectually separated on account of a zealous maintenance of a YHWH-istic worldview. Or if this is overstating the matter, at least we can say that the literal and figurative meanings were *very* closely associated. Close identification of figurative meanings with literal meanings was one way that ancients could get a handle on the mystical and irrational aspects of life.[42]

We should not be surprised then when Jouette Bassler observes that "[t]he primary reason for the Pastor's emphasis on Eve's deception, however, was not exegetical, but practical." Though there is much truth in this statement, we should understand that a modern distinction is being imposed upon the mind of an ancient author. The author of 1 Tim would never have made such a distinction: to the ancients, *all* exegesis was practical. Bassler continues, "The author stressed the connection between Eve's fall and her deception because a similar situation existed in his church . . ."[43] Though this too may be true, perhaps it would be more helpful to admit that the author is stressing the connection because the situation that arose in his church is one that arises the world over, including in the OT. Resignedly, and despite our best efforts to help complementarians avoid the culturally embarrassing argument that women are more gullible than men, we have found our way back to the observation that the biblical literature sometimes presents women as "the devil's gateway"[44] and that 1 Tim 2.14 is one of those times! In spite of the above attempts to escape taboo, our complementarian version of Paul's second argument breaks down

[41] This intriguing dynamic between a man, a woman and the proper worship of YHWH recurs throughout the biblical literature. See, for example, Carlos R. Bovell, "Gen 3.21: The History of Israel in a Nutshell?" *ExpTim* 115 (2004): 361–366; and "Symmetry, Ruth and Canon" *JSOT* 28 (2003): 175–191. It goes without saying that sex was *not* created by God in order to provide him with appropriate metaphorical terms by which he might describe our relation to him, *contra* John Piper, "Sex and the Supremacy of Christ: Part One" in *Sex and Supremacy of Christ* (ed. J. Piper and J. Taylor; Wheaton, IL: Crossway, 2005), 25–36.

[42] Compare E. R. Dodds, *The Greeks and The Irrational* (Berkeley: University of California Press, 1951) and H. and H. A. Frankfort, J. A. Wilson and T. Jacobsen, *Before Philosophy*. (Baltimore: Pelican Books, 1949). For the modern employment of metaphors, see G. Lakoff and M. Johnson, *Metaphors We Live By*. (Chicago: University of Chicago Press, 1983).

[43] "Adam, Eve, and The Pastor: The Use of Genesis 2–3 in the Pastoral Epistles" in *Genesis 1–3 in the History of Exegesis: Intrigue in the Garden* (ed. Gregory Allen Robbins; Lewiston, NY: Edwin Mellon Press, 1988), 43–66, 50.

[44] The title of the fifth chapter of John A. Phillips' *Eve: The History of an Idea*. (San Francisco: Harper and Row Publishers, 1984).

into an eloquent restatement of the traditional, stereotypical argument that women are more easily deceived than men.

How can evangelical complementarians agree with Paul's argument that women are more easily deceived than men when the argument is derived from cultural metaphors and myths? "It is based on Scripture!" comes the reply. Before responding, we should note that the focus here is on how the Scriptures can be considered authoritative in light of the non-scientificality of the argumentation it employs. By way of response, the complementarian can hold that (1) though Paul's second argument is bogus, the first is sound and that the conclusion therefore still holds. Or he might insist that (2) Paul's argument is an inspired observation that he drives home through analogous references to Adam and Eve. Or that (3) it does not matter whether the arguments hold or not (i.e., according to our sinful standards of valid argumentation): God has argued this way through Paul and we have to simply accept it. We shall briefly tend to each type of response.

With regard to (1), the complementarian who admits the impermissibility of Paul's second argument faces the same dilemma that the egalitarians faced in the first part of the chapter: 1 Tim 2.14 is no longer part of the canon. By canon, power and authority are meant: the text is not binding—it has no power or authority—on modern Christians since it employs antiquated argumentative techniques. Egalitarians have surmised the same for Paul's first argument too. Complementarians who respond with response (1) cannot fault egalitarians who are responding in the same way. With regard to response (2)—that Paul's observation is an inspired one—we should recall the degree to which cultural metaphors and myths have influenced the observation. Furthermore, a number of honest husbands (not to mention the history of the church) testify against the inspired observation. Inspired or not, the claim that women are more gullible than men will be qualified by a huge network of uninspired churches. As soon as we have found a counterexample to the observation, the evangelical search for an inspired truth in the text ensues and is conducted and concluded by various groups of uninspired men and women. In other words, for the sake of argument, the case could turn out such that *in certain (or in many) situations* women are more gullible than men, but even this hypothetical conclusion does not warrant a *universal* ban on women ministers.[45] A complementarian might counter that God has given us this command in order to save the church from possible danger, but this is a

---

[45] Compare Plato's *Republic* 452e–457c.

far cry from what the text of 1 Tim 2.13–14 appears to be saying. These complementarians have backed their way into a scientific apology for the reality of pre-modern argumentation in Scripture (which is precisely the problem this discursus purports to illuminate).

Lastly, a complementarian might opt for response (3)—that we need to remember our subordinate place to the text and that our inherent sinfulness always drives us to disobey God. This is an interesting response that seems the epitome of "God-fearingness"; however, given our inherent sinfulness, there is no guarantee that we have not sinfully mistaken this God-fearingness for plain old sinfulness, prejudice and/or laziness. The churches' subordination to Scripture is quite meaningless, if not foolish, without understanding what Scripture is saying, and how and why it is saying whatever it seems to be saying. This business is nothing less than the study and practice of hermeneutics, and hermeneutics, as we now know all too well, is a contingent undertaking that changes with time and differs by culture—it even changes over time within the same person and culture.[46] Especially given what evangelical scholars have learned and are still trying to learn from post-modern and post-secular hermeneutical theory, the days of "common sense" readings of the Bible are gone, even if many evangelicals long for their return. The most unsettling feature of the hermeneutical spiral is that there is no real way for a reader to turn back. With each new reading, old cherished readings morph in response to new critical questions. Likewise, the critical questions that are asked are likely to change in response to the pre-understanding that is brought to the text by, among a host of other things, the last reading. Furthermore, different individuals within the churches will be at different points along the hermeneutical spiral. If that were not enough, individuals' hermeneutical spirals are likely to differ as well. From this vantage, most will agree that response (3) is a healthy evangelical attitude toward Scripture, but it ceases to be a viable response to the problem at hand when taken as the only and final solution. Response (3) is more of a reminder of the humility we should have when reading Scripture than a real solution to the problem we have delineated. To urge other evangelicals to agree with the complementarian position simply because the Bible is God's Word that must be obeyed ignores the inevitable reality of hermeneutics. In fact, the hermeneutical problems that are triggered by this particular issue have even caused some to count the notion of an authoritative Bible as completely erroneous. It will surely prove disconcerting to many that the hermeneutical spiral is of-

---

[46] One might note here John G. Stackhouse, Jr., *Finally Feminist: A Pragmatic Christian Understanding of Gender*. (Grand Rapids: Baker, 2005).

ten something that resists our attempts at control. Yearning for some sort of definitive resolution, however, complementarians who opt for response (3) should take care not to overplay—or even misuse—their current theological convictions.

IV. Conclusion

The hermeneutics employed in this discursus determined that Paul resorted to a mode of argumentation that is no longer operative in Western society. Yet Paul's argument, according to evangelical theory, is contained within God's Word. The dilemma for the complementarian is that God's Word is the churches' ultimate authority: if Paul's argument is utterly nonsensical to a contemporary Western reader, how can the Bible be authoritative? Egalitarians argue that Paul's conclusion is not binding; this does not alleviate the burden of explaining what Paul's argument in 1 Tim 2.14 ramifies for an authoritative Scripture. In fact, that they confute Paul's conclusion exacerbates their task. Complementarians, on the other hand, must explain how a conclusion that is based upon an argument can persist in its validity when the supporting scriptural argument collapses. Furthermore, they must explain how the authority of a text is not impugned by its inclusion of a defunct argument.

In the present author's view the only way out of this pickle for either side is for evangelicals to suspend their predilection for scientific exactitude with regard to biblical authority and especially inner-biblical exegesis. In addition, evangelicals need to engage the problem of the incompatibility of biblical authority and the antiquated methodology (in terms of argumentation, cosmological assumptions and scriptural exegesis) that is found in the Bible. It will not do for evangelicals to cleave to one at the expense of the other. Readers should not insist on Scripture's authority by disallowing the admission that the Bible's exegetical strategies are thoroughly pre-modern and are no longer cogent. Readers will hopefully also guard against prematurely discarding their Bibles, concluding that the information contained therein is obsolete. Evangelical leaders and teachers, especially, must begin to more openly acknowledge to their students that evangelical views of the Bible precipitate a paradox such that the Scriptures' absolute authority and its sporadic incompetence (at least through contemporary eyes) must be admitted simultaneously. This, I submit, is the epitome of the younger evangelical dilemma and its resolution requires, in the eyes of a number of younger evangelicals, nothing less than a paradigm shift away from inerrancy.[47]

Evangelical leaders and teachers should not set up their youth for future disaffection by playing down or outright denying what I am decrying as the evangelical predicament. There is a great reluctance to speak candidly about these topics with younger evangelicals (or even with older ones!), but perhaps initial fears can be allayed by reassessing what is really at stake in terms of the entire Christian faith.

A very popular false impression among young evangelicals—one for whose perpetuation evangelical leaders and teachers are directly and indirectly responsible—is that believers who question inerrancy or those who go on to disbelieve it are no longer true believers—not only because they have immediately become unbelievers (or are well on their way to unbelief), but because they now represent serious spiritual threats to the rest of God's people. In order to help free younger evangelicals from the existential burden of this debilitating dilemma, I set out in the next chapter to analyze common evangelical attempts to analogously bind the doctrine of Scripture to Christ in order to most forcefully inculcate its alleged indispensability. I suggest contrarily that the construal of an inerrant Bible as essential to orthodox Christianity and especially its orthodox understanding of Christ is unfounded and accordingly should not be taught to younger evangelicals.

---

[47] For what it's worth, I currently side with complementarians on the ordination issue, but I am still wrestling with just how pre-modern the Bible's intertextuality is (along with the cultural milieu of the Bible generally). I believe that the Bible is the churches' chief authority for faith and practice but have not yet found a way to adequately describe this authority. The ETS/EPS credo no longer makes any sense to me; "error" is an entirely inappropriate category for the Bible. See chapter three below.

Recognition Three

Young Evangelicals Should Not Bind Scripture to Christ

Younger evangelicals[1] are constantly taught that Christians have always believed that the Scriptures have been in some way divinely inspired and therefore inerrant. In the words of B. B. Warfield:

> The Church, then, has held from the beginning that the Bible is the Word of God in such a sense that its words, though written by men and bearing indelibly impressed upon them the marks of their human origin, were written, nevertheless, under such an influence of the Holy Ghost as to be also the words of God, the adequate expression of His mind and will.

Warfield continues:

> It has always recognized that this conception of co-authorship implies that the Spirit's superintendence extends to the choice of the words by the human authors (verbal inspiration), and preserves its product from everything inconsistent with a divine authorship—thus securing, among other things, that entire truthfulness which is everywhere presupposed in and asserted for Scripture by the Biblical writers (inerrancy).[2]

In other words, because the Holy Spirit played such an integral role in the production of the Scriptures, it is not possible that they would contain any untruths.

In this chapter, we shall first suggest that it does not *necessarily* follow from its God-breathed property that the Bible must not contain any

---

[1] I should clarify again that "evangelicals" in this work refers to those evangelicals of whatever denomination (or non-denomination) who align themselves according to the views of Scripture promulgated by the Evangelical Theological Society, the Evangelical Philosophical Society and other like-minded affiliations.

[2] "The Real Problem of Inspiration" in *The Inspiration and Authority of the Bible*. (Phillipsburg, NJ: Presbyterian and Reformed Publishing Co., 1948), 169–226, 173.

errors. We shall then consider how the inerrancy doctrine of Scripture is frequently compared with the classic Christological understanding of the incarnation in order to determine what a Christological analogy may or may not ramify for an inerrant Bible. The conclusion will admit that it is not practically helpful, and certainly not necessary, to seek elucidation of the evangelical understanding of the Bible by comparing the dual authorship of Scripture with the dual natures of Christ, for what "preserves its product from everything inconsistent with a divine authorship" does not refer to analogous things during the course of the comparison of Christ and Scripture.

I. Geisler's Deductive Reconstructions

According to Norman Geisler, "each member of the Trinity is involved in [the Bible's] inerrancy."[3] There are thus at least three possible arguments for the inerrancy of Scripture: an argument from God the Father, an argument from God the Son, and an argument from God the Holy Spirit. In the first volume of his *Systematic Theology*, Geisler conveniently presents all three arguments as both hypothetical and categorical syllogisms (although the second appears simply as a hypothesis and conclusion) on the same page, claiming that "[t]he logic is simple and irrefutable." The three arguments are as follows: 1) "If God cannot err and the Bible is the Word of God, then the Bible cannot err"; 2) "If Jesus is the Son of God, then the Bible is the Word of God (which cannot err). Hence to deny the Bible is the Word of God is to deny that Jesus is the Son of God";[4] and 3) If the Holy Spirit cannot be in error and the Bible is an utterance of the Spirit of Truth, then the Bible cannot be in error. Geisler presents these three arguments as if they were separate and independent (although he is probably assuming *some* type of relation among them since he purports to derive them from his conception of the Trinity), but, in fact, they all singularly

---

[3] Norman Geisler, *Systematic Theology Volume One: Introduction, Bible.* (Minneapolis: Bethany House, 2002), 248.

[4] Readers should note that 2) is not an argument at all, but rather a bald hypothetical assertion. Geisler's remarks about 2)'s contrapositive only follows if the hypothesis is established as true by some *other* argument. Geisler attempts an inductive argument later on in volume one that purports to demonstrate that "the two Words of God, the Living and the written, are tied together." (271) Apparently the argument amounts to something like this: Christ was convinced that the Bible (which was what exactly during Christ's time?) was the Word of God so it *is* the Word of God. Stated this way, the argument has some force to it but certainly not the "irrefutable" logic that Geisler's deductive representation is meant to suggest.

depend on the validity of the first argument. Geisler himself gives this away when he seeks to help his readers follow his second argument by appending the parenthetical remark, "which cannot err," to the consequent of the argument from God the Son. Whether the arguments' "irrefutable logic" proves compelling or not to younger evangelicals will hinge, among other things, upon what these readers understand by the word "err" when it is applied to God and to the Bible and whether they agree that the verb is appropriate in the first place for the premises of the argument.

If younger evangelicals can muster even the slightest bit of courage to critically examine Geisler's argument from God the Father (and this is where the formative role of evangelical leaders and teachers can be so decisive), they will realize that there is a good deal of latitude here for further reflection to which Geisler does not grant sufficient attention.[5] Let us illustrate this by placing Geisler's argument from the Father side by side with what he claims that critics tend to counter-argue.

God cannot err.	The Bible contains the words of humans.
The Bible is the Word of God.	Humans err.
The Bible cannot err.	The Bible errs.

Assuming that students are willing to agree that "err" will mean the same thing each time it appears during the course of the syllogisms (which they justifiably may not), younger evangelicals should surely be given the spiritual breathing room to mull over whether it would be possible for the Bible not to err insofar as it is divine and yet err in whatever way they undeniably discover (through scholarly endeavor, etc.) *insofar as it is human.*[6] Theories of accommodation and limitation will very likely appeal to younger evangelicals (especially the former).[7] Irrespective of whether older

[5] Geisler does make the following comparison in paragraph form but does not broach the possibility of affirming the corresponding alternative to his conclusion.

[6] The point that humans do not have to err is inconsequential. The reason for doubting inerrancy in the first place is precisely because "errors" of some kind have been detected. If a younger evangelical comes to the point that he can no longer in good conscience give a satisfactory account for an alleged error, that student should be given the theological room necessary to formulate an alternate, "orthodox" position. He should not be pressured into minimizing or even denying the errors found. Again, it may very well be that "error" will prove itself an inappropriate category altogether for articulating the authority of the Bible.

[7] Geisler discounts both of these (*Systematic Theology*, 1.274–280) as options for the evangelical. Kent Sparks commends the former in his "The Sun Also Rises: Accommodation in Inscripturation and Interpretation" in *Evangelicals and Scripture: Tradition, Authority and Hermeneutics.* (ed. V. Bacote, L. C. Miguélez, and D. L. Okholm; Downers Grove, IL:

evangelicals are not generally comfortable pushing the limits of the human authorship of the Bible, younger evangelicals in their formative years are increasingly willing to. How much better would it be if they had "orthodox" leaders and teachers who did not abandon them for their decisions to do so![8] Indeed, the primary purpose for writing this book is to suggest to those in leadership within evangelical communities that it is part of their spiritual responsibility to find ways to be there for those students who jettison their beliefs in inerrancy—even when the leaders wind up strongly disagreeing with their students. Evangelical leaders and teachers should not neglect their responsibilities by deciding to let students undertake these theological investigations by themselves lest the leaders' inaction inadvertently hasten some down that infamous slippery slope toward outright unbelief.

Many teachers commendably take a first step toward giving younger evangelicals a more flexible conceptual model for what the Bible really is. Following many writers, they turn to the Incarnation to help convey the dual nature of the Bible to their students.[9] Some go so far as to (i.e., inextricably) bind Scripture to Christ via theology.[10] Others head in a rather different direction inspired by the work of Karl Barth for the elucidation of a distinct dynamic between Christ and the Bible as Word of God.[11] The rest of the present chapter engages the first group of teachers by considering whether analogical comparisons between Christ and Scripture have the merit that some assume they have. To accomplish this, we shall take an all-too-brief look at how the doctrine of the Incarnation was historically articulated and then probe into what ways this Incarnation is said to illuminate an evangelical doctrine of Scripture.

InterVarsity, 2004), 112–132.

[8] Peter van Inwagen, for example, has helpfully considered the philosophical trajectory that this line of thought might initially take. See his "Genesis and Evolution," in *Reasoned Faith: Essays in Philosophical Theology in Honor of Norman Kretzmann.* (ed. E. Stump; Ithaca, NY: Cornell, 1993), 93–127.

[9] Following trajectories set, for example, by N. T. Wright (most recently in his *The Last Word: Beyond the Bible Wars to a New Understanding of the Authority of Scripture.* [New York: HarperCollins, 2005]) and others.

[10] Following trajectories set, for example, by John W. Wenham (*Christ and the Bible.* [Downers Grove, IL: InterVarsity, 1973]) and others.

[11] Following trajectories set, for example, by evangelical essays included in *How Karl Barth Changed My Mind.* (ed. D. K. McKim; Grand Rapids: Eerdmans, 1986).

II. Christ as Divine and Human

The manner in which the Christian gospel was originally presented to Second Temple Jews eventually posed at least two pressing questions to the early church. Who was Jesus and how did he relate to YHWH? And who is YHWH and how does he relate to Jesus? The adventures of the early church and their varied attempts to work through answers to these and related questions have been recorded elsewhere.[12] Some younger evangelicals have been taught to believe that there has always been some "embattled and persecuted orthodoxy maintaining a long and finally successful struggle against insidious heresy" even if, on the contrary, "at the outset nobody had a single clear answer which had always been known in the church and always recognized as true . . ."[13] Different parties and theologians made piecemeal contributions to what would become the orthodox consensus that eventually emerged over time. Those conservative evangelicals who implicitly and explicitly communicate that a distinctly evangelical line can be traced throughout the history of the Church are asked to set aside this "Foxe's Book of Martyrs approach" to Christianity and to appreciate how an early lack of consensus with regard to the nature(s) of Christ can encourage younger evangelicals who currently lack "a single clear answer" to their questions regarding the authority of Scripture.

Before turning to the analogy between Christ and Scripture, we must remind ourselves of the orthodox consensus for both the Trinitarian and the Christological formulations, over which controversies had occupied the church for almost the first millennium of its existence. We should indeed pause to reflect upon these since the Incarnation is in fact intrinsically tied to Trinitarian thinking: it is the second person of the Trinity who has become flesh in Jesus Christ. Therefore, the Trinity and the Incarnation will prove quite relevant to our discussion of Scripture if the proposed analogy is to really prove itself analogous in some way. For our summary of the doctrine of the Trinity, we shall consult Boethius' explication in *Whether Father, Son, and Holy Spirit Are Substantially Predicated of the Divinity*:

> If, then, I ask whether he who is called the Father is a substance, the answer is that he is a substance. And if I ask whether the Son is a substance, the reply is the same. So, too, no one would doubt that the Holy Spirit is also a substance. But when, on the other hand, I take together the Father, Son, and Holy Spirit, the result is

[12] For example in R. P. C. Hanson, *The Search for the Christian Doctrine of God: The Arian Controversy 318–381.* (Edinburgh: T & T Clark, 1988).

[13] Hanson, *The Search for the Christian Doctrine of God*, 870.

not several substances but one substance. The one substance of the Three, then, cannot be separated in any way or divided, nor is it combined into one as if from parts: it is simply one.[14]

Boethius explains further:

> From these things, then, we understand that Father, Son, and Holy Spirit are not predicated of the divinity in a substantial manner, but in some other way. For if each term were predicated substantially it would be affirmed of the three Persons both separately and collectively. It is evident that these terms are relative, for the Father is some one's Father, the Son is some one's Son, the Spirit is some one's Spirit. Hence not even Trinity is predicated substantially of God; for the Father is not Trinity—since he who is Father is not Son and Holy Spirit—nor yet, by parity of reasoning is the Son Trinity nor the Holy Spirit Trinity, but the Trinity consists in plurality of Persons, the unity in simplicity of substance.[15]

The relevant facts for us include that the Son is of the same substance as the Father and that the Son is not the same person as the Father. Now to Christology.

For a summary we turn to Tertullian:

> We see plainly the twofold state, which is not confounded, but conjoined in one person—Jesus, God and Man . . . so that the property of each nature is so wholly preserved that the Spirit on the one hand did all its own things in Jesus such as miracles, and mighty deeds and wonders; and the flesh on the other hand exhibited the affections which belong to it. It was hungry under the devil's temptation, thirsty with the Samaritan woman, wept over Lazarus, was troubled even unto death, at last actually died. If, however, it was only some third thing, some composite essence formed out of the two substances, like the electrum, there would be no distinct proofs apparent of either nature. [16]

Important here is that Jesus Christ is both fully God and fully man and not "some third thing." In other words, "Forasmuch . . . as the two substances acted distinctly, each in its own character, there necessarily accrued

---

[14] See Boethius, *Tractates, De Consolatione Philosophiae*. Loeb Classical Library 74. (trans. H. F. Stewart, E. K. Rand and S. J. Tester; Cambridge, MA: Harvard University Press, 1973), 33.

[15] See Boethius, *Tractates*, 35, 37

[16] Tertullian, *Adv. Prax.* 27 cited in Johannes Quasten, *Patrology* Volume 2. (Allen, Texas: Christian Classics, 1995), 328.

to them severally their own operations . . ."[17] With this succinct doctrinal overview, we are in position to ascertain potential problems raised by proposed analogies between Christ and Scripture.[18]

III. Sin and Error as Analogous

In general agreement with B. B. Warfield who was quoted earlier, evangelicals tend to view the Scriptures as God's Word: they were inspired by the Spirit and have a divine origin. Notwithstanding, the books of the Bible were also written by people who lived at various times and in various places: they are human documents throughout. An initial similarity does suggest itself between the Scriptures and the Incarnation insofar as in both the human and divine are simultaneously present. One might go further and observe that in both God is in some way revealed. Accordingly, countless scholars have sought to employ historical understandings of the latter in order to illumine the peculiarly evangelical character of the former.

Paul Enns represents a popular approach in the *Moody Handbook of Theology* where he provides a diagram that parallels the "Living Incarnate Word" and the "Living Written Word." He labels the former, "Jesus Christ," and the latter, "the Bible." He correlates Christ's human parents to the Bible's human authors; the Holy Spirit's overshadowing of Christ's birth to his superintending of the writing of Scripture; and Christ's sinlessness to the Bible's errorlessness.[19] Another example can be found in Harold O. J. Brown's essay, "The Arian Connection: Presuppositions of Errancy," in the edited work *Challenges to Inerrancy: A Theological Response*, where he writes:

> The inerrantist position is consistent with an orthodox (Chalcedonian) understanding of the relationship between the human and the divine natures in Christ, who is "in all things like us, without sin." The errantist position would be consistent with the opposite contention—although no evangelicals among the errantists wish to make it. We are speaking of the suggestion that Jesus,

---

[17] Tertullian, *Adv. Prax.* 27.

[18] For a concise account of the historical development of the Christian understanding of Incarnation, see Oskar Skarsaune, *Incarnation: Myth or Fact?* (trans. T. R. Skarsten; St. Louis, MO: Concordia Publishing House, 1991).

[19] (Chicago: Moody Press, 1989), 168. Geisler makes similar observations in *Systematic Theology*, 1.249–250, 259, 262–265.

as human, must have been capable of mistakes and perhaps even of sin, inasmuch as all men are sinners.[20]

He explicitly connects Christology to bibliology:

> The doctrine of errancy clearly implies that God cannot so interact with what is human in a way that He preserves it from all error without destroying its essential humanness. The Christological parallel would be the suggestion that God cannot assume a human nature in Christ without totally overwhelming His essential humanness . . .
>
> . . . [T]he same theological procedure that makes one feel obliged to posit errors in no-longer-existent autographs ought also to lead one to posit errors or even sin in the God-man, Jesus Christ.[21]

These two evangelical works are representative of those inerrantists who believe that the Incarnation is a good model for our understanding of Scripture as Word of God and that, furthermore, a crucial correspondence obtains on this Scripture-Christ ratio such that human error in the former is tantamount to sin in the latter. But should error somehow point toward sin or even be the analogous counterpart to sin?

There are at least two reasons that sin and error are not analogous. First of all, the analogy seems to suggest that somehow sin and error can be directly linked, but are there not errors that have nothing to do with sin? Could Adam before the fall have thrown a rock intending to hit a tree and then hit Eve by mistake? Could he ever have mistaken a turkey buzzard in the sky for an eagle? Might Jesus have believed and talked to others about how the Earth was some kind of flat disc? Or, more to the point, might Jesus ever have given false (or misleading) information because the good obtained by doing so outweighed the consequences of the resultant false beliefs? For example, in John 7.8 (where the first occurrence of the word "yet" in the KJV and NIV is disavowed by textual critics) Jesus appears to either tell a white lie or at least deliberately give a very misleading response to a rather straightforward question.[22] Even if one were to accept Brown's, Keener's (and countless others') accounts for Jesus' brothers' misunder-

---

[20] (ed. Gordon R. Lewis and Bruce Demarest; Chicago: Moody Press, 1984), 383–401, 388–389.

[21] Brown, "Arian," 390–391.

[22] See Bruce Metzger, *The Text of the New Testament: Its Transmission, Corruption, and Restoration.* 3rd ed. (New York: Oxford University Press, 1992), 202, and C. K. Barrett, *The Gospel According to St John: An Introduction with Commentary and Notes on the Greek Text.* (London: SPCK, 1965), 258.

standing in terms of his brothers' failure to realize that Jesus "[speaks] on the level of the divine plan" and not "on the purely natural level," there are still some deliberately false beliefs resulting from Jesus' evasive response in order that he could better accomplish what he wanted when he finally did go up to the feast.[23] It could even be the case that the good accomplished was enhanced precisely because his brothers began telling people that Jesus would not be going.[24] Either way, the good achieved by Jesus' answer might be said to outweigh the bad that resulted from his brothers' false beliefs. Suffice it to say that the link between sin and error is not obviously clear. The inerrantist ploy is to involve sin and error in an all-or-nothing gambit, but these terms are open for discussion. Examples like the ones presented above raise at least two interesting questions: Do all of these cases qualify as "errors" (if they do, do they qualify in the same way), and are they all necessarily connected with sin?

Second, the contexts within which each theological proposal was introduced differ so significantly that meaningful points of contact may be forced. To take it one step further, the contexts within which the doctrine of inerrancy was articulated, especially that part of it that acknowledges the human component of Scripture, were not those in response to which the prominence of the Word of God was initially delineated. Surely Christology has always played a critical role in the Protestant understanding of Scripture; seventeenth (and sixteenth) century reformers clearly maintained a strong emphasis on the Word of God. However, early discussion concerning the Word of God took place within a different social, philosophical and theological context than that which we presently inhabit. Noted church historian Richard Muller explains that

> Reformed orthodoxy was deeply aware of the soteriological and epistemological necessity of a Mediator to bridge the gap between God and man and also of the sole and gracious initiative from God's side.[25]

When contrasting what he terms "Reformed orthodoxy" with what has been termed "neo-orthodoxy," Muller states that early Protestant theolo-

---

[23] See Raymond E. Brown, *The Gospel According to John I–XII*. Anchor Bible 29. (Garden City, NY: Doubleday, 1966), 308, and Craig S. Keener, *The Gospel of John: A Commentary Volume 1*. (Peabody, MA: Hendrickson Publishers, 2003), 704–708. Quotes are from Brown, 318.

[24] Compare the pertinent section under the entry "Deception and Lying" in John J. Pilch, *The Cutlural Dictionary of the Bible*. (Collegeville, MN: The Liturgical Press, 1999), 49.

[25] "Christ—The Revelation or Revealer? Brunner and Reformed Orthodoxy on the Doctrine of the Word of God" *JETS* 26 (1983): 307–319, 317.

gians were concerned with enabling human relations with and knowledge of God in spite of the chasm that separates the holy from the sinful and the infinite from the finite. As Muller makes clear, they were tending to both historical and ontological problems. These objectives (and others like them) caused many Reformers to conclude that ". . . Christ, the Revelation and the Revealer, is both the focus and the end of the scriptural Word and the One by whom and in whom the nature and will of God is made manifest."[26] God's ability to interact with the human was not the primary issue for their great respect for the Word. In fact, in many respects, the early Protestant theologies of the Word hearken back to the medieval debates over what (if anything) could be known of God and how these things could be known. The conclusion that the Mediator was needed in order that humans might be reconciled with God seemed in many of the Reformers' minds to require that the Mediator be present at all times when humans interact with God. This includes the times during and the means by which this need for reconciliation was communicated. The dire need of a Mediator at every instance was also a primary reason why Martin Luther insisted upon the bodily presence of Christ in the Eucharist (see chapter 4). It was within this context of mediation that Protestant theologies of the Word were originally formulated.

How does this motivation for a theology of the Word and the orthodox expression of the Incarnation combine to yield a fruitful analogy between Christ and Scripture? The constraints of the present chapter do no allow a full historical investigation into the matter, but we can helpfully compare what the ancients surmised for Christ with what Warfield surmised for the Bible. Compare Tertullian, quoted above:

> Forasmuch . . . as the two substances acted distinctly, each in its own character, there necessarily accrued to them severally their own operations . . .

with Warfield:

> All the qualities of divinity and of humanity are to be sought and may be found in every portion of and element of Scripture. While, on the other hand, no quality inconsistent with either divinity or humanity can be found in any portion or element of Scripture.[27]

---

[26] Muller, "Christ," 319.

[27] "The Divine and Human in the Bible" taken from *Evolution, Science and Scripture: Selected Writings of B. B. Warfield.* (ed. Mark A. Noll and David N. Livingstone; Grand Rapids: Baker, 2000), 51–58, 57.

It is interesting to note that Warfield makes no mention of the Incarnation in this article. He warns that neither the divine nor the human should be "exceedingly exaggerated" and that the divine and the human should not be conceived in such a way as to set the one against the other. Yet the most important thing to note for the present discussion is that Warfield explicitly claims that he was influenced toward this way of putting the matter by his reflections upon (presumably Reformed interpretations of) God's *providence* and God's *grace*: no mention is made of the Incarnation.[28]

As stated above, a prevalent Reformed understanding of the Word was that just as the Mediator was needed in order that humans might be reconciled with God seemed to require that the Mediator be present at all times when humans interact with God. Hence the Mediator must be present at all times as the Spirit communicates to believers in the Bible. Compare this line of reasoning with the early motivation for insisting upon Christ's humanity: Christians in antiquity argued that Christ must be fully human for only in this way could he identify with ordinary human beings and affect the salvation that humans so desperately need. For example, Ambrose of Milan (4th century C. E.) writes in a letter to Sabinus: ". . . so in that human form there was nothing wanting in Him so as to cause Him to be judged imperfect as Man; for He came in order to save man altogether . . . for if aught was wanting to Him as Man, then He did not redeem the whole man . . ."[29] and both Gregory of Nazianzus (4th century C. E.) and John of Damascus (8th century C. E.) write: "For that which He has not assumed He has not healed . . ."[30] Thus ancient Christian writers understood that the Mediator (1 Tim 2.5, etc.) was necessarily fully human in order that humans could be redeemed.

So what analogy might be drawn? A comparison between the Fathers and Warfield shows that a divine-human Mediator is necessary for the possibility of salvation on the one hand and for the possibility of communication on the other. Both salvation and communication require divine and human components for their successful execution. The salvation—the an-

---

[28] Compare Warfield's remarks in "The Biblical Idea of Inspiration" in *The Inspiration and Authority of the Bible.* (Phillipsburg, NJ: Presbyterian and Reformed Publishing Co., 1948), 131–166, 162–163. Kevin J. Vanhoozer follows the same Reformed trajectory when he remarks: "[N]o doctrine of Scripture without a doctrine of providence." See Vanhoozer, *First Theology: God, Scripture and Hermeneutics.* (Downers Grove, IL: InterVarsity, 2002), 131.

[29] *Letter XLVIII.* Source: http://www.tertullian.org/fathers/ambrose_letters_05_letters41_50.htm#Letter48.

[30] *Letter CI* and *On the Orthodox Faith,* III.12, respectively, cited in Thomas C. Oden, *Systematic Theology Volume Two: The Living Word.* (HarperCollins, 1992, repr. Peabody, MA: Prince Press, 1998), 128–129.

cient writers were adamant about this—was accomplished by the assumption of full humanity and by the living and dying of a real human life that was *without sin*. The communication—Warfield insists upon this—was accomplished by divinely inspired human writings in a manner adequate for the conveyance of "the mind and will of God."[31] The communication provides the soul with a "sure ground for a proper knowledge of itself, its condition, and its need, or for a proper knowledge of God's provisions of mercy for it and his promises of grace to it . . ."[32]—what Warfield equates (at least in this article) with having "invariable truth," being "infallible" and "trustworthy," and elsewhere as the equivalent of being *without errors*.

So then, without Christ's sinlessness, redemption is not possibly accomplished (II Cor 5.21, etc.); but "were there no such thing as [plenary] inspiration, Christianity would [still] be true, and all its essential doctrines would be credibly witnessed to us in the generally trustworthy reports of the teaching of our Lord and of His authoritative agents in founding the Church . . ."[33] Accordingly a dis-analogy obtains where "without sin" is requisite for salvation, but "without error" is by no means requisite for communication. The Mediator must surely be present in such a way that the humanity involved is without sin in the one case but *not* necessarily without error in the second case.

So a significant disparity exists here with regard to necessity. It is very important to note that the analogical point of comparison cannot be necessity. In fact, the point needs to be stressed because it is seldom acknowledged by conservative evangelical teachers and leaders. (Geisler illustrates the point for when he interacts with the "objection" that inerrancy is an unnecessary doctrine he simply reiterates his syllogistic argument from God the Father.[34]) And when it *is* acknowledged, evangelical leaders and teachers are wont to claim that it is obviously beneath God to provide an errant Bible.[35] The concession is valid but this fact is fre-

[31] Warfield, "The Real Problem of Inspiration" in *The Inspiration and Authority of the Bible*. (Phillipsburg, NJ: Presbyterian and Reformed Publishing Co., 1948), 169–226, 173.

[32] Warfield, "The Church Doctrine of Inspiration" in *The Inspiration and Authority of the Bible*, 105–128, 124.

[33] Warfield, "The Real Problem of Inspiration," 210.

[34] See *Systematic Theology*, 1.503–504.

[35] For example, when Grudem responds to those who suggest that "accommodation [to error] was not necessary for effective communication . . ." he complains that "this theory makes God out to be unwise." See Wayne Grudem, "Scripture's Self-Attestation and the Problem of Formulating a Doctrine of Scripture" in *Scripture and Truth*. (ed. D. A. Carson and J. D. Woodbridge; repr. Grand Rapids: Baker Books, 1992), 19–59, 55.

quently concealed from evangelical students. The concession alone would go a long way toward granting some younger evangelicals the theological and spiritual breathing room they are desperately looking for. Why burden them further by suggesting to these believers, implicitly or otherwise, that any alternate views of Scripture are invariably headed toward unbelief?

IV. Two Incommensurate Standards

It remains, then, for us to briefly examine the two main points of the proposed incarnational analogy, "sin" and "error," in order to determine what the point of analogy might actually be and ponder (since it does not involve necessity) whether it is finally helpful to draw specific attention to it.

Despite its currency, sin is an unusually difficult word to define with precision. Cornelius Plantinga reminds us that sin is not a moral term, but a theological one.[36] Very generally, sin is an offense, a severing of relations, not only against another or oneself, but also, and especially, against God.[37] Josef Pieper writes that sin is "a failure that has been committed before a superhuman judging power . . ."[38] Pieper helpfully points out how theologians have historically distinguished between the act of sin and the *macula* (stain) left by the sinful act.[39] Scripture makes at least one attempt to describe sin in James 1.14–15: "Temptation comes when anyone is lured and dragged away by his own desires; then desire conceives and gives birth to sin, and sin when it is full-grown breeds death" (REB). This is a fine translation of the Greek that provides a terse metaphorical summary of how sin is born. First, a person is "lured and dragged away" by his own desire. Next, that same desire "conceives" (συλλαβουσα) and "gives birth" (τικτει) to sin. The original desire, then, has been transformed in such a way that there now exists some new passion along side it.[40] The

---

[36] He writes, "Sin is a religious concept, not just a moral one . . . Sin is the smearing of a relationship, the grieving of one's divine parent and benefactor, a betrayal of the partner to whom one is joined by a holy bond." *Not the Way It's Supposed to Be: A Breviary of Sin.* (Grand Rapids: Eerdmans, 1995), 12.

[37] See Thomas Aquinas, *Summa Theologicae*, 2.1.72.4 where it is asked if it is fitting to classify sins into those against oneself, those against another and those against God.

[38] *The Concept of Sin.* (South Bend, IN: St. Augustine's Press, 2001), 7.

[39] *The Concept of Sin*, 84. Pieper points out that Plato identified these same two parts to sin at the end of the *Gorgias*.

[40] Precisely when desire conceives sin seems more difficult to describe. Is it only upon actually acting out some unrestrained desire or merely upon being dragged away by one's desire? The Lord's comments in Matt 5.28 seem to suggest that desire run amok can count as sin even without the act. Aquinas considers the volition of any sin to be an interior act

passion is not a second "rational will" or a distinct "soul of the flesh", but an intense "habit or necessity . . . [that] arouse a man, and withdraw him from divine and spiritual things."[41] This new passion is akin to the original desire, but not equal with it. Rather, it has its own ability to "breed" (αποκυεω) something apart from itself. "Breed" carries the idea that *that which has been pregnant* is giving birth.[42] The sense is that sin is always "pregnant" with death. Though the length of the pregnancy may vary ("when it is full-grown"), its "offspring" is inevitably death. Hence, God could say, "The day you eat from that, you are surely doomed to die" (Gen 2.17, REB). Although much more might obviously be said here, we must content ourselves with the observation that Christ was tested in every way without sin insofar as he lived his life, among other things, without ever allowing his desires to be dragged away and become an offense against God the Father.

Regarding the other point of analogy, "error" seems an equally difficult word to define. Assuming that the term error should be understood as the opposite of truth, Geisler affirms that "the Bible has no errors of any kind" and that "[t]here are no mistakes or incorrect statements in the Bible."[43] Error in this context of inerrancy means a failure to correspond with the facts or a failure to correspond "to the way things really are." Geisler goes on to say that errorlessness of Scripture should not extend "merely [to] what the author intends [since] then the Bible can be wholly true and yet contain factual errors—as strange as this may seem."[44] Alan Padgett, by contrast, is persuaded that "[t]he church needs to pay a little more attention to its own internal grammar and a bit less attention to logic, philosophy, and the sciences, in seeking to answer the question 'what is truth?'" He, in a rather Heideggerian fashion, "*understand[s] truth as the mediated disclosure of being* (or reality)."[45] Roger Nicole, in an attempt to

and concedes that "it is truer to say that a sin can be without an act; else the circumstantial acts and occasions would be essential to other actual sins" (*Summa Th.* 2.1.74.5).

[41] Origen, *De Principiis.* 3.4.4.

[42] See "αποκυεω" in *BDAG*, 3rd ed, 114. It should be observed that the REB has apparently switched the order of the participles in the preceding clause that reads εξελκομενος και δελεαζομενος (i.e, REB reads "lure and drag away" as opposed to "drag away and lure"). The REB translation was chosen for its recognition of the nuance between "give birth to" and "breed."

[43] *Systematic Theology*, 1.495.

[44] *Systematic Theology*, 1.112.

[45] Alan G. Padgett, "'I Am the Truth': An Understanding of Truth from Christology for Scripture" in *But Is It True? The Bible and the Question of Truth.* (ed. A. G. Padgett and P. R. Keifert; Grand Rapids: Eerdmans, 2006), 104–114, 106, italics in original.

articulate what a full-orbed concept of 'truth' might look like for evangelicals, writes: "*The full Bible concept of truth involves factuality, faithfulness, and completeness.*" He continues:

> Those who have stressed one of these features in order to downgrade either or both of the others are falling short of the biblical pattern. Notably, those who have stressed faithfulness, as if conformity to fact did not matter, are failing grievously to give proper attention to what constitutes probably a majority of the [biblical] passages in which the word *truth* is used.[46]

(We should point out here that while evangelical proponents of speech act theory can certainly help a younger evangelical read her Bible more judiciously, it does not prevent her from finally agreeing with Charles Augustus Briggs, the evangelical taboo in question. Speech act theory may actually *facilitate* her conversion.[47]) Dembski, for his part, claims to "change the terms of this debate" by arguing that "attributing error to Scripture is itself highly problematic—indeed, more problematic than holding to an inerrant Scripture."[48] He reminds readers that they must take sufficient account of "perspectives" when dealing with attribution of error, explaining: "[P]eople commit errors when despite intending to assert truth, they actually assert falsehood . . . In charging people with error, we must enter their perspective so that we may know precisely what they are claiming."[49] In light of these and other discussions that are *still* taking place over what it might mean for the bible to err, is it any wonder that when J. P. Moreland writes on whether belief in an inerrant Bible is rational he diplomatically sidesteps the matter of definition and rather "assumes for the sake of argument" that evangelicals "possess a clear definition of inerrancy as it is understood by, say, the Evangelical Theological Society," reasoning tongue-in-cheek that "[a]fter all, proponents and opponents of inerrancy have understood the doctrine well enough to argue about it"?[50]

---

[46] "The Biblical Concept of Truth" in *Scripture and Truth.* (ed. D. A. Carson and J. D. Woodbridge; repr. Grand Rapids: Baker Books, 1992), 287–298, 296, italics in original.

[47] Compare Nicholas Wolterstorff, "The Promise of Speech-act Theory for Biblical Interpretation" in *After Pentecost: Language and Biblical Interpretation.* Scripture and Hermeneutics 2. (ed. C. Bartholomew, C. Greene, and K. Möller; Grand Rapids: Zondervan, 2001), 73–90, 85.

[48] William A. Dembski, "The Problem of Error in Scripture" in *Unapologetic Apologetics: Meeting the Challenges of Theological Studies.* (ed. W. A. Dembski and J. W. Richards; Downers Grove, IL: InterVarsity, 2001), 79–94, 80.

[49] Dembski, "The Problem of Error in Scripture", 86.

[50] "The Rationality of Belief in Inerrancy" in *Biblical Authority and Conservative*

For the sake of the present discussion, we shall take Nicole's understanding as representative of those who adopt the inerrancy position in view here: error is that "which is not in conformity with objective truth."[51] The dimension of error of interest is that which fails to correspond to reality. So when an evangelical claims that "no errant assertion occurs" in the Bible, he means that the Bible is trustworthy in not only "salvific matters" but also "when it treats of history [and] the external world."[52] In short, an error is to "[claim] to know what is not the case."[53]

Setting our definitions side by side, it is not readily apparent in what way sin and error might be analogous terms:

- allowing desires to be dragged away and become an offense to God.

- making a claim that is not in conformity with objective truth.

An initial comparison suggests that both minimally involve failures to conform to some kind of standard: the former being God's expectations for human living and the second being the way things really are. This seems to be the point of analogy that many writers have in mind when they compare sinlessness and errorlessness, a failure to meet some standard. Recall Harold O. J. Brown's remarks above: "[T]he same theological procedure that makes one feel obliged to posit errors in no-longer-existent autographs ought also to lead one to posit errors or even sin in the God-man, Jesus Christ."[54] "Errors or even sin"—to mention the two words in this manner admits what was suggested earlier: that the one does not entail the other. It also reveals an understanding that whatever relation error and sin might have, sin is in some way an exacerbation of error. The latter (in the quote) can somehow be said to be an extreme of the former. Given that they are categorically distinct, the only apparent way that sin can be seen as more severe than error in some respect is if the aspect in mind is a failure to meet a standard. And here the analogy surrenders its serviceability for younger evangelicals. Without going into detail about how one might

Perspectives: Viewpoints from Trinity Journal. (ed. D. Moo; Grand Rapids: Kregel Publications,1997),155–165, 155.

[51] Roger Nicole, "The Nature of Inerrancy" in *Inerrancy and Common Sense.* (ed. R. R. Nicole and J. R. Michaels; Grand Rapids: Baker, 1980), 71–95, 88.

[52] See Carson's comments on a proposal that aims to restrict the Bible's inerrancy to matters that pertain to redemption in D. A. Carson, "Recent Developments in the Doctrine of Scripture" in *Hermeneutics, Authority, and Canon.* (ed. D. A. Carson and J. D. Woodbridge; Grand Rapids: Zondervan, 1986), 5–48, 31.

[53] Dembski, "The Problem of Error in Scripture", 85.

[54] Brown, "Arian", 390–391.

philosophically question the correspondence standard for error, it seems clear that whether it matters if something meets a proposed standard will ultimately depend upon the consequences that ensue for failing to meet that standard. If the consequences are not serious, then whether something has met a standard is of no concern. However, if the consequences are serious, then whether a standard is met will be of great interest.

The majority of evangelicals will agree that it is of immense import that Christ lived without sin and that he, in fact, met all of God's standards for human living. However, whether the Bible meets the standard of corresponding to reality does not have anywhere near the same urgency. The main consequence for not meeting this standard is an imposition of "a considerable hermeneutical burden on any would-be interpreter of special revelation. For he has to determine the exact limits of each kind of revelation, otherwise it may happen that the mistaken beliefs of men would be equated the special revelation of God"[55]—a consequence many younger evangelicals are more than willing to live with (but not in excommunication from their evangelical leaders and teachers).[56] Since the consequences for failing to meet these two standards are not at all commensurate in the judgment of younger evangelicals, the analogy between the Incarnation and Scripture is not nearly as compelling as some have insisted.[57]

IV. Conclusion

An ancient Jewish tradition claims that Abraham kept the whole Torah of Israel even before the Torah had been given. The Old Testament, of course, indicates no such thing. Perhaps evangelicals can take a cue from the way those who posited this tradition did so in order to legitimate an ancient religious program. Could it be that evangelical concern for the legitimacy

---

[55] Paul Helm, *The Divine Revelation: The Basic Issues.* (Vancouver: Regent College Publishing, 1982), 90. "[E]ach kind of revelation" refers to his distinction between revelation as "recording/reporting" and revelation as "disclosing/endorsing."

[56] Disagreeing, for example, with John Warwick Montgomery's assessment in "Biblical Inerrancy: What is at Stake?" in *God's Inerrant Word: An International Symposium on the Trustworthiness of Scripture.* (ed. J. W. Montgomery; Minneapolis: Bethany Fellowship, Inc., 1974), 15–42.

[57] David Wells suggests that a helpful analogy can be seen in how the function of each depends crucially on the nature of each, but as Robert Sloan points out, the Incarnation is not needed to make this point. Sloan argues rather that the authority of the Bible is secured by the truthfulness of Christianity and not by Christ's divinity. See David F. Wells, "Word and World: Biblical Authority and The Quandary of Modernity" and Robert Sloan, "Response to David F. Wells" in *Evangelical Affirmations.* (ed. K. S. Kantzer and C. F. H. Henry; Grand Rapids: Zondervan, 1990), 153–175, 177–190.

of a contemporary religious schema manifests itself in the insistence of an inerrancy doctrine? The case in point is the binding of the doctrine of Scripture to orthodox Christology in such a way that the cogency of one determines the cogency of the other. Incorporating bibliology into Christological considerations seems a well-intentioned attempt to link necessity with necessity, but as we have seen, necessity is neither here nor there for inerrancy. In the long run, employing this analogy with an aim of securing Scripture's absolute authority will not prove as helpful as its proponents seem to think. Pushed too far, it might almost become a form of spiritual abuse. The usefulness of the analogy is limited to its suggestion to students that they should guard themselves against the analogical extremes of a human-only Bible or of a divine-only Bible. Each aspect must be given its full due. How? Well, that's the million dollar question. An incarnational analogy does not help students see how to do this; it only suggests that they remain vigilant that either dimension is not suppressed.[58] But the Incarnation is not necessary for appreciating this; the providence of God will suffice.[59]

It is not mentioned often enough that the question among younger evangelicals is not whether God *could* have given an inerrant Bible, but whether he, in fact, did. This might become easier to see when contemporary concerns about the authority of Scripture are compared with those involved in other historical controversies, especially those that have nothing to do with the doctrine of Scripture. By illustrating how, very generally

---

[58] See, for example, the remarks made in the "Introduction" to *Evangelicals and Scripture: Tradition, Authority, and Hermeneutics.* (ed. V. Bacote, L. C. Miguelez, and D. L. Okholm; Downers Grove, IL: InterVarsity, 2004), 7, and Pete Enns, *Inspiration and Incarnation: Evangelicals and Problem of the Old Testament.* (Grand Rapids: Baker, 2005), 18, 168. Compare the discussion in G. C. Berkouwer, *Holy Scripture.* (Grand Rapids: Eerdmans, 1975), 195–212. Increasingly, younger evangelicals are sensing that inerrancy is not a helpful answer to the How? question.

[59] Some Dutch Calvinists may agree that Christology is a red herring for inerrancy but insist that predestinarian salvation is the model for all of God's interactions with the world, including all realms of human knowledge. My stance is this: Reason may not be enough for salvation, but it is certainly enough to judge whether Scripture is inerrant *in the way that many younger evangelicals are taught when they first learn Christ*. (I am playing here with the title of Nicholas Wolterstorff's "Is Reason Enough?" in *Contemporary Perspectives on Religious Epistemology*. [ed. R. D. Geivett and B. Sweetman; New York: Oxford University Press, 1992], 142–149.) In my defense, I extrapolate remarks made by Calvinist historian Richard A. Muller regarding the use of reason. See Muller, "Historiography in the Service of Theology and Worship: Toward Dialogue with John Frame" *WTJ* 59 (1997): 301–310. Although some Westminster-type Dutch Calvinists will censure the perceived demon of Arminius or an abject failure to grasp the epistemological problem, I can only reply that the Bible was made for man and not man for the Bible.

speaking, theological construction is heavily influenced by cultural and sociological factors, we might obtain a more objective vantage on our own preoccupation with the Bible. Such historical comparisons can help clear the air, so to speak, and enable one to see familiar scenarios in new light.

The next Recognition examines a debate involving a rather unevangelical doctrine: the sacrament of the Eucharist. Perhaps by considering parallels between the controversy over the Eucharist and the controversy over inerrancy, evangelical leaders and teachers (and younger evangelicals themselves) will grow more reluctant to so closely bind their concern for the authority of Scripture with their existential search for Christ.

Recognition Four

Young Evangelicals Can Learn from an Old Controversy

OVER THE past 15 years or so, it seems that the "battle for the Bible" has evolved in such a way that *within evangelicalism* one can discern the emergence of a conservative group, a moderate sector and a liberal constituency that vaguely resembles the parities of the old Fundamentalist era.[1] Expectedly, the three can be partially identified by their respective views on Scripture, whether divine or human traits are emphasized and in what ways. Of course, not all in each category agree with each other and there are always borderline cases, but in terms of allegiance it seems to me that, perhaps subconsciously, evangelicals are more concerned with identifying themselves by who they are *not* rather than who they *are*.

This recognition involves seeing that the pattern of disagreement with respect to the nature of Scripture follows that of many other disagreements in church history. The pattern I have in mind involves the unsuspecting collusion of a painful searching for God in the midst of a changing culture and a concomitant quest for social and ecclesial belonging. These two factors can overwhelmingly compel believers to take positions that are overly rigid and unusually insistent. This is how many have learned to avoid being "guilty by association." Unaffected by spiritual disquiet or social displacement, believers might otherwise pursue more nuanced positions, but burdened by these pressures, nuance can easily give way to a preoccupation for niceties. A simplistic description of contemporary intrachurch disputes illustrates the pattern: Fundamentalists do not want to be mistaken for moderates; moderates for liberals or fundamentalists; liberal evangelicals for either of the others, even though, theoretically, all comprise the same body of Christ. Such concern over self-identification may

---

[1] "Liberal" evangelicals have called themselves "post-evangelical" or even "post-conservative." Likewise, some classically liberal Christian writers have moved on to become "post-liberals." Among the many recent accounts, Gary Dorrien's *The Remaking of Evangelical Theology* (Louisville, KY: Westminster John Knox Press, 1998) is especially recommended.

stem from many factors, but charitably we proffer the widespread belief that "one's fellowship is indicative of where one's heart is."[2]

To help understand this pattern, it may prove helpful to compare the current situation with a controversy that arose during the Reformation over the Eucharist. That the Eucharist meal from its very institution would be a perpetual source of division amongst and within Christian churches is evinced as early as Paul's attempt to explain the meal in his first letter to the Corinthians. As many church historians have remarked, the ramifications of the fact that the Lord Jesus had never given his followers a proscriptive manual for church government, practice and discipline continue to beleaguer Christendom. To this day, a variety of opinions persist regarding the Lord's Supper with respect to its status as a sacrament, its purpose, its efficacy, its frequency, its manner of presentation and distribution, its constituency (i.e., who can rightfully partake), and so on. Although it is difficult to adequately apprehend the differences between the times of the Reformation and the present, we shall revisit one side of the Eucharist controversy—that which centers upon Martin Luther—in an attempt to gain some perspective on squabbles that persist even today over the place and nature of Scripture and, more importantly, the need to discriminately identify believers.

I. A Medieval Harbinger

It is fascinating to observe how concern over what can or cannot be believed is always at least tacitly defined by what competing groups believe or disavow. Personal spiritual predicaments and socio-ecclesial relations have an often underappreciated impact upon what Christians believe. Martin Luther's view of the real presence in the Lord's Supper proves no exception when examined in light of his painful existential plight, his consequential insistence upon the Word and the socio-political order that were for him embodied in the rival views of the Roman church and those of the other Reformers. Perhaps, the most peculiar feature of Luther's Eucharistic view is better understood through medieval categories.

The Lutheran view of the Eucharist is known as consubstantiation. The *Dictionary of Doctrinal and Historical Theology* defines "consubstantiation" as "the coexistence of the Real Presence of Christ's Body and blood and the bread and wine."[3] However, *The Encyclopedia of the Lutheran*

---

[2] B. Ramm, *The Evangelical Heritage: A Study in Historical Theology.* (Grand Rapids: Baker, 1973), 108.

[3] (ed. John Henry Blunt; London, Oxford and Cambridge: Rivingtons, 1871), 151.

Church points out that definitions such as these are incorrect, or at best misleading, insofar as they might imply that it is *upon consecration* that the elements are joined with the Real Presence. *The Encyclopedia* clarifies that only *upon reception* does the joining occur.[4] This idea of consubstantiation is sometimes associated with Martin Luther himself. Although one might be tempted to view Luther in light of modern day Evangelical Lutheranism, it will prove more helpful to trace the contours of the argument from the other direction.

In the ninth century C.E. there was a dispute involving two Benedictine monks at Corbie. One monk, Radbertus, had written a book that explicitly argued that the sacrament of the Eucharist "through the consecration of his sacrament by his invisible power, effects in the substance of the bread and wine the flesh and blood of Christ."[5] As Everett Ferguson has pointed out, throughout the early church two main strands of thought with regard to the Eucharist had coincided without apparent conflict.[6] Ferguson considers Ambrose and Augustine to be representatives of the two dominant understandings of the Lord's Supper in the early church: the former emphasized an actual "metabolism" and the latter focused upon symbolism. Without subjecting Ferguson's interpretation of the history of this sacrament to scrutiny, it can be granted that Radbertus sought "to combine the religious conceptions of the church at large with the theory of Augustine."[7] In other words, Radbertus conjoined metabolism and symbolism. He asserted that there was a reality present in the elements, the reality of the body of Christ, and that "this body is in substance the same body in which Christ was born, suffered, rose from the dead, and which he still possesses in heaven."[8] At the same time, Radbertus empha-

---

[4] (ed. J. Bodensieck; Minneapolis: Augsburg, 1965).

[5] *De Corpore et Sanguine Domini* 3.4 as cited in R. Seeburg, *The History of Doctrines*, 2.41.2, (trans. Charles E. Hay; Grand Rapids: Baker, 1978).

[6] "The Lord's Supper in Church History: The Early Church Through the Medieval Period" in *The Lord's Supper: Believers Church Perspectives*. (ed. Dale R. Stoffer; Scottdale, PA: Herald Press, 1997), 21–45.

[7] Seeburg, *The History of Doctrines*, 2.41.2.

[8] Seeburg, *The History of Doctrines*, 2.41.2, In 2.14.1, Seeburg also mentions that in the early church "two methods of presenting the subject [the Lord's Supper] are found side by side without any attempt at discrimination." Compare Ralph W. Quere, "Changes and Constants: Structure in Luther's Understanding of the Real Presence in the 1520's," *The Sixteenth Century Journal* 16 (1985): 45–76, 46. The sixteenth century Catholic theologian, Cardinal Thomas Cajetan, explained that "one should, however, note that whenever these ancient writers say that the sacrament is a sign or figure of the body of Christ, or something to this effect, they do speak the truth . . . but have not as a consequence denied the reality

sized that the elements of the sacrament were symbols of a greater reality in that although the bread and the wine never cease to appear, feel and taste like bread and wine, a spiritual effect is exacted:[9]

> They are called sacraments either because they are secret in that in the visible act divinity inwardly accomplished something secretly through the corporeal appearance, or from the sanctifying conse-cration, because the Holy Spirit, remaining in the body of Christ, latently accomplishes for the salvation of the faithful all these mys-tical sacraments under the cover of things visible.[10]

We should point out here that, among other things, Radbertus' two emphases introduce an underlying tension between the ordinary workings of the natural world and the extraordinary workings of the divine realm. The tension was such that another monk, Ratramnus, who was from the same order, was asked to respond to Radbertus' theory.[11] Ratramnus iso-lated two points in his response. He addressed the manner in which Christ was present in the sacrament and the relation between his presence in the Eucharist and his historical presence in his earthly body. Radbertus, as we saw above, identifies Christ's presence in the sacrament with his historical, earthly body. Ratramnus, for his part, agreed with Radbertus insofar as he (Radbertus) held that the Lord's Supper "exhibits one thing outwardly to the human sense and proclaims another thing inwardly to the minds of the faithful."[12] This distinction in Ratramnus' mind, though, called for a further distinction between the body of Christ as it was present in the ele-ments and the historical body of Christ that actually walked the earth. On this latter point the two Benedictine monks differed in their opinions.

---

contained beneath the figure." See his "Errors on the Lord's Supper—Instruction for the Nuntio, 1525" in *Cajetan Responds: A Reader in Reformation Controversy.* (ed. and trans. Jared Wicks, S.J.; Washington, D.C.: The Catholic University of America Press, 1978), 153–173, 172. Citing *De Corpore* 1.2; 4.3; 21.9.

[9] This view later developed into the metaphysical theory of transubstantiation.

[10] *Corp* 3.1, quoted in Ferguson, "Lord's Supper," 36.

[11] For a brief overview of the affair, including its broader connections to Carolingian hermeneutics and ecclesiology, see Willemien Otten, "Carolingian Theology" in *The Medieval Theologians.* (ed. G. R. Evans; Malden, MA: Blackwell, 2001), 65–82 of which 73–76 pertain to the present topic. Ratramnus' book, incidentally, had the same title as that of Radbertus.

[12] Ratramnus, *Corp* 9, quoted in Jaroslav Pelikan, *The Growth of Medieval Theology (600-1100).* The Christian Tradition: A History of the Development of Doctrine 3. (Chicago: University of Chicago, 1978), 76–77.

The outcome of the dispute[13] is of less interest to us here than the observation that there were competing understandings of the relation between an ordinary natural world in which things happen in accord with a certain order and an extraordinary divine realm in which the given order of things can be superceded. This is not to suggest that medieval theologians (or the Reformers) entertained some version of naturalism *vis-à-vis* supernaturalism, but the observation does broach an ongoing discussion concerning the relation between what was later brought to the fore by Gabriel Biel in terms of God's *potentia absoluta* and God's *potentia ordinata*.[14] As Oberman points out, these terms became formative in theological discussions beginning with Duns Scotus;[15] however, the concepts were present much earlier and touched upon everything from Christology to Mariology to ecclesiology.[16] In any event, many of the disputes that broke out later during the Reformation are illuminated by the historical observation that the Church had for some time been arguing over how to relate the manner in which God *has chosen* to work with the fact that God *is able* to work in ways other than those which he has chosen.[17] In other words, what does the fact that God *has chosen* to operate in a certain fashion indicate with regard to how God *is able* to operate and what does the fact that God *can* operate in any fashion that he pleases ramify with respect to how God *has chosen* to operate? Or again, in what ways, if any, has God bound himself to do things in accord with the means that he has chosen? And in what ways do God's absolute freedom, authority and power relativize, diminish, or minimize those means by which he has chosen to accomplish his will?

Any reader familiar with the literature on the Eucharist controversy during the Reformation knows that scholarly discussions tend to focus upon different understandings of symbols and their relations with the realities they signify. We have opted to pursue another point of departure in order to connect the Reformation dispute with those among present day evangelicals. The relation of the two orders (*ordinata* and *absoluta*) will

---

[13] The dispute was not as serious as later theologians, especially the Reformers, have made it out to be. See Otten, "Carolingian Theology."

[14] See Heiko Oberman, *The Harvest of Medieval Theology: Gabriel Biel and Late Medieval Nominalism.* rev. ed. (Grand Rapids: Eerdmans, 1967).

[15] *The Harvest of Medieval Theology*, 36.

[16] See, for example, Pelikan, *The Growth of Medieval Theology*, 66–80. Oberman (p 473) mentions that the medievals offered this distinction solely to aid theological discourse and not as an attempt to describe what actually exists.

[17] See, for example, St. Anselm's *Why God Became Man* and *On the Incarnation of the Word*.

provide us with a helpful vantage from which to perform our proposed comparison.[18]

II. Luther's Theological Concerns

As with every doctrinal disputant, Martin Luther's understanding of the Lord's Supper cannot be fully understood in isolation from his personal theology, from the political and social climate of the time, or from his paralyzing, existential angst that was effectively dispelled by his "tower experience." Below we shall briefly outline the Reformer's theology in light of the Reformer's own emotional and spiritual struggles. The political and social climate will be considered in the next section.

In 1545, Luther reflected upon a powerful conversion experience that he underwent some twenty-five or so years earlier. He recounts:

> Though I lived as a monk without reproach, I felt that I was a sin-ner before God with an extremely disturbed conscience. I could not believe that he was placated by my satisfaction. I did not love, yes, I hated the righteous God who punishes sinners, and secretly, if not blasphemously, certainly murmuring greatly, I was angry with God and said, "As if, indeed, it is not enough, that miserable sinners, eternally lost through original sin, are crushed by every kind of calamity by the law of the Decalogue, without having God add pain to pain by the gospel and also by the gospel threatening us with his righteousness and wrath!" Thus I raged with a fierce and troubled conscience.[19]

The despair that had overcome Luther during that time was such that the German monk maintained a very strong belief in God and all that God had purposed to accomplish in the cross of Christ. Yet his belief involved a terrible God before whom Luther felt all but condemned. "For I hated that word, 'righteousness of God,' which, according to the use and custom of all the teachers, I had been taught to understand philosophically regard-ing the formal or active righteousness . . . with which God is righteous and

---

[18] In this way, Pelikan's application of the two orders to the dispute over the virgin birth is very suggestive.

[19] *LW* 34:336–337. Compare *LW* 54:193–194, 308–309. Wherever possible the Luther citations have been taken from *Luther's Works*. 55 Vols. (ed. Jaroslav Pelikan and Helmut T. Lehmann; Philadelphia: Muhlenberg Press, 1955–76). A regular exception regards the *Table-Talk* where *The Table-Talk of Martin Luther*. (trans. William Hazlitt; Philadelphia: The United Lutheran Publication House, n.d.) was used instead and is cited by entry. Occasionally, when a parallel was found in *LW*, such a reference is provided.

punishes the unrighteous sinner."[20] One can easily detect in these words an intense awareness of God's holiness and righteousness; however, the God that Luther knew was so glorious that the Reformer found himself "raging with wild and disturbed conscience" over the fact that there seemed to be no hope of sinners escaping his holy wrath.

Luther never lost sight of this holy God, but he did manage to complement his understanding with a second perspective. Although in Luther's *Table-Talk* appears the following anecdote: "When one asked, where God was before heaven was created? St. Augustine answered: He was in himself. When another asked me the same question, I said: He was building hell for such idle, presumptuous, fluttering and inquisitive spirits as you,"[21] Luther could now continue:

> After he had created all things, he was everywhere, and yet he was nowhere, for I cannot take hold of him without the Word. But he will be found where he has engaged to be. The Jews found him at Jerusalem by the throne of grace, (Exod. xxv.) We find him in the Word and faith, in baptism and the sacraments; but in his majesty, he is nowhere to be found.

The majestic God who so troubled Luther earlier is still one who is beyond the reach of sinners; however, Luther had since discerned a way in which God can be known and worshipped by Christians. As Vilmos Vatja points out, Luther believed that

> God indeed is present everywhere, but he cannot be found everywhere, at least not as the God of love and mercy. There is a significant difference between his omnipresence and his "presence-for-us." The latter is a presence in the Word. God can be found only where he adds the Word to his work.[22]

From the material covered in the last chapter it should be easy to see that the same mediatory role that the Word plays in so many of Luther's writings seems to be that which Scripture plays in the writings of contemporary evangelicals. Perhaps, and without being unfair, a difference can be found in that in many ways the incarnated Christ himself and his *historical* plight played a noticeably stronger role in Luther's theology. For example, in his *Larger Catechism*, Luther explained:

---

[20] *LW* 34:336.

[21] *Table-Talk*, lxvii. Compare *LW* 54:377.

[22] *Luther on Worship: An Interpretation*. (trans. U. S. Leupold; Philadelphia: Muhlenberg Press, 1958), 87.

> These articles of the Creed, therefore, divide and separate us Christians from all other people upon earth. For all outside of Christianity, whether heathen, Turks, Jews, or false Christians and hypocrites, although they believe in, and worship, only one true God, yet know not what His mind towards them is, and cannot expect any love or blessing from Him; therefore they abide in eternal wrath and damnation. For they have not the Lord Christ, and, besides, are not illumined and favored by any gifts of the Holy Ghost.[23]

According to Luther, those who "have not the Lord Christ" are subject to God's wrath.[24] In the *Table-Talk*, we read:

> [H]e that does not take hold on Christ by faith, and comfort himself herein, that Christ is made a curse for him, remains under the curse . . . for where he is not known and comprehended by faith, there is not to be expected either advice, help, or comfort, though we torment ourselves to death.[25]

Only in relation to Christ could anyone rightfully set aside their fears of God exacting his judgment upon them. Luther here refers to Christ *in the flesh* as we shall see below.[26]

On the other hand, and in agreement with contemporary evangelicals, Luther was persuaded that Christ is available only through the Scriptures:

> I know nothing of Jesus Christ but only his name; I have not heard or seen him corporally, yet I have, God be praised, learned so much out of the Scriptures, that I am well and thoroughly satisfied; therefore I desire neither to see nor to hear him in the body.[27]

Thus, we see that the Word, i.e., the Scriptures, takes on for Luther a very integral role with regard to his relation to Christ.

Since it is impossible to do justice to Martin Luther's understanding of the gospel, not to mention its development throughout the course of

---

[23] Article III.

[24] Apparently, Luther counted himself among those under God's wrath until he began to study the book of Romans and the Psalms. See *LW* 34:336 and also Philip Melancthon, "The History of the Life and Acts of Luther. 1548." Prepared by Dr. Steve Sohmer 1996. Translated by T. Frazel 1995. Cited 10 April 2003. Source: http://www.iclnet.org/pub/resources/text/wittenberg/melan/lifec-01.txt.

[25] CCI.

[26] For a warm expression of his understanding of Christ's nature, see *Table-Talk* CXXXI.

[27] *Table-Talk* CXXXII. Compare XLVIII.

his life, in the allotted space, we shall only raise one last point here. The place of the creeds in theological formulation and construction during the history of the church, including the Reformation, can hardly be overestimated. It had long been believed in accord with the creeds that the life of Christ began when he was born of a virgin and ended when he ascended into heaven. *Luther, however, did not see Christ's ascension as the termination of his earthly ministry.*[28] He seems to have welcomed the gospel (and, especially, the incarnation) so openly and heartily that he refused to view Christ's ascension as the end of a wonderful ministry that purposed to set sinners free. When the incarnate Christ came into the world, so did the gracious gospel; conversely, if the incarnate Christ were to leave the world, then so would Luther's precious gospel. After all the life-changing soul-searching that Luther had done, he was not about to let the gospel get away from him (or any of God's people for that matter). He understood that Christ's humanity was crucial to the gospel's validity and efficacy. He also understood that when Christ promised that he would be with his disciples always, even to the end of the age, and that he would be in the midst of two or three that gathered in his name, Christ was not claiming that he would be present in some spiritual way only, but that Christ as incarnate Christ, *the Christ that the disciples knew*, would somehow be there in accordance with his promise.

It must be pointed out that the same anxiety that overtakes Luther at the thought of an Incarnate Christ not being present to him in the sacrament is very similar to that anxiety that seems to overwhelm evangelicals when they consider the thought of an inerrant Bible not being available to them. The former was not about to relive his Tower Experience; perhaps the latter are not about to give up their own spiritual niche and be swept away by naturalism, secularism, relativism and so on.

In sum, we have highlighted three salient features found in Martin Luther's personal theology. First, Luther understood that the God of the Bible had determined judgment for all persons and that this judgment could not be averted by humans. Second, he understood that Christ the Lord had brought good news (i.e., the gospel) to the effect that he was making a way for sinners to receive forgiveness of sins and blessings from God. Third, he saw a crucial connection between the duration of the earthly incarnation and the efficacy and availability of the proffered gospel. With these three points in mind we shall review Luther's understanding of the Lord's Supper. Certain aspects of his position will be cast in light of his

---

[28] For this point see David C. Steinmetz, "Scripture and the Lord's Supper in Luther's Theology," *Int* 37 (1983): 253–265, 262.

disposition towards his contemporaries and then his doctrine of the real presence will be cross-examined by a handful of his critics.

III. Luther's View of the Eucharist

Most studies that investigate the various views of the Lord's Supper that were held during the Reformation begin with a discussion regarding theories of signs and how and whether they actually relate to what they signify.[29] The present inquiry, by contrast, will, as far as possible, omit such discussion, in order that we might eventually detect the relation between God's *potentia ordinata* and God's *potentia absoluta* in Luther's position and in those of his opponents. This will allow our parallel to contemporary disputes regarding Scripture. We shall forego, therefore, the customary prefatory introduction.

Socially and politically Luther primarily identified himself over against two groups of contemporaries. The first is mentioned early in his writings, for example in his *Letter to Pope Leo X* (1518), and is comprised of corrupt Roman Catholic priests:[30]

> There was just one means which they used to quiet opposition, to wit, the protection of your name, the threat of burning at the stake, and the disgrace of the name "heretic." It is incredible how ready they are to threaten, even, at times, when they perceive that it is only their own mere silly opinions which are contradicted . . . I am not much moved, however, by the fact that they envy me the privilege granted me by the power of your Holiness, since I am unwillingly compelled to yield to them in things of far greater moment, viz., when they mix the dreams of Aristotle with theological matters, and conduct nonsensical disputations about the majesty of God, beyond and against the privilege granted them.[31]

[29] The reader is directed to a number of works on the Eucharist debate. See B. A. Gerrish, "Discerning the Body: Sign and Reality in Luther's Controversy with the Swiss," *The Journal of Religion* 68 (1988): 377–395; Ralph W. Quere, "Changes and Constants: Structure in Luther's Understanding of the Real Presence in the 1520's," *The Sixteenth Century Journal* 16 (1985): 45–76; John Stephenson, "Martin Luther and the Eucharist," *SJT* 36 (1983): 447–461; Kenneth R. Craycraft, Jr., "Sign and Word: Martin Luther's Theology of the Sacraments," *Restoration Quarterly* 32 (1990):143–164.

[30] This group, of course, eventually expanded to include the entire Roman Catholic infrastructure, not least the pope himself.

[31] This English translation is taken from Martin Luther, "Letter to Pope Leo X, Accompanying the "Resolutions" to the XCV Theses 1518" in *Works of Martin Luther* (trans. and ed. Adolph Spaeth, L.D. Reed, Henry Eyster Jacobs, et al.; Philadelphia: A. J. Holman Company, 1915), 1:44–48. Source: http://www.iclnet.org/pub/resources/text/

Luther is disgusted with a prevalent misuse and outright abuse of priestly authority along with a disproportioned co-mingling of Aristotelian philosophy and theological construction and reflection.

The second group over against which Luther identified himself was one whom he commonly branded as "Radicals," "Evangelicals," or "Heretics." Perhaps, a genuine fear can be detected in certain of Luther's writings that reveals just how seriously he wished to dissociate himself from this broad and, in his mind, hetero-Christian movement. His rationale is understandable considering the political associations that attended the more extreme ranks within the group. Martin Luther's volatile relationship with his one-time colleague, Andreas Karlstadt, is well-known.[32] As Euan Cameron writes, "It is impossible to separate the strife of ideas over the Eucharist from the context and the personalities which produced it." He continues:

> Luther, already disgusted with Karlstadt because of his precipitate moves in altering worship at Wittenberg and his tactlessness, despised him yet more on this issue. When Luther heard that Karlstadt's ideas were gaining adherents in Switzerland he was at once predisposed to listen no further.[33]

According to Cameron, Luther associated a whole family of ideas pertaining to the Eucharist with Karlstadt. His disdain for the man attached itself to his ideas and, in one fell swoop, extended to all who entertained or promulgated ideas that bore even the slightest semblance to his, whether they had been influenced by him or not. One major reason for this was what culminated in Karlstadt's personal involvement in the Peasants' Revolt of 1524/5. Toward this uprising and the social and political attitudes that incited it, Luther had nothing but the strongest contempt:

> For baptism does not make men free in body and property, but in soul; and the Gospel does not make goods common, except in the case of those who, of their own free will, do what the apostles and disciples did in Acts 4 [:32–37]. They did not demand, as do our insane peasants in their raging, that the goods of others—of Pilate and Herod—should be common, but only their own goods. Our

wittenberg/luther/nine5-pope.txt. The original can be found in *WA* 1:527–529.

[32] For a brief biography, one might start with Alejandro Zorzin, "Andreas Bodenstein von Karlstadt (1486–1541)" in *The Reformation Theologians.* (ed. Carter Lindberg; Malden, MA: Blackwell, 2002), 327–337.

[33] For Karlstadt's ill-timed reforms, see Euan Cameron, *The European Reformation.* (New York: Oxford University Press, 1991), 163–164, 210–214, and Owen Chadwick, *The Reformation.* (New York: Viking Penguin, 1972), 50–62.

peasants, however, want to make the goods of other men common, and keep their own goods for themselves. Fine Christians they are! I think there is not a devil left in hell; they have all gone into the peasants. Their raving has gone beyond all measure.[34]

Clearly, though, Luther had already begun to despise him after his return to Wittenberg in 1522. Violence, iconoclasm, and extreme mysticism had earlier proved (at least theoretically) appealing to Karlstadt, who had, in Luther's judgment, "devoured the Holy Spirit feathers and all."[35] Luther's former colleague had allowed a dangerous subjectivism to obscure and gradually overtake his sense of judgment.[36] Karlstadt, of course, was not the only one who had developed and accepted the opinions of the "radicals" nor was he the most radical. Others, notably Thomas Muntzer,[37] also emphasized the immediacy of the Christian experience, innovatively stressing individualism, egalitarianism and certain mandatory social justices in the name of the Holy Spirit.[38] As it became more and more clear that the followers of these Christian activists had set themselves to the institution of their reforms by violently upsetting the civil and social order, Luther began to associate the leaders' theological schemas with that segment's anarchic activity. His abhorrence of both the former and the latter went hand in hand and often conflated in his mind.[39]

[34] *LW* 46:51–52.

[35] *LW* 40:83.

[36] One example is related in the *Table Talk*: "Our burgomaster here at Wittenberg lately asked me, if it were God's will to use physic? for, said he, Doctor Carlstad has preached, that whoso falls sick, shall use no physic, but commit his case to God, praying that His will be done" (DXCIII).

[37] Karlstadt apparently did not initially endorse Muntzer's radicalism; however, they eventually joined in common cause (at least in a manner of speaking) in the so-called Peasants' War. For an overview of the series of outbreaks, see Euan Cameron, *The European Reformation*, 202–209.

[38] Deeply troubled by social injustices, Muntzer complained, "What possible chance does the common man ever have to welcome the pure word of God in sincerity when he is beset by such worries about temporal goods?" *The Collected Works of Thomas Muntzer* (trans. and ed. Peter Matheson; Edinburgh: T. & T. Clark, 1998), 151, cited in Gottfried Seebass, "Thomas Muntzer (c. 1490–1525)" in *The Reformation Theologians*. (ed. Carter Lindberg; Malden, MA: Blackwell Publishers, 2002), 338–350, 346.

[39] Luther's un-nuanced grouping of his opponents into stark Roman or Radical categories was unfortunate (such as identifying a Karlstadt with a Muntzer). Inevitable inconsistency in this regard is evident in his close friendship with Melanchthon, for example. Such black-and-white thinking helped Luther reduce matters in a way that made the theological and political landscape appear unrealistically uncomplicated. For example, Luther writes, "Anyone who has failed to grasp the faith may thenceforth believe whatever he likes,

Luther, then, sought to articulate his understanding of the Eucharist along the trajectory set by his own broader theological program. However, he always went about his theological business with an eye toward the formulations that were proffered by the "papists" and the "radicals." The social and political dynamic was such that in order for Luther's Reformation to succeed he could not be mistaken for either group. In other words, Luther was forced in many ways to react to transubstantiation as well as the Radicals' symbolic understanding of the sacrament. The former could be interpreted as the Roman insistence upon the appropriation of Aristotle and the legitimacy and cruciality of the priesthood and the papacy; the latter a forthright repudiation of the Word and a devilish desire to commune with God immediately and directly, i.e., without the Word (understood as the Scriptures and, most importantly, Christ) but also without priests (understood as almost every type of church leadership—in other words, anarchy).

Luther, for his part, developed his own theology of the sacraments in keeping with his broader theological emphases, but always in light of his opponents' positions.[40] One point of contention involved the vital role of the Word in God's dealings with his people. The Radicals claimed that on account of believers' possession of the Holy Spirit, it was not always necessary for the Word to play such a central role in the Christian's life, much less clergymen.[41] Rome, for its part, had centuries before annexed an entire sacramental system to their understanding of how Christ mediated God to believers that seemed to relegate the Word to the periphery of Christian worship and living and helped elevate (even if inadvertently) the position of the priests. For Luther, however, the Word was absolutely crucial to any interaction with God; he also appropriated the Word in a

---

it makes no difference. Just as when someone is on the point of drowning, whether he drowns in a brook or in the middle of a stream, he is drowned just the same. So I say of these fanatics: if they let go of the word, let them believe whatever they like . . ." (*LW* 36:336–337). He acknowledges "that six or seven sects have arisen over the sacrament," but he repeatedly categorically dismisses them as one (*LW* 34:162, 379).

[40] "Now that [Satan] sees he cannot subdue us from the left side, he rushes over to the right side. Formerly he made us too papistic; now he wants to make us too evangelical. But God commanded us many times in the Scriptures to keep on the straight path and not to turn either to the right or to the left" (*LW* 36:237; compare 54:43). It has been reported that Luther candidly explained, "The reading of the Bible would never have lead me to the understanding I have unless I had been instructed by the actions of my adversaries" (*LW* 54:274).

[41] *LW* 54:97. Of course, not every Radical promulgated this view, but in Luther's mind, a Radical was a Radical. See n. 40 above.

way that sought a balanced role for the ministry of clergymen. It is very important to keep this in mind when discussing any of Luther's beliefs.[42]

Luther, in many religious matters, was content to leave decisions up to individual consciences. For example, though Luther believed that all believers were entitled to partake of both elements of the Eucharist, he neither thought it fitting to compel parishioners to partake of one without the other nor to require that they partake of both. He only demanded that the church offer both to the laity in order that they could partake in accordance with their conscience. He also appealed to the conscience of a believer with regard to the adoration of the sacrament. This can be seen through his encounter with the Bohemian Brethren, for example.[43] Luther even went so far as to permit churchgoers to retain their beliefs in transubstantiation if they preferred to do so. He wrote:

> My one concern at present is to remove all scruples of conscience, so that no one may fear being called a heretic if he believes that real bread and real wine are present on the altar, and that every one may feel at liberty to ponder, hold, and believe either one view or the other without endangering his salvation.[44]

Martin Luther upheld Christian liberty to the greatest extant that he could. He, however, would not tolerate those views of the Eucharist that in some way denied the bodily presence of the Christ.[45] He adamantly insisted, "So we say, on our part, that according to the words Christ's true body and blood are present when he says, 'Take, eat; this is my body.'"[46] Luther held this to be no "minor matter" on which Christians were free to disagree since "God's Word is God's Word." Neither reason nor experience could dissuade Luther of his position. Though he regarded one particular argument to be "the strongest of them all," Luther could not change his mind even on account of the fact that his doctrine might become "burdensome to the people" in that "it is difficult to believe that a body is at

[42] Unfortunately, many scholars tend to preoccupy themselves with Luther's peculiarities with respect to the Eucharist at the cost of his broader theological concern. By contrast, see Thomas J. Davis, "'The Truth of the Divine Words': Luther's Sermons on the Eucharist, 1521–28, and the Structure of Eucharistic Meaning" *Sixteenth Century Journal* 30 (1999): 323–342.

[43] *LW* 36:271–305.

[44] *LW* 36:30.

[45] Luther's contempt for Zwingli, for example, is famous. When reflecting upon how Zwingli had died with weapon in hand, he is reported to have remarked, "If God saved him [Zwingli], he has done so above and beyond the rule." See *LW* 54:152.

[46] *LW* 37:25.

the same time in heaven and in the Supper."[47] Luther believed that "philosophy understands naught of divine matters" and that reason was "mere darkness" if not "in the hands of those who believe."[48] Difficulty of belief, after all, was not a test of truth. In any event, Luther was always suspect of a "spirit [that] will not believe what the Word of God says, but only what he sees and feels."[49]

In all fairness to Luther, it is improper to focus exclusively or even predominantly on Luther's understanding of the bodily presence of Christ in the bread and the wine.[50] After all, "up to now I have not preached very much about the first part [what one should believe about the sacrament], but have treated only the second [its proper use], which is also the best part," wrote Luther in 1526.[51] In other words, Luther's understanding of the real presence, though crucial, was not considered by him to be the most significant part of his doctrine and not one with which he would ordinarily occupy himself during preaching.[52] In *The Babylonian Captivity of the Church*, Luther's "first captivity of the sacrament" was the fact that "the sacrament does not belong to the priests, but to all men."[53] The second "captivity" referred to the real presence and "is less grievous as far as the conscience is concerned." Luther then claimed that the third "captivity" (that the mass was a sacrifice) was "by far the most wicked abuse of all." Granted, this was one of his earliest works to address the sacrament, yet, as Quere points out, "even though it changed its place in the structure, the function and power of the Word remained the same" throughout the Eucharistic controversy.[54]

---

[47] *LW* 37:74–75. See also *LW* 54.91–92, 284.

[48] *Table-Talk*, XLVIII; LXXVI. Compare *LW* 54:183–184, 377–378.

[49] *LW* 40:216.

[50] On the other hand, it is understandable since 1) Luther's understanding of the sacrament underwent several changes throughout his career. The real presence is one of the few features that remained constant. 2) It was the real presence against which so many of his critics focused their energies.

[51] *LW* 36:335.

[52] Luther continued: "But because the first part is now being assailed by many. . .so that in foreign lands a large number are already pouncing upon it and maintaining that Christ's body and blood are not present in the bread and wine, the times demand that I say something on this subject also." *LW* 36:335. Yet his absolute insistence upon the real presence of Christ in the sacrament is demonstrated, for example, in his inordinacy on the subject during the ecumenical venture of Philipp of Hesse (1529).

[53] *LW* 36:27, written 1520.

[54] "Changes and Constants," 75. It is well known that Luther's view of the Eucharist changed with time. Quere writes, "While I tend to agree with Althaus that the real presence

Why did Luther retain the Word as the core of his sacramental theology throughout his career? Because, as noted earlier, there is no other way to commune with God but through the incarnate Christ, according to Luther. Or as Davis puts it: "If one would know God, one must know Christ; what's more, one must know Christ in his humanity."[55] Therefore, whether Christ's body and blood were considered by Luther (as they were during various times throughout his career) as the sign, the *res*, the vehicle, or the vessel of the Church's incorporation into the body of Christ and/or of the Church's forgiveness of sins,[56] without the real presence of Christ he would not have been able to teach, for example, "'Here my Lord has given me his body and blood in the bread and wine, in order that I should eat and drink. And they are to be my very own, so that I may be certain that my sins are forgiven, that I am to be free of death and hell, have eternal life, and be a child of God and an heir of heaven.'"[57]

This section aimed to show that Luther was heavily influenced by his personal spiritual journey as well as the positions of rivaling factions as he constructed and modified his Eucharistic theology during the course of his ministry. It is always easier to see such influences operating in historical figures and controversies than in contemporary ones. So before rendering a brief comparison between the Eucharistic dispute and that among evangelicals, let us pause to examine how Luther dealt with certain competing arguments.

IV. Luther's Critics' Chief Argument

The controversies in which Luther found himself enmeshed primarily arose on account of how he could hold that the elements of the sacrament are both the body and blood of Christ and the bread and wine at the same time. We have endeavored to show that though this was crucial for Luther it did not comprise the core of his teaching on the Eucharist. Nevertheless, the real presence had achieved such attention from his opponents that he was driven to contend fiercely for its validity as more and more theologians

---

had no significant theological function in the early 1520s, it might be more accurate to say that it had a clearer place in the new structure in the late 1520s." (74) See also, Davis, "The Truth of the Divine Words."

[55] Davis, "The Truth of the Divine Words," 338. He continues, "There is no other God for us, Luther stated, than the one who comes in 'swaddling clothes.'"

[56] See Quere, "Changes and Constants."

[57] *LW* 36:350–351. The objectivity of the sacrament can provide a powerful assurance.

inveighed against him. We shall consider here what Luther deemed the "strongest [argument] of all": that the belief was a burden to the people.

That the real presence of Christ is too difficult for the ordinary person to believe ranked as the chief objection for Luther, especially given his sensitivity to the consciences of believers. The argument is actually a family of arguments that capitalizes on the belief's affront to simple, everyday reasoning. One version of the argument Luther credits to "the subtle Wycliffe and the sophists" and it maintains "that two distinct beings cannot be one, nor can one being be confused with the other."[58] Another, quoted earlier, complained of the difficulty in believing that Christ was both in heaven (at the right hand of the Father) and on earth (in the bread) at the same time. We shall examine these criticisms in light of the concepts of God's *potentia ordinata* and his *potentia absoluta* introduced above.

Whether a theologian would charge another that his belief in the real presence is absurd can depend in great measure on that theologian's understanding of the relation between God's *potentia ordinata* and his *potentia absoluta*. An interesting question to ask is what did a particular theologian seem to think with regard to what God *could* do (but did not opt to do) and what God *did* do? For example, Cajetan explained:

> It is first clear that in the words "This is my body," the pronoun "this" indicates neither the bread nor the body of Christ, since an indication of the bread would go against the truth of what is. Then the sense would be that this, this bread, is my body—which is patently false. This bread is not the body of Christ, neither at the end of the words, nor afterwards, nor before, since bread is never the body of Christ. However, once the sacrament is confected and while it continues to be, it is true that what was bread is the body of Christ. Nonetheless it is never true that bread is the body of Christ.[59]

Cajetan's wording is very interesting. Luther's understanding of the Eucharist is not "absurd" (as Zwingli charged) but rather "goes against the truth of what is." Perhaps Cajetan is intimating that since God can do all things, the Lutheran sacramental view is not impossible for God: it is simply not the way that God has chosen to constitute the sacrament.[60]

[58] *LW* 37:299.

[59] "Errors on the Lord's Supper—Instruction for the Nuntio, 1525" in *Cajetan Responds: A Reader in Reformation Controversy*. (ed. and trans. Jared Wicks, S.J.; Washington, D.C.: The Catholic University of America Press, 1978), 153–173, 166.

[60] In other words, this need not entail a logical contradiction given its physical impossibility. For the medieval resolution of the apparent contradiction that attends the real presence,

Zwingli, by way of contrast, may have considered Luther's version of the real presence as logically impossible and therefore without both God's *potentia ordinata* and his *potentia absoluta*.[61] Zwingli might have thought along these lines:

> [I]f the finite humanity of Christ is at the right hand of God, then it cannot be in the eucharistic elements. Christ stands at the right hand of God to intercede for the church. But if he is *there*, he cannot be *here*. *It is not possible for a finite body to be in two places at the same time*.[62]

Oecolampadius seems to have reasoned in a similar fashion. Against him, Luther writes,

> Since God can do more than we understand, we must not say without qualification, simply on the basis of our own deduction and opinion, that these two propositions are contrary to each other: Christ's body is in heaven, and in the bread. For both are God's words.[63]

It is apparent, at least from Luther's vantage, that Oecolampadius' stumbling block was his misidentification of the real presence as a logical contradiction and therefore without God's *potentia absoluta*.

Luther, for his part, saw the matter very differently. In fact, Luther argued not only that the real presence was within God's *potentia absoluta*, but that given the way that Christ was able to appear at will wherever he wanted after his resurrection, [64] the real presence was actually within God's *potentia ordinata*. What God *did* do and what God *can* do and their relation form a big part of the question concerning the Eucharist. Not only that, but what *others* think about these matters is also pertinent to the question. Without denying the primacy given to arguments from Scripture for each of these theologians, the relation of God's *potentia ordinata* and his *potentia absoluta* with respect to the Eucharist and with respect to contrary positions held by opponents played an important role in the formulation of Luther's position.

see Oberman, *The Harvest of Medieval Theology*, 271–280; Steinmetz, "Scripture and the Lord's Supper," 260–261.

[61] Though see *LW* 37:156, 171.

[62] Steinmetz, "Scripture and the Lord's Supper," 260 (emphasis mine).

[63] *LW* 37:276. Luther sees no contradiction "just as it is no contradiction that Christ sat with his disciples after his resurrection, Luke 24 [:44], and yet at the same time was not with them, as he himself says, 'These things I spoke to you, while I was still with you.' Here we find 'with you' and 'not with you,' and yet there is no contradiction . . ."

[64] Steinmetz, "Scripture and the Lord's Supper," 261. See, for example, *LW* 54.92–93.

V. Application

It was said above that we would not occupy ourselves here with arguments over the relation between "signs" and "signifieds." Rather, we took great pains to incorporate arguments over the relation between God's *potentia ordinata* and his *potentia absoluta*. In this way, the above account can be helpfully appropriated in such a way that we might better understand current disputes over the nature of Scripture.

Could God arrange for a Scripture to be written without error? Would not most evangelicals—even the most liberal—reply, "Yes, there must have been a way for God to do this."[65] This first question does not appear to be a contentious one among most evangelicals. Did God in fact inspire Scripture in this way? The answers to this question are what divide. "Yes, I think He did" might be said to be the answer of both fundamentalists and moderates. The difference between them can be explained by virtue of whether God doing so was on account of his *potentia ordinata* or his *potentia absoluta*. Fundamentalists would categorize the inspiration of Scripture with the former and moderates with the latter. Liberals, for their part—perhaps not all— would answer, "No, though He might have done things this way, He did not choose to so inspire the Scriptures."

Viewed in this way, the break among the three camps is not as severe as commonly depicted since all answer, "Yes," to the first question. That said, on account of personal and spiritual journeys that color discussions and decisions that bear upon the topic of Scripture, it may not prove easy to live comfortably with these familial resemblances. For example, fundamentalists may be so scared of what they categorically denounce as "liberalism" that they refuse any (or allow only limited) interaction with either of the other two camps—even though they are both evangelical. Moderates, on the other hand, may not be taken seriously by either of the other two groups being mistaken by the others for that camp that lies on the opposite end of the spectrum. Lastly, so many "post-evangelicals" happen to be either former moderates or former fundamentalists—non-evangelical liberals incidentally are often former evangelicals—and have no desire for any thing that even smells of the burdens of their pasts.

Surely there is much to learn from the Eucharist controversy by way of how intra-church disputes unfold. To believe that "whatever the Bible

---

[65] Contemporary crusades against "methodological naturalism" or the older "secular humanism" may overlook the fact that many Christians, evangelical and otherwise, are often very willing to concede that God *could* have done things a certain way; it is simply that he chose not to.

ultimately says is what I believe"—even though it describes the rhetoric of every European Reformer—does not wholly describe the motivation and rationale for why Luther believed what he did. To believe that Luther was unqualifiedly true to this sort of creed is a mistake that bespeaks untold consequences for evangelical churches today. Evangelicals should be mature enough to reason by parity that if it was not unqualifiedly the case for Luther that "whatever the Bible ultimately says is what I believe," it is most certainly not the case among contemporary evangelicals, irrespective of one's camp. May the Lord grant grace to his churches as we try to live with each other!

VI. Conclusion

There were a host of factors that contributed to the development of Martin Luther's position in the Reformation debates over the Eucharist just as there are a host of factors that contribute to the various evangelical positions regarding Scripture. This chapter recounted some of Luther's existential, socio-political and theological influences. It also sought to show, among other things, that by approaching the debate from a perspective that considers the relation between God's *potentia ordinata* and his *potentia absoluta*, there is more to learn than the differing theories of signs and things signified: Luther, evangelicals and believers everywhere hold the beliefs that they do, at least in part, on account of a response to their perception of the spheres of God's activity, their level of personal spiritual angst and the degree to which they experience socio-ecclesial strife. A major step can been taken by showing younger evangelicals how doctrines of Scripture do not simply fall out of heaven but are rather constructed in relation to a host of this-worldly factors. The ETS/EPS doctrines of Scripture cause younger evangelicals to be unusually resistant to the full force of this realization. My experience suggests that when an appreciable amount of headway is made here, a fundamental spiritual crisis ensues and that younger evangelicals are often tempted to spiritually retreat to the historical certainty of a biblical canon. Unfortunately, however, the next logical (and also most devastating) recognition is that these cultural and historical insights also apply—with all of their cumulative force—to evangelicalism's sacrosanct canon itself.

Recognition Five

Young Evangelicals Need to See the Openness of the Canon

IF YOUNGER evangelicals[1] begin to realize how much mystery attends the faith; how equivocation subtly lurks in affirmations of inerrancy; how efforts to bind doctrines of Scripture to Christology are not as helpful as one might hope; and how evangelicals themselves contribute via cultural and personal pressures to their own views of Scripture, they may believe that they can always bear down—if even as a last resort—on the implicit notion of biblical canon. Though philosophical reflection may reveal equivocation and theological reassessment a protective oversimplification, surely the objective and historical fact of canon can be called upon to champion younger evangelicals. However, it may be the case that young evangelicals have intimated that many Christians believe in a divinely sanctioned, *ahistorical* canonical process. An ahistorical view of the canonical process can elicit a very profound sense of trust from younger evangelicals but can potentially do the greatest spiritual damage to them. In these last few chapters of the book, a providentially *open* canon is shown to be that which can be historically discerned. A closed, once-and-for-all canon from which all subsequent theory must be drawn is not so easily found. To wit, the mere idea of an ultimately authoritative source for the faith proves to be an imaginative chimera. I posit that no other recognition can prove more devastating to evangelical spiritual formation.

Recently, a number of scholars have deliberately involved themselves in the debate over the roles of Scripture and canon within ancient Judaic and Christian communities. It is hoped that the demonstration proffered here will convince (or remind) evangelical leaders and teachers of the complex historical processes to which the biblical canon was

---

[1] For readers who did not read the introduction, "evangelicals" in this work refers to those Christian believers of whatever denomination (or non-denomination) who affirm the views of Scripture associated with the Evangelical Theological Society, the Evangelical Philosophical Society and other like-minded affiliations.

subjected. These two chapters also purport to mitigate extreme positions held by both "maximal" and "minimal" polemicists regarding the role of canon in the early church. This recognition involves realizing that both the ideas of the absolute or ultimate authority of Scripture and of the mere sociological function of canon are necessarily empty. Indeed, there is much to be learned from the similar attitudes that were resident among the views of several prominent religious leaders of both late Judaism and early Christianity. Hillel, Paul, James, Justin Martyr, and Irenaeus are adduced below as evidence that it had unwittingly been discerned that a symbiotic relation obtained amongst the varied components of religious "tradition."

With respect to the early church, Ralph E. Person defines "tradition" as "everything (teachings, rites, customs, etc.) Christ had delivered to the apostles and the apostles had delivered to the church and the church had faithfully preserved and passed on from generation to generation."[2] Since Scripture is easily conceived as a functional part of this composite deposit of the church, a methodological choice has been made here to subsume arguments over canon into a larger historical rubric where both theological and sociological insights are admitted. By doing this, it is hoped that scholars and students alike might be helped on their way to a more constructive perspective from which to discuss and teach the nature of canon.

Readers should know at the outset that these chapters do not comprise an original study *per se*. Rather summative citations are employed to mark out one promising direction which discussions of tradition and canon might take.[3] Even a perfunctory read will show that this study relies heavily upon secondary literature and is, to that extent, more of a collation of scholarly conclusions than an offering of ground-breaking, primary research. The motive for such an approach stems from both the trends that the author has discerned in existing studies on Scripture and canon and what these chapters set out to accomplish:

1. Too often contributions to the topics of canon, tradition and Scripture provide otherwise competent, in-depth, primary studies in such a way that they, nevertheless, somehow lack something by way of reflective synthesis.

---

[2] "The Mode of Theological Decision Making at the Early Ecumenical Councils: An Inquiry into the Function of Scripture and Tradition at the Councils of Nicaea and Ephesus." (Th.D. dissertation, University of Basel; Friedrich Reinhardt Kommisionsverlag: Basel, 1978), 7.

[3] Of course, not all authors cited argue for consensual positions.

2. Conversely, contributions that aim at synthesis many times fall short in terms of analyses to the effect that semi-scholarly readers may find themselves pondering how well authors' wide and sweeping conclusions fit with the primary data and, more importantly, how scholars and others from other fields can intelligently apply published conclusions to contemporary ecumenical discussions.

3. These chapters will attempt a middle path, and, in order to arrive at this, duly range over a very broad selection of the literature—not only to meet the expected quota for analysis, but especially to set the necessary ancient and contemporary backdrop for the synthesis that follows. In this way, it is hoped that both specialist and non-specialist readers can gain a fuller appreciation of the "two horizons"—the ancient world and the contemporary scholarly landscape—within which the present argument has taken its form.

To this end and for the sake of space, biblical and patristic *scholars* are cited in lieu of the biblical and patristic *writers* themselves. Summative citations are employed to propel the argument along in order that a variegated chorus of published scholarly analyses might be rendered more apprehensible to a wider readership.[4] Recent scholarly discussions given to canon, tradition and Scripture have proven productive and will continue (it is hoped) along lines such that an ecumenical space can be enlarged wherein open dialogue among the churches and academicians can flourish and (within evangelical circles) younger evangelicals can explore their own bibliological stomping grounds as it were.

I. The Role of Scripture During the Second Temple Period

J. Arthur Baird may have gotten ahead of himself when he immediately considered the *logia* of Jesus as the fountainhead from which the New Testament and the Christian church eventually developed.[5] In very obvious ways, he is right as far as it goes. However, perhaps it is more proper to begin a study on the early church's conception of Scripture with the

[4] As mentioned, a benefit to frequent reference to the secondary literature includes the creation of a context within which to understand otherwise isolated studies. One downfall, though, may include a false sense of consensus on certain of these topics. For this reason, where practical, mention is made in the notes of pertinent contemporary disputes.

[5] *Holy Word: The Paradigm of New Testament Formation.* JSNTSup 224 (ed. Craig A. Evans and Stanley E. Porter; Sheffield: Sheffield Academic Press, 2002).

destruction of the first temple in Jerusalem in 587/6 B.C.E. A major reason for this is that so many religious changes were predicated upon this momentous event. Chief among these was the manner in which it was perceived that God communicated with his people. William N. Schniedewind, for example, observes in a study of the period that "[p]ost-exilic biblical literature . . . reflects a transition in the meaning of the 'word of God.'" He explains:

> The "word of God" in the pre-exilic literature is truly "living and active." It comes directly from God to the prophet who in turn speaks to the people. After the exile, the "word of God" becomes the received traditions—Scripture—which an inspired interpreter makes alive for the people.[6]

The understanding of a prophet as a person who interprets the received tradition in order to communicate God's plans for his people marks a shift with respect to a primary way through which God was seen to interact with his people. The inspired interpreters of sacred traditions came to be those who perpetuated the prophetic call in Second Temple Judaism. This transformation of the image of those who carried on the prophetic heritage and the corresponding transition in what was understood to constitute YHWH speaking to his people Israel most certainly laid the seeds of what the early church would eventually conceive as the "apostolic tradition."

Of course, this does not mean to imply that prophets in the "classic" sense were totally extinct, but rather that hagiographers, apocalypticists and others, such as the writers at Qumran, were all increasingly seen as prophets insofar as they were prophetic *interpreters* of the common traditions that had been received, accepted and compiled over the history of Israel's existence. Examples of the shift abound. Alejandro Diez Macho observes at least the following four examples. Although Daniel is commonly understood to be a prophet, he is not presented as a prophet as such in the book that bears his name, but rather as a sage, a wise man. Enoch, in the Pseudipigrapha, is no prophet in the "classic" sense, but rather a wisdom figure who knows heavenly things. Similarly, Ezra is a scribe and not a prophet, and the figure of Jeremiah is eclipsed by Baruch, his scribe.[7] The present point is generally agreed upon and is summarized well by Joseph Blenkinsopp:

---

[6] *The Word of God in Transition: From Prophet to Exegete in the Second Temple Period.* JSOTSup 197 (Sheffield: Sheffield Academic Press, 1995), 11.

[7] Paraphrasing (and translating) *Apocrifos Del Antiguo Testamento.* T1. (Madrid: Ediciones Cristianidad, 1984), 83.

If prophetic activity was to continue in the basically different social and political circumstances obtaining in the postdisaster period, it would necessarily be of a different kind and would be perceived differently among the survivors of the disaster . . . What it amounted to was a much stronger conviction that, at least in the normal course of events, God does not communicate directly but has revealed his will and purpose in past communications whose bearing on the present situation remains to be elucidated.[8]

With the destruction of the first Temple, the people of Israel were forced to reconsider the ways in which their God, YHWH, could be said to be among them. The response was to first establish the fact that YHWH had indeed been with and among the people at one time in the past. Utter certainty on this point was crucial in the minds of Second Temple Jews.[9] Only then was it natural (and expedient) to understand that in this past YHWH had not only revealed himself to the people of those earlier times, he also had the subsequent generations in mind as well. The question was how was a past encounter with God to be translated into a present (or future) encounter with God? Enter the inspired exegetes: the hagiographer, the apocalypticist, and the scribe, among others.

At this point, it may be helpful to broadly introduce the notion of "canon." Canon, for our purposes, will mean simply "a collection of books that were widely accepted as authoritative for religious purposes."[10] Such a vague definition allows for the possibility that there may exist different *kinds* of collections of books that were widely accepted as authoritative for religious purposes. John Barton, for example, has insisted upon a very useful distinction between *inclusive* and *exclusive* canonical understandings.[11]

---

[8] *A History of Prophecy in Israel.* rev and enl. (Louisville, KY: Westminster/John Knox, 1996), 227. See also James L. Kugel, "Interpreters of Scripture" in J. Kugel and R. Greer, *Early Biblical Interpretation.* (Philadelphia: Westminster, 1986), 52–72.

[9] On the paramount role that the figure of Moses plays with respect to the Jewish Scriptures and tradition, see, for example, David Noel Freedman, "The Formation of the Canon of the Old Testament" in *Ancient Israelite History and Religion: Selected Writings of David Noel Freedman.* Divine Commitment and Human Obligation Vol. 1 (ed. John R. Huddleston; Grand Rapids: Eerdmans, 1997), 470–484; Rolf Rendtorff, "Some Reflections on the Canonical Moses: Moses and Abraham" in *A Biblical Itinerary: In Search of Method, Form and Content: Essays in Honor of George W. Coats* (ed Eugene E. Carpenter; Sheffield: Sheffield Academic Press, 1997), 11–19.

[10] Much more will be said about "canon" at the end of the next chapter. For now open canon refers to an *inclusive*, authoritative collection of sacred writings and closed canon refers to an *exclusive*, authoritative collection of sacred writings. See below.

[11] "The Significance of a Fixed Canon" in *Hebrew Bible/Old Testament: The History of Its Interpretation. Volume I: From the Beginnings to the Middle Ages (Until 1300).* (ed. Magne

The former regards the general acceptance of a particular writing as holy; the latter pertains to the widespread rejection of a particular writing as holy. Barton wisely cautions against the assumption that the former somehow entails the latter or that the former requires some sort of definitive list of which writings were holy.[12] He writes:

> The "inclusive" sense of "canon" mattered a great deal: scriptural, authoritative, in this sense "canonical," books were interpreted very differently from profane ones. But the 'exclusive' idea of a canon—"these books and no others"—seems weakly attested, and is a comparatively minor factor where interpretation is concerned. Reflection on the fact that particular books are *not* canonical, or on those that are as a kind of *maximum* that may be believed in or interpreted, seems on the whole alien to Judaism of ancient times.[13]

We shall see below that the same also held, *at least practically*, for the early Christian church and that this understanding of Scripture opened the way for the admission of manifold sources of sacred teaching. In light of the fact that inclusively canonical books were considered to have a divine origin, ancient readers believed that all sacred writings were relevant to present concerns. In addition, as Barton notes, "The scriptural status of these books meant that whatever they said about God had to be taken as having universal relevance. Anything true of God at one point in Israel's history must be true of him at all times."[14] For these reasons, the inspired exegete of whatever class or type felt the obligation to and was expected to render the sacred traditions relevant for the current generation. As important and widespread as this practice would become, we should remember Cohen's observation that during this period "Jewish sects composed and/or pre-

---

Saebo; Gottingen: Vandenhoeck and Ruprecht, 1996), 67–83. Kraft warns of failing to distinguish between what he calls a "Scripture consciousness" and a "canon consciousness" (compare Zevitt's notions of implicit and explicit canons). See Robert A. Kraft, "Scripture and Canon in Jewish Apocrypha and Pseudepigrapha" in Magne Saebo, *Hebrew Bible/Old Testament*, 199–216; and Z. Zevitt, "The Second-Third Century Canonization of the Hebrew Bible and Its Influence on Christian Canonizing" in *Canonization and Decanonization: Papers Presented to the International Conference of the Leiden Institute for the Study of Religions (LISOR), Held at Leiden 9–10 January 1997*. (ed. A. van der Kooij and K. van der Toorn; Boston: Brill, 1998), 133–160, 138.

[12] For one such view of canon, see Guy G. Stroumsa, "Hermeneutical Revolution and Its Double Helix" in *The Use of Sacred Books in the Ancient World*. CBET 22. (ed. L. V. Rutgers, P. W. van der Horst, H. W. Havelaar and L. Teugels; Leuven: Peeters, 1998), 9–28, esp. 16.

[13] Barton, "Significance," 83.

[14] "Significance," 75.

served works that they alone considered authoritative, but this activity was not apparently essential either to their self-definition or to the way in which they were defined by their opponents."[15] In other words, with respect to our discussions about canon, we should take care not to overstate the case and understand that Scripture did not operate in such a way that it alone defined various groups of believers or unified the Jewish people as a whole. We shall briefly attempt to set forth a case that the culture was such that Scripture could not have even *fundamentally* served in this capacity. Scripture maintained a vital role, to be sure, but there were clearly always other authoritative factors (including other texts) at work: the canon functionally remains open.

In what follows we shall draw upon Jack N. Lightstone's notions of open and closed boundaries with regard to perceptions of the social, cultural and political world.[16] These correspond roughly and respectively to the "inclusive" and "exclusive" canons mentioned earlier, but the former pertain not only to texts: they extend beyond written texts to include all manner of spatial, temporal, cultic and inter-personal spheres of religious and non-religious existence.[17] Expanding our horizons beyond the sacred texts of Second Temple Judaism seems highly appropriate considering that the "people of the book" were hardly people of the book in the way that modern people often tend to think.[18] This is primarily because, as Susan Niditch has pointed out, there then existed a complex interplay between a widespread culture-cache that she terms an "oral register" and the production of written texts that is very difficult for modern persons to fully appreciate or apprehend without a bit of effort on our part.[19] Niditch explains:

> The written text provides a portion of tradition that becomes set,
> an icon, perhaps a sacred object that may be ritually studied sequentially or read for special occasions, or copied when the old

[15] Shaye J. D. Cohen, *From the Maccabees to the Mishnah*. (Philadelphia: Westminster Press, 1987), 133–134.

[16] *Society, The Sacred, and Scripture in Ancient Judaism: A Sociology of Knowledge.* Studies in Christianity and Judaism 3. (Waterloo, Ontario: Wilfrid Laurier University Press, 1988).

[17] William J. Abraham also refuses to restrict the idea of canon to texts. See his *Canon and Criterion in Christian Theology: From the Fathers to Feminism.* (New York: Oxford University Press, 1998), 27–83.

[18] Compare Jacob Neusner's complaint against what he terms the "book-religion model" of Rabbinic Judaism: "The model's framework categorizes ancient rabbis so much in our image and after our likeness that it begs more questions than it answers." See Jacob Neusner, *Rabbinic Judaism: Structure and Content.* (Minneapolis: Fortress, 1995), 32.

[19] *Oral World and Written Word: Ancient Israelite Literature.* (Louisville, KY: Westminster John Knox Press, 1996).

papyrus begins to succumb to age. The stories, the customs, the rituals, and the proverbs live, however, in the oral culture, in the lives and words of people. A work such as the Hebrew Bible, richly traditional and informative as it is, is just a slice of, a collection of freeze frames in an even richer tradition.[20]

The oral culture from which the Hebrew Bible eventually emerged did not disappear with the advent of the holy writings. On the contrary, it survived as a dominant cultural context within which the Hebrew Bible began to exist.[21]

The fact that various sacred traditions had now been written or compiled and collected did not stem the oral avenue of cultural influence. If anything, the written collection made the oral factor all the stronger since, in Delwin Brown's words, "the genius of canon may be precisely in the fact that it imposes a material integration upon what is incorrigibly diverse."[22] In other words, with respect to an emergent Hebrew Bible, the gradual production and acceptance of a body of holy writings contributed to the broader cultural milieu from which it emanated in such a way that the trajectory of the oral culture's growth and development had become more directed and distinctive. Brown explains:

> Tradition is cultural negotiation circumscribed by a canon, a more or less explicit field of play formed in history. The field, the canon, may be defined as a list of documents, a set of stories, a complex of myths, a body of doctrine or concepts, a cluster of symbols, a group of rituals, a pattern of cultivated sensibilities, and so forth, or combinations of these . . . The boundedness of canon creates the tentative and proximate identity of a negotiating process, the identity of a tradition. To negotiate or play within and with these boundaries is what it means to be a participant in the tradition.

The oral register and the written word stand in a dialectic relation such that it is not possible for what is written to be an "ultimate" or "absolute" authority. The amorphous and patently historical oral register that exists prior to, during and subsequent to the production of such writings might be given a very broad direction with respect to which communities will begin to modify or develop their various traditions, but it never subjects

---

[20] *Oral World*, 77.

[21] For a comprehensive treatment, see David M. Carr, *Writing on the Tablet of the Heart: Origins of Scripture and Literature.* (New York: Oxford University Press, 2004).

[22] *Boundaries of Our Habitations: Tradition and Theological Construction.* (Albany, NY: State University of New York Press, 1994), 77.

itself absolutely to writings insofar as granting them "absolute" authority. Additional support for this is found in the persistence of oral cultures in various parts of the world today in spite of the production of written records. One example is taken from Kenneth E. Bailey's research involving the contemporary transmission of oral traditions in the Middle East. Bailey observed how storytellers are both allowed great liberties in their retellings of stories and socially constrained by the bounds that naturally attend the establishment of traditions. He termed such bounded liberty "controlled flexibility,"[23] and concluded that "[t]he writing down of the material (particularly in a second language) did not halt the oral recitation of that same material nor curtail its controlled flexibility."[24]

In the next section, we shall examine particular examples of this paradoxical interplay between "control" and "flexibility" or open and closed boundaries. We shall find that authorized interpreters were called upon (or felt called upon) to interpret inclusively canonical texts in accord with what they believed God was doing among his people.

II. The Role of Interpretation During the First Century

We shall begin our investigation of Second Temple interpretation of Scripture by reproducing in its entirety an old rabbinic parable as presented by Ben Zion Boksur:[25]

> On one occasion a fierce debate ensued between Rabbi Eliezer and his colleagues on a complicated problem of law. Rabbi Eliezer cited a variety of arguments but his colleagues remained unconvinced. Finally he invoked divine intervention to corroborate his opinion. "'If the law is in accordance with my view,' he exclaimed, 'may this carob tree offer testimony' [by divine miracle]. The carob tree moved a hundred [or, as others related, 400] cubits from its place. They replied to him: 'No proof can be cited from a carob tree.' Thereupon he exclaimed, 'If the law is in accordance with my views, may this stream of water offer testimony.' The stream moved backward from its normal course. They replied to him: 'No proof can be cited from water-channels.' Then he exclaimed,

---

[23] Eugene Ulrich writes of the concept in terms of a faithful creativity in "The Canonical Process" in E. Ulrich, *The Dead Sea Scrolls and the Origins of the Hebrew Bible.* (Grand Rapids: Eerdmans, 1999), 51–78

[24] "Informal Controlled Oral Tradition and the Synoptic Gospels" *AJT* 5:1 (1991), 34–54, 47.

[25] *Judaism and the Christian Predicament.* (New York: Alfred A. Knopf, 1967), 70–71, as related in *Bava Metzi'a* 59b.

'If the law is in accordance with my views, may the walls of this Academy offer testimony.' The walls of the Academy began caving in and were already on the point of collapsing when Rabbi Joshua rebuked, them, 'If the students of the Torah contend with one another what concern is it of yours?' Out of respect for Rabbi Joshua they did not collapse, but out of respect for Rabbi Eliezer they remained aslope. Finally Rabbi Eliezer pleaded, 'If the law is in accordance with my views, may testimony be offered from the heavens above.' Whereupon a heavenly voice announced, 'What have you against Rabbi Eliezer? The law is in accord with his views.' Rabbi Joshua at once rose to his feet and announced, 'It is not in heaven' [Deuteronomy 30:12]. What did he mean by this? Said Rabbi Jeremiah: 'That the Torah had already been given at Mt. Sinai; we pay no attention to heavenly voices, because long ago it was declared at Sinai [Exodus 23:2] that one must follow the majority.' Rabbi Nathan met Elijah and asked him: 'What did the Holy One praised be He do in that hour?" He replied: 'He laughed with joy, saying, "My sons have defeated me, My sons have defeated Me."'

As Bokser observes, the final court of appeal with respect to interpretation according to the parable always lay in the judgment of the Torah's official interpreters.[26] Notwithstanding conscious attempts that were being made to legitimate and stabilize a specific group of recognized, authoritative religious teachers at the end of the first century C.E.,[27] it was generally understood that the Torah had been given to Israel and its teachers were the ones who had to decide what it meant for the people in light of their history and traditions. In other words, the canon was open-ended,[28] if not with regard to what constituted Torah (and not necessarily what did not), then at least in light of how Torah could be variously construed. In this respect, God's "sons" were most certainly in a position where they could "defeat" his intent.

[26] Torah here refers to divine revelation; torah refers to general religious instruction.

[27] See, for example, Patrick Tiller, "Anti-apocalyptic Apocalypse" in For a Later Generation: The Transformation of Tradition in Israel, Early Judaism, and Early Christianity. (ed. Randal A. Argall, Beverly A. Bow, and Rodney A. Werline; Harrisburg, PA: Trinity Press International, 2000), 258–265.

[28] Eugene Ulrich maintains that it is simply not helpful to speak of an "open canon." We do so in keeping with Barton's idea of an "inclusive canon" which we find especially useful. Perhaps, Ulrich unduly restricts his definition in response to the ambiguity that has begun to attend the term. See his "The Notion and Definition of Canon" in The Canon Debate. (ed. Lee Martin McDonald and James A. Sanders; Peabody, MA: Hendrickson, 2002), 21–35.

It is well known that torah teachers interpreted in light of an accumulating oral Torah; less known is the degree to which some torah teachers circumvented the written Torah in their halakic pronouncements. The widespread rabbinic concern that sought to trace all traditions to Scripture apparently did not arise until about the turn of the first century C.E. with Rabbi Akiba and his contemporaries.[29] According to D. R. Schwartz, Hillel, for example, who flourished some one hundred years before, "did not have to search the Scriptures for the answers to all problems which arose. Contrary to Ben Bag-Bag (m.Ab 5:22) and Akiba, Hillel did not assume that everything was to be found in it."[30] Schwartz continues: "If scribes—*sopherim*—directed their attention to the details of Scripture (cf. b.Kid 30a), Hillel did not teach 'as one of the scribes'; he taught either directly out of Scripture, or on the basis of tradition, or, most characteristically, 'as one who had authority.'" Schwartz quotes here from Mk 1.22, comparing Hillel to Jesus Christ in the way that he taught without deferring to Scripture. Suffice it to say that Jesus "did not train His disciples to be 'well-plastered cisterns, never losing a drop'—the ideal set before the pupils of the rabbis—but rather to be his apprentices, sharing His ministry with His own creative freedom."[31] In other words, both Jesus and Hillel did not see themselves as strictly bound by Torah, but were free to teach and pronounce judgments in keeping with what they "took to be its basic, charitable purpose,"[32] even if it conflicted with earlier rulings or with Torah itself. The role of interpretation was such that it operated on a much broader plane than that of written texts (though it obviously included

---

[29] For the following, see D. R. Schwartz, "Hillel and Scripture: From Authority to Exegesis" in *Hillel and Jesus: Comparative Studies of Two Major Religious Leaders* (ed. James H. Charlesworth and Loren L. Johns; Minneapolis: Fortress, 1997), 335–362. In addition, based on the transmission of texts, James A. Sanders surmises that "the Jewish understanding of the authority of scripture gradually but firmly shifted from a kind of shamanistic or dynamic view of inspiration (the message of scripture), to verbal inspiration (the words), and the literal inspiration (the letters)." He dates each of the phases at first century B.C.E., the end of the first century C.E., and third century C.E. respectively. See James A. Sanders, "The Issue of Closure in the Canonical Process" in *The Canon Debate*. (ed. Lee Martin McDonald and James A. Sanders; Peabody, MA: Hendrickson, 2002), 252–263, 256.

[30] Schwartz, "Hillel," 360.

[31] F. F. Bruce, *Tradition: Old and New.* (Grand Rapids: Zondervan, 1970), 27, citing Pirqe Abot 2:8. Particularly telling are Bruce's comments regarding the "Deuteronomic loophole" that was later added to Jesus' teaching on divorce.

[32] Schwartz, "Hillel," 360.

these). Much rather, interpretation oftentimes was driven by what teachers thought to be God's overall purpose for his people and his creation.[33]

One can glean similar traits in the New Testament writings of Paul. Peter Richardson, for example, has examined I Cor 7 which contains an extended section wherein Paul enunciates his own halakah.[34] He points out that whereas many rabbis were known to base their arguments on written Torah to the extent that they could, only then deferring to oral Torah and custom, Paul bases his arguments on his own personal authority. Paul, according to Richardson, passes over midrash in favor of halakah.[35] In fact, he allows what the Lord's command prohibits, based on his own spiritual insight.[36] Richardson observes how Paul was not reluctant to relativize a given Torah command in the interest of what was best for the situation at hand.

Another New Testament writer, James, is pertinent to our discussion of the relation of Torah to a teacher's specific teachings.[37] James' letter does not provide any instances of halakah akin to those of Paul: the occasion that elicited his letter differed from that of Paul's. Comments upon his letter will be restricted, therefore, to his citation of what Davids calls "the wider collection of traditional embellishments and theological reflection, which he assumes his reader knows."[38] James' style of writing was such that he incorporated popular biblical narratives into his argument to enjoin his

---

[33] Thus Jacob Neusner's complaint that the torah of Jesus is quite incompatible with the Torah of Moses misses the mark. See Neusner, *A Rabbi Talks with Jesus*. rev. ed. (Ithaca: McGill-Queen's University Press, 200). The idea that one should understand Scripture as a storyline that tells of God's interaction with Israel is usefully employed in the work of N. T. Wright, for example, in his *The New Testament and the People of God*. Christian Origins and the Question of God Volume 1. (Minneapolis: Fortress, 1992), 215–243.

[34] Peter Richardson, "'I Say, Not the Lord': Personal Opinion, Apostolic Authority and the Development of Early Christian Halakah". *TynBul* 31 (1980): 65–86.

[35] "I Say, Not the Lord," 85.

[36] "I Say, Not the Lord," 86.

[37] As mentioned in chapter two above.

[38] Peter H. Davids, "Tradition and Citation in the Epistle of James" in *Scripture, Tradition, and Interpretation: Essays Presented to Everett F. Harrison by His Students and Colleagues in Honor of His Seventy-fifth Birthday*. (ed. W. Ward Gasque and Willaim Sanford LaSor; Grand Rapids: Eerdmans, 1978), 113–126, 113. For an example of recourse to extant exegetical traditions in the very production of the Gospel story itself, see William Richard Stegner, "The Temptation Narrative: A Study in the Use of Scripture by Early Jewish Christians." *BR* 35 (1990): 5–17; idem, "The Use of Scripture in Two Narratives of Early Jewish Christianity (Matthew 4.1–11; Mark 9.2–8)" in *Early Christian Interpretation of the Scriptures of Israel: Investigations and Proposals*. JSNTSup 148. (ed. Craig A. Evans and James A. Sanders; Sheffield: Sheffield Academic Press, 1997), 98–120.

readers to incline themselves toward sustained charity and faithful perseverance. As mentioned above in Recognition Two, his use of the stories of Abraham, Rahab, Job and Elijah all depend in differing degrees on extrabiblical traditions that had come to attend the biblical stories. James' use of these traditions was such that Davids writes:

> The freedom with which James combines the canonical with the extra-canonical means that he apparently had no firm boundary in his mind between the two. The amount of reliance on the oral tradition varies: in the case of Job it is probable that the extra-canonical materials are the primary reference our author has in mind, but in the case of Rahab his dependence may be minimal. So for James the apocryphal and canonical are not sharply divided, and his apparent biblical references are not so entirely biblical at all.[39]

James, though not as flagrantly as Paul, also extends beyond written Torah in order to guide his readers in the Way. He was comfortable enlisting extrabiblical traditions that could contribute to the effective communication of his understanding of God's overall will for his people. Though James does not explicitly ground his argument in his own spiritual discernment (as Paul did), he nevertheless appeals to prevalent traditions, a collective discernment, as it were, that were not based on Scripture.[40]

Interpretation of what God was doing amidst his people, then, was of crucial import during the first century. In light of the above applications and interpretations of Torah during this period of Second Temple Judaism, it is not hard to see that religious teachers conducted their activities under the auspices of an open canon at best. Those who surmise that they have conclusively demonstrated the "closing" of a canon prior to the first century C. E. perhaps have mistaken the formation of an open canon for a closed one as Barton suggests.[41] Lieman, for example, writes "there is no evidence that normative Judaism ever again considered adding

---

[39] "Tradition and Citation," 122.

[40] Again, to argue that the traditions can be derived from Scripture misses the point.

[41] Barton, "The Significance of a Fixed Canon," 68–70. For an early closing of the canon, see Sid Z. Leiman, *The Canonization of Hebrew Scripture: The Talmudic and Midrashic Evidence.* 2nd ed. (New Haven: The Connecticut Academy of Arts and Sciences, 1991) and, with an even earlier date, Roger Beckwith, *The Old Testament Canon of the New Testament Church.* (Grand Rapids: Eerdmans, 1985). Sanders muses over how the evidence that drove Leiman to his conclusions was the same that caused him to come to an opposite one. See Leiman, "The Issue of Closure," 253–254. See also James C. Vanderkam, "Revealed Literature in the Second Temple Period" in his collection of essays, *From Revelation to Canon: Studies in the Hebrew Bible and Second Temple Literature.* (Boston: Brill, 2002), 1–30.

a book to the biblical canon. Since no books were added to the biblical canon, it was closed."[42] However, we have endeavored to suggest examples of religious leaders who utilized the sacred writings in such a way that they complemented, supplemented, and even trumped Scripture's teachings with their own or those of oral traditions. In addition, the canonical store available to these teachers was not restricted to what became the Hebrew Bible.[43] The situation mirrored that which arose within the history of the transmission of the sacred texts. Sanders explains:

> In the early history of transmission tradents of the text, both scribes and translators, could focus on the need(s) of the community to understand the messages of the text, even to the extent of modestly altering or clarifying archaic or out-moded expressions so that their community could understand what it might mean to them.[44]

We have suggested above that the needs of the situation at hand allowed Torah teachers flexibility with their open canon,[45] bounded ultimately by their personal (or collective) understanding of how God was presently working among his people. In this regard, quoting Sanders again:

> the primary character of canon was still its relevance to the communities it served. Once the text could no longer be modified to show relevance, hermeneutic rules were devised to break open the frozen text . . . When stories could no longer be added . . . the stabilized canon was subjected to new ways of reading . . .[46]

We shall attempt also to show that the early church did not break from this model, but, on the contrary, always had new stories to tell and, if not

---

[42] *Canonization*, 132.

[43] With respect to the idea that no other books were considered inspired and authoritative, Vanderkam offers *Jubilees* and *I Enoch* as counterexamples. See Vanderkam, "Revealed Literature," 20–29.

[44] Sanders, "The Issue of Closure," 256–257.

[45] Jack N. Lighthouse, whose idea of "open" and "closed" boundaries we have loosely adapted, has recently argued that the fact that the generic Judaism of the time did not have a "closed" canon did not prevent each individual community from accepting a pervasive "canonical principle." Nevertheless, he admits that the principle was "counterbalanced" by claims to additional revelation. See his essay, "The Rabbis' Bible: The Canon of the Hebrew Bible and the Early Rabbinic Guild" in *The Canon Debate*. (ed. Lee Martin McDonald and James A. Sanders; Peabody, MA: Hendrickson, 2002), 163–184.

[46] Sanders, "The Issue of Closure," 259.

new textual adjustments to make,[47] new hermeneutical innovations to introduce. The issue at hand is not whether the early church had a high view of the authority of Scripture or whether they generally understood the Scriptures to be without error.[48] Rather we claim that to understand that the early church held the Bible to be the "ultimate" or "absolute" authority represents an underappreciation of the practices of the times.[49]

III. Excursive Remarks on the Role of the LXX as Scripture

A major development that proved crucial to Christian trajectories of canon, Scripture and tradition, a development that we can but touch upon here, is the production of the LXX.[50] One difficulty that frustrates almost

---

[47] The New Testament writers, for example, are notorious for their adaptation and modification of Scriptural texts in the interest of contemporariness and relevance. See E. E. Ellis, "Quotations in the NT" in *ISBE* rev. ed. (ed. G. Bromiley; Grand Rapids: Eerdmans, 1979–1988), 4.18–25; and for the role of apologetics: Bart Ehrman, *The Orthodox Corruption of Scripture: The Effect of Early Christological Controversies on the Text of the New Testament.* (New York: Oxford University Press, 1997), and Wayne C. Kannaday, *Apologetic Discourse and the Scribal Tradition: Evidence of the Influence of Apologetic Interests on the Text of the Canonical Gospels.* (Atlanta: Society of Biblical Literature, 2004).

[48] Woodbridge has already made a case against an earlier claim to the contrary. See John D. Woodbridge, *Biblical Authority: A Critique of the Rogers/McKim Proposal.* (Grand Rapids: Zondervan, 1982). Yet the question itself seems a bit misguided since "inerrancy" for the ancient church would not have (and could not have, given their pre-modern intellectual milieu) meant the same thing that it does in certain Post-Reformation Protestant circles. See D. H. Williams, *Evangelicals and Tradition: The Formative Influence of the Early Church.* (Grand Rapids: Baker, 2005), 88–92.

[49] This is William Abraham's main point in *Canon and Criterion.*

[50] Readers should be reminded that "LXX" is an amorphous designation that different authors use to refer to different things. It is most commonly employed as a catch-all phrase that encompasses loosely "the Greek translation of the Hebrew Scriptures." The classificatory problems ensue when one inquires into precisely which Greek translation (or its revisions) one is referring or which books among the Hebrew Scriptures comprise the LXX. For example, Tov and many others acknowledge a distinction between the LXX and the Old Greek while Menken and Greenspoon, among others, identify the LXX with the Old Greek. See E. Tov, "The Septuagint" in *Mikra: Text, Translation, Reading and Interpretation of the Hebrew Bible in Ancient Judaism and Early Christianity.* CRINT 2.1. (ed. M. J. Mulder; Philadelphia: Fortress, 1988), 161–188, 161 and "Jewish Greek Scriptures" in *Early Judaism and Its Modern Interpreters.* (ed. R. A. Kraft and G. W. E. Nickelsburg; Atlanta: Scholars, 1986), 223–237, 230; M. J. J. Menken, "Old Testament Quotations in the Gospel of John" in *New Testament Writers and the Old Testament.* (ed., J. M. Court; London: SPCK, 2002), 29–45, 32; L. Greenspoon, "Hebrew into Greek: Interpretation In, By and Of the Septuagint" in *A History of Biblical Interpretation Vol. 1: The Ancient Period.* (ed. A. J. Hauser and D. F. Watson; Grand Rapids: Eerdmans, 2003),

every discussion of the LXX is that, with the discovery of at least one new Hebrew *Vorlage* among the Judean desert scrolls, scholars have realized that the process that eventuated in the LXX was far more complex than previously believed and that some claims that detect Septuagintal influence in the NT, for example, must now be reconsidered while others, at the very least, should remain tentative.[51] James Barr, for example, has complained of an over-reliance on the part of scholars upon a few standard works (namely, Ellis and Swete [whom Barr says Ellis seems to have followed]) to the effect that whatever weaknesses attended these seminal studies infect by derivation the entire corpus that was subsequently produced.[52]

Fortunately for us, germane to our study of canon, tradition and Scripture is the simple fact that the LXX was viewed as Scripture in the early church. For example, it is widely recognized that there are instances in the New Testament where an author seems to deliberately quote from the LXX and where that quoted Septuagintal text differs from the original Hebrew.[53] For example, Longenecker lists a handful of Jesus' citations

80–113. Tov suggests that a scholar's use of terminology may depend upon his place of training (i.e., in America, Europe, etc.). Since the level of the present study does not require that we get bogged down with terminology, we shall be content with following convention and use "Septuagint" and "LXX" interchangeably to mean simply "the Greek translation of the Hebrew."

[51] Silva writes, "Indeed, the textual transmission of the Greek Old Testament, when set against any other piece of ancient literature, almost certainly ranks first in complexity." See Silva, "The New Testament Use of the Old Testament" in *Scripture and Truth*. (ed. D. A. Carson and John D. Woodbridge; Grand Rapids: Baker, 1992], 147–165, 148–149.) See also Ralph W. Klein, *Textual Criticism of the Old Testament: The Septuagint After Qumran*. (Philadelphia: Fortress, 1974).

[52] James Barr, "Paul and the LXX: A Note on Some Recent Work." *JTS* 45 (1994): 593–601. For context, see E. Earle Ellis, *Paul's Use of the Old Testament*. (Grand Rapids: Eerdmans, 1957; repr. Grand Rapids: Baker, 1981; repr. Wipf and Stock, 2003) and H. B. Swete, *Introduction to the Old Testament Greek*. (Cambridge University Press, 1914; repr. Peabody, MA: Hendrickson, 1999). Sidney Jellicoe's *The Septuagint and Modern Study* (New York: Oxford University Press, 1968) updates Swete in many ways but does not attend to the use of the LXX in the NT.

[53] As Craig A. Evans notes, "Some of its differing readings appear in the NT, whose authors follow the LXX in more than one-half of their quotations of the OT." See his *Noncanonical Writings and New Testament Interpretation*. (Peabody, MA: Hendrickson, 1992), 73–74. Some vehemently resist this claim or are at least resistant to the more developed claim that the LXX was favored among Christians. For resistance to the latter, see Brevard Childs, *Introduction to the Old Testament as Scripture*. (Minneapolis: Fortress, 1979), 661–667; Christopher Seitz, "Two Testaments and the Failure of One Tradition-History" in *Figured Out: Typology and Providence in Christian Scripture*. (Louisville: Westminster/John Knox, 2001), 35–47.

in Matthew and Mark that depend on the LXX over against the MT[54] for their main points; L. T. Johnson has studied Acts to the effect that "the MT would have been useless for [the evangelist's] purposes";[55] Jostein Adna, among others, has specifically argued that the wording of the LXX was necessary for James' conclusion regarding Gentiles in Acts 15;[56] and a number of scholars have commented upon how the author of Hebrews seems also to have relied heavily upon the LXX for his argumentation.[57]

[54] Without spilling over into the niceties of textual criticism, we shall follow convention and refer to "the original Hebrew" as "MT."

[55] Luke Timothy Johnson, *Septuagintal Midrash in the Speeches of Acts.* (Milwaukee: Marquette, 2002), 14, approvingly summarizing the work of Jacques Dupont. See Richard N. Longenecker, *Biblical Exegesis in the Apostolic Period.* 2nd ed. (Grand Rapids: Eerdmans, 1999), 45–46. See also Gert J. Steyn, *Septuagint Quotations in the Context of the Petrine and Pauline Speeches of the Acta Apostolorum.* CBET 12. (Kampen: Kok Pharos, 1995); Huub van de Sandt, "The Quotations of Acts 13.32–52" *Bib* 75 (1994): 26–58; idem., "Acts 28.28: No Salvation for the People of Israel? An Answer in the Perspective of the LXX" *ETL* 70 (1994): 341–358; Joseph Fitzmyer, "The Use of the Old Testament in Luke-Acts" in *To Advance the Gospel: New Testament Studies.* 2nd ed. (Grand Rapids: Eerdmans, 1998), 295–313. The *absence* of a quote on the basis of the LXX's omission of key phrases is postulated in Fredrick C. Holmgren, *The Old Testament and the Significance of Jesus: Embracing Change—Maintaining Identity.* (Grand Rapids: Eerdmans, 1999), 52–53.

[56] "James' Position at the Summit Meeting of the Apostles and the Elders in Jerusalem (Acts 15)" in *The Mission of the Early Church to Jews and Gentiles.* WUNT 127. (ed. J. Adna and H. Kvalbein; Tubingen: Mohr, 2000), 125–161, 148. See also van de Sandt, "An Explanation of Acts 15.6–21 in the Light of Deuteronomy 4.25–29 (LXX)" *JSNT* 46 (1992): 73–97.

[57] The claim that there are Septuagintal citations/allusions in Hebrews is not universally accepted. See Roy E. Gane, "Re-Opening Katasma ('Veil') in Hebrews 6:19" *AUSS* 38 (2000): 5–8; Norman H. Young, "Where Jesus Has Gone as a Forerunner on Our Behalf" *AUSS* 39 (2001): 165–173; Richard M. Davidson, "Christ's Entry 'Within the Veil' in Hebrews 6:19–20: The Old Testament Background" *AUSS* 39 (2001): 175–190; Young, "The Day of Dedication or the Day of Atonement? The Old Testament Background to Hebrews 6:19–20 Revisited" *AUSS* 40 (2002): 61–68; Davidson, "Inauguration or Day of Atonement? A Response to Norman Young's 'Old Testament Background to Hebrews 6:19–20 Revisited' *AUSS* 40 (2002): 69–88. Acknowledging disagreements, Silva uses Hebrews as his test case in "The New Testament Use". And see now, Radu Gheorghita, *The Role of the Septuagint in Hebrews: An Investigation of Its Influence with Special Consideration to Use of Hab 2:3–4 in Heb 10:37–38.* WUNT 160. (Tubingen: Mohr, 2003). For additional NT texts that evince OT citations/allusions (including many that are not strictly Septuagintal), one might peruse: C. H. Dodd, *According to the Scriptures: The Sub-Structure of New Testament Theology.* (London: Fontana Books, 1962), 28–110; Swete, *Introduction,* 381–405. Scholars have been known to cull through *Old Testament Quotations in the New Testament.* (ed. R. E. Bratcher, et. al.; United Bible Societies, 1987) for suggestions; students and ministers the indices provided in their Greek New Testaments. For a catalogue of references in the DSS, see the appendices in James Vanderkam and Peter Flint, *The Meaning of the Dead Sea Scrolls: Their Significance for Understanding the Bible, Judaism, Jesus*

When one examines the broad picture, it is not difficult to see that the LXX had quickly become the preferred Old Testament for Christians from virtually every quarter.[58] Below, we shall briefly consider how the church incorporated a panoply of texts into its collection of holy Scriptures.[59]

Scholars were once of the opinion that the LXX was a fanciful rendering of the MT wherein the translators either did not know their Hebrew, were not concerned with providing an accurate, literal translation, or were so encumbered by Greek ways of thinking that their theological sensibilities were such that they felt compelled to affect changes to their texts in order to render them more acceptable to Greek readers (e.g., by de-anthropomorphizing references to God). As early as 1937, however, it became apparent to some, on the basis of a close comparison between the LXX

---

and Christianity. (New York: HarperCollins, 2002).

[58] Disavowals by Childs, Seitz and others stem in part, I think, from different emphases rather than different presuppositions (as Seitz unhelpfully suggests). David G. Dunbar also mentions how faulty presuppositions are governing the investigations of those who disagree with him. See his "The Biblical Canon" in *Hermeneutics, Authority and Canon.* (ed. D. A. Carson and J. D. Woodbridge; Grand Rapids: Zondervan, 1986), 299–360. Instructive in this regard may be the dialogue between Stanley E. Porter and Robert W. Walls over the proper roles of historical criticism and theological concerns respectively. Though they do not discuss the LXX, their discussion illustrates how two related emphases concurrently command the attention of scholars in overlapping fields. See Porter, "Pauline Authorship and the Pauline Epistles: Implications for Canon" *BBR* 5 (1995): 105–123; Wall, "Pauline Authorship and the Pauline Epistles: Response to S. E. Porter" *BBR* 5 (1995): 125–128; Porter, "Pauline Authorship and the Pauline Epistles: Response to R. W. Wall's Response" *BBR* 6 (1996): 133–138. Perceived, and real, theological issues involving the role of the LXX may be deemed problematic; this may help explain the clamor over presuppositions. The sentiment may very well be, "If these theological problems do not disturb you, your presuppositions must have gone awry (i.e., you have lost a particular form of theological sensitivity)." Along these lines, Silva's "The New Testament Use" was specifically commissioned to address particular expressions of these concerns. Sanders, for his part, suspects that Childs' approach is essentially a product of the Reformation, and if he is right, then Ulrich's question becomes an especially pointed one: "[I]f Jerome or the translators in the early Reformation period had had Hebrew texts available like 4QpaleoExod, 4Qsam, 1QIsa, and 4QJer alongside 'the Hebrew' they knew (namely, the MT), would they have chosen the MT?" See his "Double Literary Editions of Biblical Narratives and Reflections on Determining the Form to Be Translated" in Ulrich, *The Dead Sea Scrolls*, 34–50, 43.

[59] For concise introductions to the LXX and related concerns, see Roger Ledeaut, "The Greek Bible: Hidden Treasure for Jews and Christians" in *Renewing the Judeo-Christian Wellsprings.* (ed. V. A. McInnes; Crossroad: New York, 1987), 53–71; Julio Trebolle Barrera, *The Jewish Bible and the Christian Bible: An Introduction to the History of the Bible.* (New York: Brill, 1998), 301–323; and Mogens Müller, "HEBRAICA SIVE GRAECA VERITAS: The Jewish Bible at the Time of the New Testament and the Christian Bible" *SJOT* 1 (1989): 55–71.

and the New Testament, that the LXX was not a "sloppy" translation at all, but rather, in all likelihood, following, at certain points, an alternate text than the one then available to scholars.[60] As time went on, and as is well known today, more and more scholars began to appreciate that the LXX need not be deemed a sloppy translation, for it does, in several instances, follow a non-MT text and sometimes actually preserves the earlier reading, in effect correcting the MT.[61] In fact, some scholars are so impressed with the integrity of the LXX that they have concluded that the LXX was specifically designed to replace the existing Hebrew texts for readings in the synagogue.[62] If this is true, it would stand to reason to suppose that the LXX translators exercised an extraordinary amount of care as they completed their task. Though these considerations have considerably increased its usefulness for text-critical questions, it is safe to say that the importance of the LXX has moved beyond text critical matters.

The (Greek) Christian culture that had begun to take root during the first centuries of the Common Era was largely influenced by the LXX.[63] An obvious way in which this occurred was the role that the LXX played in proselytizing. Common sense agrees with Sperber's remarks: "In order to appeal to the prospective Christians . . . both Testaments had to be presented in Greek." [64] It is not difficult to imagine that the same would

[60] See, for example, Sherman E. Johnson, "The Septuagint and the New Testament" *JBL* 56 (1937): 331–345.

[61] See Natalio Fernández Marcos, *The Septuagint in Context: Introduction to the Greek Versions of the Bible.* (trans. W. G. E. Watson; Boston: Brill, 2001), 66–70, and also Heriberto Haber, "The LXX and the Bible: Matter for Thought" *JBQ* 24 (1996): 260–261. "Sloppy" is meant to encapsulate "fanciful," "incompetent," and "ideological." Marcos (or at least his translator with whom he collaborated) uses the word "tendentious."

[62] See Staffon Oloffson, "The Septuagint and Earlier Jewish Interpretive Tradition— Especially as Reflected in the Targums" *SJOT* 10 (1996): 192–216; Mogens Müller, "The Septuagint as the Bible of the New Testament Church: Some Reflections" *SJOT* 7 (1993): 194–207; F. F. Bruce, *The Canon of Scripture.* (Downers Grove, IL: InterVarsity, 1988), 44.

[63] An interesting question, not pursued here, is how classical traditions of interpretation affected early Greek Christian culture. For example, with respect to our immediate discussion, the classical idea that a culture must be based upon written texts likely facilitated the prominent position that Christians allotted to the LXX. For this and other points, see Frances M. Young, *Biblical Exegesis and Formation of Christian Culture.* (Cambridge University Press, 1997; repr. Peabody, MA: Hendrickson, 2002).

[64] Alexander Sperber, "New Testament and Septuagint" *JBL* 59 (1940): 193–293, 195–196. Not only that, but, as Schaper writes, "Greek translations of biblical books were used by Palestinian Jews as a means of religious propaganda amongst their brethren in the diaspora." See J. Schaper, "The Rabbinic Canon and the Old Testament of the Early Church: A Social-Historical View" in *Canonization and Decanonization: Papers Presented to*

have held for successful engagement with the wider Greek culture (the case of Philo comes readily to mind).[65] Though pragmatic concerns such as these may seem theologically embarrassing to some, the stuff of history is, in great measure, comprised of unavoidable practicalities. The appeal of the LXX to the early church (not to mention Jews, particularly prior to the advent of Christian sects) was a natural development. It should be noted, though, that the LXX differs from the MT in 1) the order and titles of its books, 2) in the order and contents of the material contained within many of these books, and 3) in the number of books that were chosen for inclusion within the respective collections. These have, from the beginning, proven to be very thorny issues.[66] Whereas 1) and 2) can be at least partially explained by way of reference to a non-MT *Vorlage*,[67] 3) has (especially recently) been a matter of interminable dispute. Even so, it was really the first two that especially troubled ancient Jewish and Christian adherents.[68]

---

the *International Conference of the Leiden Institute for the Study of Religions (LISOR), Held at Leiden 9–10 January 1997.* (ed. A. van der Kooij and K. van der Toorn; Boston: Brill, 1998), 93–106, 95.

[65] For suggestions regarding the import of the LXX with respect to the contemporary cultural milieu, see Young, *Biblical Exegesis*; Lamin Sanneh, *Translating the Message: The Missionary Impact on Culture.* (Maryknoll, NY: Orbis, 1989); W. Richey Hogg, "The Scriptures in the Christian World Mission: Three Historical Considerations" *Missiology* 12 (1984): 389–404, 393; James L. Kugel, *Traditions of the Bible: A Guide to the Bible as It Was at the Start of the Common Era.* (Cambridge, MA: Harvard University Press, 1998), 515–516, 653–654; C. H. Dodd, *The Bible and the Greeks.* (London: Hodder & Stoughton, 1964).

[66] Consider, for example, the early apologetic efforts on behalf of the LXX that prompted the *Letter of Aristeas* and, especially, its subsequent embellishments. For the differences between the LXX and the MT, see J. Lust, "Septuagint and Canon" in *Biblical Canons.* (ed. J. M. Auwers and H. J. de Jonge; Leuven: Peeters, 2003), 39–55; for the *Letter* and its embellishments, see Marcos, *The Septuagint*, 35–52.

[67] J. Lust, "Septuagint and Canon", 43, for example, accounts for the "minuses" in LXX Ezekiel this way and generalizes, "Many of the divergences are clearly due to the Hebrew Vorlage used by the Greek translators, and not to changes brought in by the translators or later redactors, nor to errors in the course of the transmission of the text." See also Ulrich, "Multiple Literary Editions: Reflections Toward a Theory of the History of the Biblical Text" in *The Dead Sea Scrolls*, 99–120. The issues raised here obviously take us well beyond the range of the present essay. For starters, the reader might consult Karen H. Jobes and Moisés Silva, *Invitation to the Septuagint.* (Grand Rapids: Baker, 2000). Barr cautions, though, that Jobes and Silva unduly downplay the import of the LXX in favor of the MT. See James Barr, review of Karen H. Jobes and Moisés Silva, *Invitation to the Septuagint, Review of Biblical Literature* [http://www.bookreviews.org] (2002). This review now includes an appended response by Jobes and Silva.

[68] See, for example, Ulrich, "The Canonical Process," 60: "[T]he multiplicity of 'titles' and

That the LXX contained books not found in the MT does not seem to have been a major item of debate.[69] It would seem that, from a Jewish perspective, the Bible (Old Testament) persisted as an open canon and the LXX was simply viewed as a legitimate variation. Either way, all books contained within the LXX, even those in excess of the MT, were of traditional Jewish stock and highly regarded (if not thought of as inspired). Most of the tension would build rather around those books which were common to all traditions, but the reason for this was textual and hermeneutical and surely not canonical.[70]

Conversely, the church was not apparently bothered by the fact that its LXX contained extra books. In fact, some scholars surmise that the inclusion of additional books was deliberately done by the Church in order to maintain the greatest measure of continuity possible between the churches and contemporary Jewish communities. Schaper explains that the church "demonstrated what it perceived as its unbroken continuity with Israel by accepting all the books contained in the rabbinic canon"— even those that were of no avail (S of S, Esther, etc.). In addition, Schaper notes, by accepting books that were without the rabbinic canon, "[t]he Church thus attempted to accommodate not only Palestinian groups and their messianic traditions, but also the more philosophically minded and more thoroughly 'Hellenized' communities in the Diaspora."[71] In essence, "[t]he canon of the Christian Septuagint can be described as a compromise solution intended to establish Christian unity through the representation of all or nearly all (Jewish) Christian 'Old Testament' traditions."[72]

---

the general lack of concern about expressly naming and delimiting the contents forcefully indicate that the many authors who referred to this anthology of literature with such diverse and generic designations were obviously unconcerned about the issue concerning which later Jews and Christians made decisions and still later called canon."

[69] Barrera, *The Jewish Bible*, 511, does list "the extent of the canon" as an item of dispute, but he interestingly passes over the item in the enumeration that follows.

[70] Ulrich cites Talmon to the effect that "[t]he limited flux of the textual transmission of the Bible appears to be a legitimate and accepted phenomenon in ancient scribal tradition" and stresses that "it was books, not specific textual forms of the books, that were canonical." See Ulrich, "Plurifomity in the Biblical Text, Text Groups, and Question of Canon" in *The Dead Sea Scrolls*, 79–98, 93 n.37, citing S. Talmon "The Textual Study of the Bible—A New Outlook" in *Qumran and the History of the Biblical Text*. (ed. F. M. Cross and S. Talmon; Cambridge, MA: Harvard University Press, 1975), 321–400. Text forms (in this case, LXX vs. MT) did, however, become an issue when Christians began to commandeer the LXX for their own purposes.

[71] J. Schaper, "The Rabbinic Canon," 103.

[72] J. Schaper, "The Rabbinic Canon," 104.

The "extra" books within the LXX (a fact that tends to bother modern Christians) were not evidently an issue between Jews and Christians in antiquity. However, the disparate texts that comprised the books of the LXX and the MT (a fact that does not seem to bother modern Christians) eventually became a major source of contention. For one thing, it aggravated early Christian apologetic efforts on several accounts. [73] First, Christians had been taught via *testimonia* [74] or otherwise that the Greek Jewish Scriptures provided proof that the apostolic teaching about Jesus was fulfillment of prophecy. Second, the majority of Christians seem to have believed that the LXX was inspired by God. Third, many Christians understood that they had inherited the LXX as the Scriptures that the Apostles had used and that Christians, therefore, had a religious duty to uphold the accuracy of the LXX. For these and other reasons, it was inconceivable to early Christians that the LXX could actually differ from the MT. Nevertheless, as Jews began to produce LXX revisions that were more in line with the MT, Christians were soon confronted with just such a possibility. The majority of them responded, in turn, by strictly denying the possibility (Jerome, in his time, being a notable exception) that the LXX really differed from the MT.[75] Instead, they accused their Jewish interlocutors of tampering with the sacred texts and deliberately de-Christianizing the Old Testament without due reference to the MT. As Müller points out: "[T]he moment the question of the true wording of the Old Testament was raised, the Septuagint was declared [by Christians] to be the genuine Bible text."[76] In this way, Old Testament Scriptural proofs of the Christian gospel, such as the famous virgin birth "prophecy" of Isaiah 7.14, were repeatedly caught up in the fray over whether the LXX or the MT provided legitimate readings.[77]

---

[73] For the following, see Mogens Müller, "GRAECA SIVE HEBRAICA VERITAS? The Defence of the Septuagint in the Early Church" *SJOT* 1 (1989): 103–124.

[74] See Joseph A. Fitzmyer, "'4QTestimonia' and the New Testament" in *Essays on the Semitic Background of the New Testament.* (Scholars, 1974, as *The Semitic Background of the New Testament*; repr. Grand Rapids: Eerdmans; Livonia, MI: Dove, 1997), 59–89.

[75] See William Adler, "The Jews as Falsifiers: Charges of Tendentious Emendations in Anti-Jewish Christian Polemic" in *Translation of Scripture: Proceedings of a Conference at the Annenberg Research Institute, May 15–16, 1989.* (Philadelphia: Annenberg Research Institute, 1990), 1–27.

[76] Muller, "The Septuagint," 195.

[77] This controversy continues today with many Christians arguing that the events that befell Jesus literally fulfill specific Old Testament prophecies or, at the very least, that aspects of the life, death and resurrection of Jesus correspond to various portions of the Old Testament when viewed as a "composite prophecy" or when interpreted in terms of

In sum, when it comes to the import of the LXX to the early church, Sanders' surmise cannot be gainsaid: "Focus on the MT leaves the NT, whose Scripture was the Septuagint, out in the cold for the most part."[78] The role of a Greek *translation* as the Scripture of the Apostles and the early Church certainly implies a degree of variability and preferentiality[79] inherent in the relation among canon, Scripture and tradition that should certainly elicit further scholarly attention by evangelicals.

IV. The Role of Scripture in the Early Church

Geoffrey W. Bromiley emphasizes in a pertinent article that "as the Word of God given by the Spirit of God, Scripture had for the Fathers the status of a primary authority in the life, teaching, and mission of the church. Deriving from God and enshrining the truth of God, it had indeed the authority of God himself."[80] Interestingly enough, in this study of the role of Scriptures in the writings of the Apostolic Fathers, Bromiley discovers, among other things to be sure, nothing other than the Reformation principle of *sola scriptura*:

> First, the coexistence of the oral and written Word or tradition must not mean their equation, for the two must be differentiated as well as identified and the former subordinated to the latter. Second, the presence of the Holy Spirit in the life and work of the church does not imply the church's exemption of Holy Scripture . . . Third . . . no agreed interpretation, however ancient or as-

a "cumulative exegesis." See, for example, F. F. Bruce, "Paul's Use of the Old Testament in Acts" in *Tradition and Interpretation in the New Testament: Essays in Honor of E. Earle Ellis for His 60th Birthday*. (ed. G. F. Hawthrone and O. Betz; Grand Rapids: Eerdmans, 1987), 71–79, where Paul is understood, in places, to offer initially unrelated prophetic texts conjunctly as a "composite prophecy"; Homer Heater, Jr., "Matthew 2:6 and Its Old Testament Sources" *JETS* 26 (1983), 395–397, where Matthew is said to rely upon a combination of unmentioned Old Testament texts that would have naturally come to mind if a "cumulative exegesis" is employed. More balanced, in the eyes of the present author, is Fitzmyer, "Old Testament Quotations in Qumran and the NT" in *Essays*, 3–58.

[78] James A. Sanders, *From Sacred Story to Sacred Text: Canon as Paradigm*. (Minneapolis: Fortress, 1987; repr. Eugene: Wipf and Stock), 166.

[79] Hengel points out that textual disparities comprised only a secondary problem. A more fundamental problem must be admitted: disagreement over *how* the Jewish Scriptures should be interpreted. See also Müller, "GRAECA". Those desiring a fuller treatment should see Hengel, *The Septuagint as Christian Scripture: Its Prehistory and the Problem of Its Canon*. (New York: T & T Clark, 2002). Above reference to Hengel, *The Septuagint*, 9.

[80] "The Church Fathers and Holy Scripture" in *Scripture and Truth*. (ed. D. A. Carson and John D. Woodbridge; Grand Rapids: Baker, 1992), 195–220, 207.

sured, can be described as definitive . . . Fourth, the dogmas of the church do not form, even at the hermeneutical level, a body of teaching comparable in status to Holy Scripture . . . they are always historical interpretations and as such they can have only relative normativeness and not the absolute normativeness that, under God, Holy Scripture itself enjoys.[81]

To be sure, these four points are, according to Bromiley, ones "that the Fathers sensed but did not always formulate as explicitly as one could desire." Notwithstanding, he adamantly claims that these indeed were paramount concerns of the early church. In spite of an open acknowledgement and critique of non-Reformation attitudes and interpretive practices that are present in the Fathers, Bromiley could not resist involving himself in "the search for sola scriptura in the early church."[82] Before proceeding we should confess that if someone of Bromiley's stature could not refrain from seeking to legitimate his own tradition in his study on the early church,[83] it is unlikely that the present chapters can claim any more innocence. Nevertheless, we shall self-consciously press further and attempt to ascertain whether the above pattern continued into the post-apostolic era.

---

[81] "The Church Fathers," 219.

[82] On this general phenomenon, see D. H. Williams, "The Search for Sola Scriptura in the Early Church." *Int* 52 No. 4. (Oct 1998): 354–366.

[83] Can the same be said for T. F. Torrance? See, for example, T. F. Torrance, "The Deposit of Faith," *SJT* 36 (1983): 1–28.

Recognition Six:

Young Evangelicals Need to Appreciate the Canonical Dialectic

THUS FAR it has been suggested that it is helpful to govern an inspection of the role of Scripture in the early church in terms of inclusive and exclusive canons and open and closed boundaries. The cultural and social situations during the Second Temple period were such, it was argued, that the introduction of holy writings in no way stifled the flourishing of a rich oral complex. If anything, these writings gave more direction to the oral and other cultural traditions and became part of the living history of Israel. It was then posited that there existed a number of religious teachers during the first century C.E. who operated within the parameters of a broad and diverse religious and cultural tradition that suggested to them differing outlines of what God was planning for his people. These leaders, it was observed, were content to teach in line with what they saw to be God's overall purposes and at times saw it fit to rule against the scriptural mandates (in the case of halakah) or to reference embellished interpretive traditions as if they were Scripture (in the case of haggadah). Below, we shall compare and contrast the uses of Scripture in two of the early church fathers with those of their predecessors.

I. The Early Church as an Extension of Second Temple Developments

During the Second Temple period, it cannot be disputed that manifold tradition histories and oral torahs existed upon which religious teachers, and even the biblical writers themselves, drew in learning and teaching Torah. What counterpart existed with respect to the earliest church? The new Christian groups, for their part, could boast of oral gospel traditions, including different versions of Jesus' *logia*, the interpretive traditions of the Jewish Scriptures, including the Scriptures themselves, and their own catechisms, baptismal or otherwise.[1]

On the latter, Philip Carrington has provided a fascinating study.[2] Beginning with the advent of proselyte baptism in Second Temple Judaism, Carrington examines the role of the Holiness Code (Lev 17–20) in terms of a Jewish, and eventually, though modified, Christian, proselytizing and teaching tool. He suggestively describes this catechetical emphasis as "the Christian tradition of walking (*halakah*) or consecration."[3] The main points are: "(1) Not to walk as the gentiles: Lev. xviii, 1–5. (2) To avoid the (three) major sins: Lev. xvii–xviii. (3) The reception of the Spirit is a call to holiness: Lev. xix, 2. (4) Love one another: Lev. xix, 18."[4] He traces the phrases "do not walk as the gentiles," "fornication, covetousness, idolatry" (the three major sins), and others through the letters of Paul, Peter and James, the Acts and other New Testament and contemporary Christian literature. Especially convincing is his comparison of his proposed summary of the Holiness Code with I Thess 4 and I Pet 1.[5] For our purposes, his summary of the religious understanding of these early Christians' communal identity is particularly instructive:

> Outside was the dark gentile world whose unclean practices were renounced; baptism cleansed its recipient from defilement (the word *hamartia*, sin, is never free from this conception) and was the occasion on which he received the Holy Spirit. This was not, however, an individual or subjective experience; it was, rather, the incorporation or adoption of the convert into the community in which the Holy Spirit lived, the brotherhood which was the sanctuary of God

---

[1] For a fuller, though speculative, catalog, see David L. Tiede, "Religious Propaganda and the Gospel Literature of the Early Christian Mission." *Principat* 25.2 (Berlin: Walter de Gruyter, 1984), 1705–1729.

[2] *The Primitive Christian Catechism: A Study in the Epistles.* (Cambridge: Cambridge University Press, 1940).

[3] *The Primitive Christian Catechism*, 12.

[4] *The Primitive Christian Catechism*, 12.

[5] *The Primitive Christian Catechism*, 16–29. He then proceeds to adduce further common material (not without variation) amongst many of the New Testament works, emphasizing order, appearance of key Greek words, the context in which they appear and their continuity with Jewish precedents. Willy Rordorf, for example, writing almost sixty years later, confirms (even if in passing) a thesis similar to Carrington's in his essay, "The Bible in the Teaching and the Liturgy of Early Christian Communities" in *The Bible in Greek Christian Antiquity*. (ed. and trans. Paul M. Blowers; Notre Dame, IN: University of Notre Dame Press, 1997), 69–102, 82–84.

himself, whose spirit consecrated it in love. The divine community
of Leviticus is the pattern and progenitor of the new.[6]

Notice how the proposal is an outline of Christian halakah and not primarily a summary of beliefs. Although some may perceive a lack of continuity here with the later "rule of truth,"[7] Carrington's proposal does boast
a "Jewishness" that was characteristic of much of early Christian teaching.[8]
Especially in light of how so many Christians today take pride in how
they can distinguish their religion from all others by observing that it is
what Christians *believe* (and not what they *do* per se) that sets them apart,
Carrington's focus upon Christian halakah is most illuminating.

Carrington's work coincides with recent attempts that re-conceive
the full breadth of the church's "canonical material" in terms of its "use in
the Church to bring people to salvation, to make people holy, to make believers proficient disciples of Jesus Christ and the like."[9] This is not to deny
the truth contained in the common portrayal of a conflict-driven, doctrinally sensitive Church whose self-understanding was heavily determined by
conflict and its concomitant quest to guard the "faith once delivered to the

---

[6] *The Primitive Christian Catechism*, 21.

[7] One can still affirm, for example, that "at the centre of Christian believing , teaching
and confessing stood, from the start, Jesus, through whom God is working for the world's
salvation" or that "the early formulas therefore include . . . a recital of his way from birth to
cross, resurrection, exaltation and on to his expressed return." See "The Apostolic Faith in
the Scriptures and in the Early Church." Report of a Faith and Order Consultation held in
Rome, 1–8 October 1983. *Ecumenical Review* 36 (Jl 1984): 329–37, 333. For an in-depth
study, see J. N. D. Kelly, *Early Christian Creeds*. 3rd ed. (New York: Longman, 1972).

[8] See, for example, *The Didache* and The Shepherd of Hermas, *Mandate*. For a brief account
of the development of baptismal catechisms in the early church, see Paul W. Harkins,
"Chrysostom's Postbaptismal Instructions" in *The Heritage of the Early Church: Essays in
Honor of The Very Reverend Georges Vasilievich Florovsky*. Orientalia Christiana Analecta
195. (ed. D. Neiman and M. Schatkin; Rome: Pont. Institutum Studiorum Orientalum,
1973), 151–165.

[9] William J. Abraham, *Canon and Criterion*, 51. Abraham paraphrases 2 Tim 3.16 and
applies the description to all that he includes in his construal of canon. Training for intact
Christian living was in a very important sense *the* purpose of God. With respect to the study
of Scripture, see Allan E. Johnson, "The Methods and Presuppositions of Patristic Exegesis
in the Formation of Christian Personality." *Di* 16 (Sum 1977): 186–90. With respect to
the use of the gifts of the Holy Spirit, see M. Parmentier, "The Gifts of the Spirit in Early
Christianity" in *The Impact of Scripture in Early Christianity*. (ed. J. Den Boeft and M. L.
Van Poll-Van De Lidonk; Leiden: Brill, 1999), 58–78. With respect to the formulation of
doctrine, D. M. Stanley, "'Become Imitators of Me': The Pauline Conception of Apostolic
Tradition" in *Studia Biblica et Orientalia Volumen II: Novum Testamentum*. Analecta Biblica
11. (Roma: Pontificio Instituto Biblico, 1959), 291–309.

saints."[10] However, such emphases tend to obscure the pastoral and other practical (and spiritual) concerns of many of the leaders, not to mention laypersons, of the early church. An example of this can be seen in the formation of the New Testament itself. New Testament scholar Koester insists that "[w]hatever attested the events of salvation and told the shared story and whatever proved useful for the building of communities was acceptable."[11] As uncomfortable as this statement may be for many evangelicals, Koester at least reminds us that sacred writings alone never constituted the gospel. What constituted the gospel was "the saving message that created and sustained the Christian faith."[12] Without submitting to a false dichotomy, there is a real danger of construing canon in epistemological terms only.[13] Contrast this epistemological emphasis with Herbert T. Mayer's list of Scripture, exegesis, tradition, the rule of faith, the Holy Spirit and the bishops as those factors which determined theological authority in the early church.[14] We might add to this the "spiritual discernment for every day living"[15] characteristic of Hillel, Jesus and Paul as seen above. In the face of the rise of the Montanist movement, it may seem absurd to emphasize such a factor on behalf of the early church. Nevertheless, we shall examine two fathers to see to what extent they can be said to be in line

---

[10] According to Robert B. Eno, "Throughout this development, there is the presumption of a certain static and set nature of revelation. God has revealed his plan for the world and Jesus has carried it out, all basically in the past. The ongoing life of God's people is also a part of the sacred history but the most important actions of God are the two comings of Christ . . . The task of the present is to hold tight to the past so that nothing may be lost or added in anticipation of that future . . . In this schema, the principal agency for the mediating of the word is the official ministry of the Church." See Eno, "Authority and Conflict in the Early Church." *EgT* 7 (Ja 1976): 41–60, 45.

[11] Helmut Koester, "Writings and the Spirit: Authority and Politics in Ancient Christianity." *HTR* 84:4 (1991): 353–72, 370. Koester's assessment fits well with James' use of extracanonical sources above. See also, Lee M. McDonald, *The Formation of the Christian Biblical Canon*. Rev. ed. (Peabody, MA: Hendrickson, 1995), 289. For a different view, see D. Moody Smith, "When Did the Gospels Become Scripture?" *JBL* 119.1 (2000): 3–20.

[12] Koester, "Writings and the Spirit," 366.

[13] See Abraham, *Canon and Criterion* and John Webster, *Holy Scripture: A Dogmatic Sketch*. (New York: Cambridge University Press, 2003).

[14] "Scripture, Tradition, Authority in the Early Church." *CTM* 38 (Ja 1967): 19–23. Mention of the Holy Spirit bespeaks a concern to legitimate the Lutheran tradition of the writer, as Mayer himself intimates.

[15] For an example of this from a later period, see François Neyt, "A Form of Charismatic Authority." *ECR* 6 (Spr 1974): 52–65.

with the trajectory established thus far. The church fathers to be examined are Justin Martyr and Irenaeus.

II. The Role of Scripture in Two Church Fathers

Justin Martyr

Justin Martyr is slightly earlier than Irenaeus and was possibly his teacher for a time.[16] A salient feature of Justin's writings is a prophecy-fulfillment emphasis.[17] As a matter of fact, the Hebrew prophets to whom Justin repeatedly defers not only predicted all that took place with respect to the specifics of the Christian revelation (i.e., Christ), they also predicted all that the Greek philosophers would ever eventually come to discover. In his *First Apology*, for example, we find this astounding claim:

> And so, too, Plato, when he says, "The blame is his who chooses, and God is blameless," took this from the prophet Moses and uttered it. For Moses is more ancient than all the Greek writers. And whatever both philosophers and poets have said concerning the immortality of the soul, or punishments after death, or contemplation of things heavenly, or doctrines of the like kind, they have received such suggestions from the prophets as have enabled them to understand and interpret these things. And hence there seem to be seeds of truth among all men; but they are charged with not accurately understanding [the truth] when they assert contradictories. So that what we say about future events being foretold, we do not say it as if they came about by a fatal necessity; but God foreknowing all that shall be done by all men, and it being His decree that the future actions of men shall all be recompensed according to their several value, He foretells by the Spirit of prophecy that He will bestow meet rewards according to the merit of the actions done, always urging the human race to effort and recollection, showing that He cares and provides for men.[18]

---

[16] W. H. C. Frend, *The Rise of Christianity*. (Philadelphia: Fortress, 1984), 244.

[17] Cullen I. K. Story, *The Nature of Truth in "The Gospel of Truth" and in the Writings of Justin Martyr: A Study of the Pattern of Orthodoxy in the Middle of the Second Christian Century*. NovTSup 25. (Leiden: E. J. Brill, 1970). It is not to be thought, on account of our failure to mention it above, that Irenaeus did not also share this preoccupation. See Rodrigo Polanco Fermandois, *El Concepto de Profecía en la Teología de San Ireneo*. (Madrid: Biblioteca de Autores Cristianos, 1999).

[18] *1 Apol.* 11.44.

All of history and all that men think and do can be accounted for by Justin's concept of prophecy. As James Pan notes, Justin writes in this way on the basis of his "assumption that everything true and good must have come from revelation through the Logos in which all humanity participated."[19] Pan concludes that in spite of Justin's intention to integrate church tradition with Hellenistic philosophy in order to establish Christianity's reasonableness to outsiders, he has compromised the biblical vision and especially the uniqueness of the Incarnation. Irrespective of whether Pan is right or not,[20] we can observe that Justin's portal that allowed him to interact to such an extant with Greek philosophy seems to be his innovative concept of "seeds of the word" ("seeds of truth" in the above quotation). Recognizing that Justin is here borrowing a Stoic idea, Neuhauser explains how it has also been transformed by him: "This human logos is 'engrafted' (emphytos) in all mankind. It is 'seminal' (spermatikos), a seed. But it is a seed of the true and real Logos, Christ."[21] Corresponding to these seeds of the Word were demons who accomplished precisely the opposite of what the Word enabled. The demons operated in the world of falsehood and deceived people into abandoning ethics. Only the seed of the Word could secure an individual from the activity of demons.[22] How did the seeds of the Logos affect Justin's view of Scripture? In order to suggest an answer to this, we shall turn our attention to his *Dial*.

One scholar has challenged the consensus that Justin considers certain New Testament writings as equally authoritative as the Old Testament. Notably, Charles H. Cosgrove has argued for precisely the opposite based upon the fact that Justin does not make a case for the New Testament writings as Scripture. He writes, "The fact is, he does less than fail to defend

[19] "Contextualization: A methodological Enquiry With Examples from the History of Theology." *South East Asia Journal of Theology*, 21 no 2–22 no 1 (1980–1981): 47–64, 52.

[20] For a different view, see Henry Chadwick, *Early Christian Thought and the Classical Tradition: Studies in Justin, Clement and Origen*. (New York: Oxford University Press, 1966), 9–23.

[21] Friedrich Neuhauser, "The Doctrine of the 'Seeds of the Word' in the Apologies of St. Justin Martyr" in *Research Seminar on Non-Biblical Scriptures*. (ed. D. S. Amalorpavadass; Bangalore: National Biblical, Catechetical and Liturgical Centre, 1975), 190–209, 193. Though a passage from Justin's *1 Apol.* was quoted above in order to introduce the idea, the phrase "seeds of the Word" appears only in his *2 Apol.* See also A. H. Armstrong and R. A. Markus, *Christian Faith and Greek Philosophy*. (London: Darton, Longman and Todd, 1960), 143–144.

[22] Neuhauser, "Seeds of the Word," 197–198. According to Grant, "The notion of *daimones* as standing between God or the gods and humanity was apparently developed by the Platonic philosopher Xenocrates." See Robert M. Grant, *Greek Apologists of the Second Century*. (Philadelphia: The Westminster Press, 1988), 63.

their authority; he actually dethrones them from what scriptural authority they may have been attaining by his use of the designation 'memoirs'."[23] The term "memoirs" is allegedly meant to convey, "purely historical documents" and not "authorities."[24] However, Cosgrove's argument does not rest upon this point: he only requires that the *Dial.* be written to Christians.[25] Justin's intended audience is a disputed question, though. Barnard does not seem to have been of the opinion that Justin had written primarily with Christians in mind.[26] Allert, too, does not believe that the work was written for Christians,[27] but the matter is by no means settled.[28]

In any event, for our purposes, we shall briefly examine the role that Scripture plays for Justin. Neither Justin nor Trypho give evidence of knowing any Hebrew whatever.[29] This seems a reasonable conclusion based upon how Justin restricts his biblical quotations to the LXX.[30] However, he was knowledgeable with respect to many details that pertain to Jesus' life and ministry that were not included in the canonical Gospels.[31] Justin was certainly privy to oral traditions, but as we saw in his *Apologies*, he

---

[23] "Justin Martyr and the Emerging Christian Canon: Observations on the Purpose and Destination of the Dialogue with Trypho." *VC* 36 (1982): 209–232.

[24] Cosgrove, "Justin Martyr," 223.

[25] Cosgrove, "Justin Martyr," 211.

[26] L. W. Barnard, "The Old Testament and Judaism in the Writings of Justin Martyr." *VT* 14 No. 4 (1964): 395–406. For a reading of the *Dial.* that differs from that of Barnard with respect to the nature of Jewish-Christian dialogue, see Daniel Boyarin, "Justin Martyr Invents Judaism." *Church History*, 70 No. 3 (2001): 427–461.

[27] Craig D. Allert, *Revelation, Truth, Canon and Interpretation: Studies in Justin Martyr's Dialogue with Trypho*. VCSup 64. (Leiden: Brill, 2002). See his extensive critique of the Cosgrove article on pp. 15–29.

[28] See H. P. Schneider, "Some Reflections on the Dialogue of Justin Martyr with Trypho" in *Torah and Other Essays: A Symposium in Honour of the 80th Birthday of H. L. Ellison*. (Ramsgate, Kent: International Hebrew Christian Alliance, 1983), 64–72; Graham Stanton, "Other Early Christian Writings: *Didache*, Ignatius, *Barnabas*, Justin Martyr" in *Early Christian Thought in its Jewish Context*. (ed. John Barclay and John Sweet; New York: Cambridge University Press, 1996), 174–190; John Barton, *Holy Writings, Sacred Texts: The Canon in Early Christianity*. (Louisville, KY: Westminster John Knox Press, 1997), 53–62.

[29] Barnard, "The Old Testament," 399–400; David E. Aune, "Justin Martyr's Use of the Old Testament." *Bulletin of the Evangelical Theological Society*, 9 No. 4 (1966): 179–197.

[30] For an overview of the texts and their recensions, see H. B. Swete, *Introduction to the Old Testament in Greek*. (Cambridge University Press, 1914; repr. Peabody, MA: Hendrickson Publishers, 1989), 417–424. Swete gives the same information for Irenaeus on pp. 414–417.

[31] See L. W. Barnard, *Justin Martyr: His Life and Thought*. (New York: Cambridge University Press, 1967), 53–74. For an overview of his familiarity with extra-biblical Jewish practices and beliefs, see Barnard, "The Old Testament," 400–404.

was mainly concerned with interacting with those who had the fullest portions of the logos. In his *Dialogue*, we read how Justin was moved by these words:

> There existed, long before this time, certain men more ancient than all those who are esteemed philosophers, both righteous and beloved by God, who spoke by the Divine Spirit, and foretold events which would take place, and which are now taking place. They are called prophets . . . Their writings are still extant, and he who has read them is very much helped in his knowledge of the beginning and end of things, and of those matters which the philosopher ought to know, provided he has believed them.[32]

Allert expounds, "The Prophets saw and heard. In Justin's eyes this qualified them to communicate knowledge about God . . . Through the incarnate *Logos*, the Apostles saw the fulfillment of God's will . . . and his actions . . . this is the significance of their writings."[33] There is no question of the import of the Old Testament prophecies for Justin.[34] However, his prophecy-fulfillment schema tended to lend more weight to the apostolic writings through which the Old Testament had to be understood.[35] In order to accomplish this, Justin pursued many of the "Church's *pesher* texts" and other testimonia to retrieve his Christological results.[36] Scholars would contend that Justin was not as "free" in his use of the Old Testament as perhaps Hillel, Paul and James were; however, he proved sufficiently non-strict that Aune could say:

> Unfortunately, he is rarely satisfied with taking over the valid New Testament teachings about the Old Testament without adding to, and thus almost inevitably detracting from those teachings . . . Justin, in spite of his philosopher's cloak, was in reality a zealous missionary who sought by all the means at his disposal to persuade Jews and Gentiles to believe in the true God through the revelation of the incarnate Logos, Jesus Christ.[37]

[32] *Dial.*, 7.

[33] Allert, *Revelation*, 217.

[34] To Justin, the Torah and other sections of Scripture were considered prophecies.

[35] Justin, of course, is not the first to subordinate the Old Testament to portions of the New. See George Soares-Prabhu, "The Inspiration of the Old Testament as Seen by the New and Its Implication for the Possible Inspiration of Non-Christian Scriptures" in *Research Seminar on Non-Biblical Scriptures*. (ed. D. S. Amalorpavadass; Bangalore: National Biblical, Catechetical and Liturgical Centre, 1975), 99–116.

[36] Barnard, *Justin Martyr*, 63–74; Story, *The Nature of Truth*, 208–214.

[37] Aune, "Justin Martyr's Use of the Old Testament," 197.

In other words, whatever worked to his advantage, he did not hesitate to use. Thus, Justin's exegesis was broadly in keeping with Jewish and Christian practice of the time. Let us then move on to the second church father of our study.

Irenaeus

Irenaeus was recently the subject of controversy with regard to his view of the episcopacy and Scripture.[38] Paice, for example, in order to stem a contrary opinion, argues that though "Irenaeus undeniably does regard episcopal succession as important . . . he did not believe there to be an inherent quality in the office apart from teaching."[39] Paice reviews the relation among the three sources of authority for Irenaeus (Scripture, the rule of truth, and the episcopacy) and surmises that Scripture was always his ultimate authority. Or in the words of one committee, with respect to the church fathers generally: "The basis of the whole process of teaching and learning in the struggle to preserve, transmit and commend the apostolic faith remained the scriptures, even though the complete settlement of the canon took time. Every formula of faith had to be measured against the scriptures."[40]

According to W. H. C. Frend, "For [Irenaeus], Christianity rested on revelation, on tradition, and on the power of the Holy Spirit."[41] But he goes on to write that Irenaeus "pointed out that the faith was based on the tradition of the gospels handed down to the apostles and 'is guarded by the succession of the elders in the churches.' There were no 'hidden mysteries' to which the Gnostic leaders could claim access. The Bible alone had authority."[42] Still it seems that Irenaeus' main work, *Against Heresies*, can be

---

[38] See R. J. R. Paice, "Irenaeus on the Authority of Scripture, the 'Rule of Truth' and Episcopacy (Part 1)." *Chm* 177 No. 1 (2003): 57–70.

[39] "Irenaeus", 58. Paice intends a contrast between Irenaeus and Ignatius. For a fuller discussion of Ignatius' conception of authority, see C. E. Hill, "Ignatius and the Apostolate: The Witness of Ignatius to the Emergence of Scripture" in *Studia Patristica* Vol. XXXVI (ed. M. F. Wiles and E. J. Yarnold; Leuven: Peeters, 2001), 226–248.

[40] "The Apostolic Faith in the Scriptures and in the Early Church." Report of a Faith and Order Consultation held in Rome, 1–8 October 1983. *Ecumenical Review* 36 (Jl 1984): 329–37, 334.

[41] *The Rise of Christianity*. (Philadelphia: Fortress, 1984), 244. Frend mentions the Holy Spirit in light of the validation of the episcopacy by their possession of the Spirit. (249–250).

[42] *The Rise of Christianity*, 245, to be taken in context to be sure, for he reiterates in his summary of the period: "In any event, the canon of Scripture took its place with episcopacy, the Rule of Faith, and the liturgy to provide the basis for a disciplined and unified church."

read in various ways such that one could conceivably attribute the status of "ultimateness" to the Scriptures, the Rule of Faith, or the episcopacy respectively. For example, one could conceivably argue (as many in fact do) for the primacy of Scripture for Irenaeus since in his preface he explicitly lodges his main grievance against his opponents with the following words: "The men falsify the oracles of God, and prove themselves evil interpreters of the good word of revelation."[43] But just as easily, one might insist that Irenaeus plainly states that he is writing because "certain men have set the truth aside" and that he accordingly grants primacy to the rule of faith.[44] A very strong argument indeed can be made that Irenaeus' main concern is that the heretics have replaced the true faith (i.e., the rule of faith) with a false one.[45] Or, conversely, one might observe how ultimate priority is seemingly given to the episcopacy in *Against Heresies* and argue on this basis that although the other two forms of authority are very important to Irenaeus absolute authority resides in the officiating bishops:

> Wherefore it is incumbent to obey the presbyters who are in the church,—those who, as I have shown, possess the succession from the apostles; those who, together with the succession of the episcopate, have received the certain gift of truth, according to the good pleasure of the Father.[46]

(251) See also Bruce M. Metzger, *The Canon of the New Testament: Its Origin, Development, and Significance.* (New York: Oxford University Press, 1987), 154–156.

[43] *Haer.* Preface.1. In 1.8.1, for example, Irenaeus complains that certain of the Gnostics "gather their views from other sources than the Scriptures" and then try to piece together Scriptural support so that "their scheme may not seem altogether without support." For an examination of Gnostic interpretation, see Louis Painchaud, "The Use of Scripture in Gnostic Literature." *JECS* 4 No. 2 (1996): 129–147; Francisco García Bazán, "Ricos y Pobres: Las Gratificaciones del Injusto Mammon: El Testimonio de la Verdad (CNH IX, 3, 68.3–4)." *RevistB* 57 No. 1 (1995): 29–39.

[44] The opening words of *Haer.* Preface 1. On Irenaeus' use of "truth", see Thomas C. K. Ferguson, "The Rule of Truth and Irenaean Rhetoric in Book 1 of *Against Heresies*." *VC* 55 No. 4 (2001): 356–375.

[45] Tertullian, for example, in *Praescr.* 3, says that a believer who turns to heresy is one who has "fallen from the rule of faith."

[46] *Haer* 4.2. Paice's denominational opponents heavily emphasize this line of thinking in Irenaeus. See R. J. R. Paice, "Irenaeus on the Authority of Scripture, the 'Rule of Truth' and Episcopacy (Part 1)." *Chm* 177 No. 1 (2003): 57–70. Protestant writers are generally speaking extremely uncomfortable conceding the important role played by the episcopacy in the early church. D. H. Williams, for example, in his *Retrieving the Tradition and Renewing Evangelicalism: A Primer for Suspicious Protestants* (Grand Rapids: Eerdmans, 1999), claims, for example, that "Irenaeus's appeal to the sufficiency of Tradition alone, or to the vindication of apostolicity by tracing Episcopal succession, were polemical tactics he used when pushed to the extreme" (90).

Given the considerable ambiguity that characterizes Irenaeus' work, it would not be unreasonable for a reader of *Against Heresies* to deem a draw amongst these three competing interpretations of authority.[47]

Along these lines, a very interesting proposal for getting a better handle on Irenaeus' view of Scripture has been suggested by Blanchard. After combing Irenaeus' work for the various ways by which he refers to Scripture, Blanchard observes that Irenaeus has certainly moved beyond the Christian apologists before him and extended their seemingly "bipartite" view of Scripture to include a tertiary component.[48] The said bipartite understanding of Scripture supposes that Christian Scriptures were very early on comprised of the Law and the Prophets on the one hand and the teachings of the apostles on the other. The teachings of the apostles are understood as (among other things to be sure) hermeneutical guidelines passed on from Jesus through the apostles according to which the Law and the Prophets can be properly understood. Sensing the inadequacy of this bipartite schema for Irenaeus' complex understanding of Scripture, Blanchard and others[49] insist upon a tripartite schema of Scripture along the lines of Prophets, Teachings of the Lord, and Teachings of the Apostles. In support of this almost pedantic modification, Blanchard poignantly argues that although "the Law" and "the Prophets" might be used interchangeably to refer to Jewish Scripture, the difference between dominical and apostolic teaching as understood by Irenaeus is such that the two are not interchangeable and are better delineated as distinct "testimonies."[50]

Out of necessity for Irenaeus, the teachings of the apostles, the third wave of testimony as it were, must extend in some manner to the teachings of the ones who are passing on those very teachings. As Blanchard points out, the unity of the threefold testimony is not guaranteed "internally."

---

[47] Robert B. Eno's presentation of Irenaeus' view of authority as a "synthesis" is akin to the "draw" of which I speak. See his *Teaching Authority in the Early Church*. Message of the Fathers of the Church 14. (Wilmington, DE: Michael Glazier, Inc., 1984). Incidentally, a number of scholars have suggested that Irenaeus was not as clear a thinker as many of the other early church fathers. In defense of Irenaeus, see Thomas C. K. Ferguson, "The Rule of Truth and Irenaean Rhetoric in Book 1 of *Against Heresies*." *VC* 55 No. 4 (2001): 356–375; Mary Ann Donovan, *One Right Reading? A Guide to Irenaeus*. (Collegeville, MN: The Liturgical Press, 1997); Robert M. Grant, "Irenaeus and Hellenistic Culture." *HTR* 42 No. 1 (1949), 41–52.

[48] Yves-Marie Blanchard, *Aux sources du canon, le témoignage d'Irénée*. (Paris: Les Editions du Cerf, 1993), 132–145.

[49] Blanchard, for example, is indebted to B. Sesboüé, "La Preuve par les Écritures chez saint Irénée" *Nouvelle Revue théologique* 103 (1981): 872–887.

[50] Blanchard, *le témoignage d'Irénée*, 136–137.

Young hits on this same point when she describes the religious context within which Irenaeus writes: "Disputes about the contents of scripture, disputes about the reference of prophetic texts and about the status of the Jewish law, alerted [Irenaeus] to the fact the scriptures were not self-sufficient, the reader not competent without instruction to construct a coherent view of their direction."[51] The external instruction that informs a believer of the direction that a reading of Scripture should take is an intricate extension of Blanchard's third testimony, "the teaching of the apostles." For Irenaeus, the rule of faith and the apostolic succession reciprocally provide whatever Scriptures he refers to during the course of his writing with a unity that they would not possess on their own.[52] If the Bible alone has authority for Irenaeus as Frend remarks, then what Irenaeus understood by "Bible" is certainly not what we today would understand by the word (or is it?[53]).

Perhaps a creative comparison with what Carmelo J. Giaquinta's observes with respect to a very different aspect of early church activity—evangelism—can analogously instruct us.[54] To paraphrase Giaquinta, a dialectical evangelistic matrix existed such that a) once the gospel is offered to all, b) then God provides every necessary means, c) in order that the gospel can be offered to all.[55] In other words, the early proclamation depended upon persons who could competently proclaim it, but the persons who did the proclaiming were utterly dependent on the holy proclamation.[56] The dialectic was such that neither the proclamation nor the

[51] Frances Young, *Virtuoso Theology: The Bible and Interpretation*. (Cleveland: The Pilgrim Press, 1993), 48. Compare John J. O'Keefe and R. R. Reno, *Sanctified Vision: An Introduction to Early Christian Interpretation of the Bible*. (Baltimore: Johns Hopkins University Press, 2005).

[52] For specific examples, the reader is directed to Young, *Virtuoso Theology*, 53–65. On the problem of the unity of the canon, see the various essays in C. Helmer and C. Landmesser, ed., *One Scripture or Many? Canon from Biblical, Theological and Philosophical Perspectives*. (New York: Oxford University Press, 2004).

[53] I have argued this from another angle in chapter 2 above. The term "Bible" will always refer to both the book itself *and* the implicit tradition within which an evangelical interprets it. See Brian Malley, *How the Bible Works: An Anthropological Study of Evangelical Biblicism*. (Lanham, MD: AltaMira Press, 2004). As Eno observes, when it comes to issues of authority, "[t]he difficulty then as now is not the supremacy of Scripture but what that means in practice. All parties to every dispute claim to base their position on Scripture." See Eno, *Teaching Authority in the Early Church*, 21.

[54] "¿Aristocracia o Pueblo de Dios? Opción Evangelizadora de la Iglesia Patrística" *Criterio* 47 No. 1705–06 (24 dec 1974): 715–722.

[55] "¿Aristocracia o Pueblo de Dios?," 722.

[56] Compare Martin Anton Schimdt, "Tradition, Apostolic and Ecclesiastical."

proclaimer was threatened by the other or should be considered superior to the other. Each component was a necessary part of a complex dialectical process—evangelization. Evangelization depends on both the message and the messenger; the one without the other cannot accomplish its end. Hence, it is *practically* meaningless to speak of primacy or ultimateness with respect to either aspect.

Applied to the case of Irenaeus, the Scriptures, rule of faith and apostolic succession can all be considered inseparable aspects of a divinely authoritative complex that he conceived conjointly as apostolic tradition. Hence, an interpretation of Irenaeus that assigns one specific aspect of the apostolic tradition ultimate authority will always seem partly justified, at least in a sense, by duly recognizing the authority of a respective aspect of the authoritative complex in Irenaeus' thought; however, since each is necessary to the other, an insistence upon absoluteness will inevitably lead to distortion. Certainly, Tavard was right in his summary of Irenaeus' conception of authority:

> Not only has the written Gospel been entrusted to the bishops by the Apostles, the Churches have been similarly placed under their care . . . Both the Scriptures and the apostolic sees stand or fall together on the ground of an apostolic tradition. The sees are keepers of the writings; and the writings do not remain undefiled when cut off from the sees. Thus the Irenaean view does not sponsor a dichotomy of Scripture and tradition. It holds fast to the priority of an apostolic charism in which the Scripture and the Church universal, epitomized in the apostolic bishoprics, form one uncleft whole.[57]

Even if Baird and others are right and the Church Fathers constantly returned to "the words of Jesus as the final test of their theological authority,

Reconsiderations: Roman Catholic/Presbyterian and Reformed Theological Conversations 1966–1967. (New York: World Horizons, 1967), 26–42, 28, 29, 31: "I think that there is general agreement that ecclesiastical tradition is *in some way* secondary to divine and apostolic tradition. Without apostolic tradition, ecclesiastical tradition would be without its origin." "[E]cclesiastical tradition in all its acts is so dependent on the fullness of apostolic tradition that whichever gift it transmits, it is the apostolic truth so transmitted (apostolic truth *in actu*)." "The real problem among us does not concern the greater or lesser importance of the Church. It rather lies in the tension between apostolic truth seen as a gift to the Church and apostolic truth seen as a task for the Church . . ."

[57] George H. Tavard, *Holy Writ or Holy Church.* (London: Burns and Oates, 1959), 9.

and the basis of their hermeneutic"[58] and claimed to *theoretically* proceed along these lines,[59] *practically speaking*, a final test is difficult to deduce.[60]

It has been pointed out that throughout the *Haer*, the church father mentions "scripture" some 165 times, cites the Old Testament 629 times and the New Testament 1065 times.[61] In no way, therefore, says Osborn, can Irenaeus be interpreted as seeing tradition "as a saving supplement which rescues the inadequacy of scripture."[62] Irenaeus is commonly linked to the establishment of a fourfold Gospel[63] and there is clearly evidence that he rejected certain writings as apocryphal.[64] But what does all this entail for the *practical* role that Scripture played in Irenaeus' thought? Osborn observes how Irenaeus' position on the four Gospels was "not the result of an ecclesiastical decision but of his own rational acceptance of the rule of faith which embodies the new testament message."[65] In Torrance's words:

> What he did was to trace back the preaching and teaching of the Church in all its main centres to their common source in the apostolic foundation, to show that their preaching and teaching which had come down to us in the Gospels and Epistles, together with the Acts and the Apocalypse, were grounded from beyond themselves in the Words of the Lord and indeed in Jesus Christ himself as Truth . . .[66]

---

[58] J. Arthur Baird, *Holy Word*, 212.

[59] Although, see Helmut Koester, "Written Gospels or Oral Tradition?" *JBL* 113 No. 2 (1994): 293–297, who minimizes the sanctity and authoritativeness of the writings in favor of their practical conveniences with respect to social and administrative purposes. Eric F. Osborn approaches the rule of faith in a similar way. See his "Reason and the Rule of Faith in the Second Century AD" in *The Making of Orthodoxy: Essays in Honour of Henry Chadwick*. (ed. Rowan Williams; New York: Cambridge University Press, 1989), 40–61.

[60] Even in the famous case of Serapion and the Gospel of Peter, the case could easily be made that the dialectic is already at work. For the story as related by Eusebius, see C. F. D. Moule, *The Birth of the New Testament*. 3rd ed. (London: A & C Black, 1981), 251–252, and, more recently, Bart Ehrman, *Lost Christianities: The Battles for Scripture and the Faiths We Never Knew*. (New York: Oxford University Press, 2003), 14–16.

[61] Eric Osborn, *Irenaeus of Lyons*. (New York: Cambridge University Press, 2001), 172.

[62] *Irenaeus*, 172.

[63] For an argument in favor of the existence of a non-canonically ordered four-Gospel codex already in circulation by the time of Irenaeus, see T. C. Skeat, "Irenaeus and the Four-Gospel Canon." *NovT* 34 No. 2 (1992): 194–199.

[64] An account of one such infancy narrative can be found in Robert M. Grant, "Like Children." *HTR* 39 No. 1 (1946): 71–74.

[65] *Irenaeus*, 179.

[66] Thomas F. Torrance, *Divine Meaning: Studies in Patristic Hermeneutics*. (Edinburgh: T

If this is true, then it must be the case that this rule of faith must have developed such that it was at least in some way independent of the Scriptures.[67] Clearly, we are met with a dilemma: how could a "canon" (i.e., closed collection) be submitted (according to Osborn) by Irenaeus that was in his mind in accord with the rule of faith if the rule of faith had been formulated earlier in terms of the submitted canon? It seems safe to say that Irenaeus, Tertullian and others did believe that the rule of faith to which appeal was constantly made was in some sense independent of the Scriptures. Yet on the other hand, scholars also surmise that the same church fathers believed that the rule of faith was utterly dependent upon the Scriptures.

We have apparently run into a paradox here, one very similar to Giaquinta's dialectical evangelistic matrix. In the face of this paradox, Kelly proposed the following:

> The whole point of his teaching was, in fact, that Scripture and the Church's unwritten tradition are identical in content, both being vehicles of the revelation. If tradition as conveyed in the "canon" is a more trustworthy guide, this is not because it comprises truths other than those revealed in Scripture, but because the true tenor of the apostolic message is there unambiguously set out.[68]

Again, we are met with the idea that the contents of Scripture are made all the more intelligible by means of apostolic tradition. Yet as Young points out, the rule of faith seems rarely to provide a recognizable summary of the story of the Bible.[69] Although canon is commonly thought of as the final arbiter in disputes, for Irenaeus the case is not so cut and dried. Canon does not appear to be the deciding factor in *Against Heresies*. There is rather a complex interaction amongst the variegated authoritative components of

and T Clark, 1995), 126.

[67] Bertrand de Margerie, *An Introduction to the History of Exegesis: Volume I The Greek Fathers.* (Petersham, MA: Saint Bede's Publications, 1993), 53; J. N. D. Kelly, *Early Christian Doctrines.* rev. ed. (San Francisco: HarperCollins, 1978), 37.

[68] *Early Christian Doctrines*, 39. He continues, "Tertullian's attitude does not differ from Irenaeus's in any important respect." "Canon" in the above quotation is short for "canon of faith," our "rule of faith." R. P. C. Hanson offers another solution: "The most probable conclusion from the statements of both these writers [Irenaeus and whoever penned the Muratorian Canon] is that though they were perfectly ready to reproduce single items of miscellaneous historical information independent of the Bible they do not imagine that any significant or important information about the Christian faith exists in their day outside the Scriptures." See Hanson, *Tradition in the Early Church.* (Philadelphia: The Westminster Press, 1962), 46.

[69] Young, *Virtuoso Theology*, 50, 52.

the composite apostolic tradition to which justice cannot be done by way of undue emphasis upon a closed canon.

We shall now attempt an integrative summary that endeavors to do justice to the historical material presented above and hone in on the open and closed notions of canon with which these chapters contended.

III. Summative Remarks

Let us begin by stating upfront that these two chapters do not purport to question the fact that all Christians of the early church held "that there was one traditional authority which was an authority in the full sense, a body of teaching in which the fullness of universal truth was contained and with which it was not permissible to disagree, though of course it had to be interpreted rightly and intelligently."[70] Nor do they deny the fact that "for practically all Christians the Bible stood alone and unchallenged as the one traditional authority in the full sense."[71] Neither do they assert that individual church fathers or bishops were so involved with the transmission of the apostolic tradition that their writings were on a par with Scripture.[72] The claim that *is* being made is that one traditional authority, the Bible, has always operated (and continues to operate) as part of such a powerful cultural dialectic that it is not helpful to speak of it as an ultimate authority, especially in terms of practicalities. In the space that remains, we shall revisit the rubrics of open and closed canons and identify certain characteristics that each of the periods covered seem to share.[73]

---

[70] A. H. Armstrong, "Pagan and Christian Traditionalism in the First Three Centuries A.D." in *Studia Patristica* Vol. 15 (ed. Elizabeth A. Livingstone; Berlin: Akademie-Verlag, 1984), 414–431, 414.

[71] Armstrong, "Pagan and Christian," 115.

[72] The practice of explicitly quoting fathers apparently did not begin until the fourth century. See Mark Vessey, "The Forging of Orthodoxy in Latin Christian Literature: A Case Study." *JECS* 4 (1996): 495–513.

[73] As the works on canon are voluminous and a full-fledged digression into the subject would take us too far afield, only scattered references are made to the contemporary debates. Though Sanders was cited approvingly above, it should also be noted that Childs' presentation of the Old Testament as "Scripture" also seems similar in many respects to the picture painted above. See Childs, *Introduction*, 75–81. For the affinity that exists among these and many "canon critics", see Magne Saebo, "From 'Unifying Reflections' to the Canon" in his collection of essays, *On the Way to Canon: Creative Tradition History in the Old Testament*. JSOTSup 191. (Sheffield: Sheffield Academic Press, 1998), 285–307, first published as "Vom 'Zusammen-Denken' zum Kanon: Aspekte der traditionsgeschichtlichen Endstadien des Alten Testaments" in *Zum Problem des biblischen Kanons*. (JBT, 3; Neukirchen-Vluyn: Neukirchener Verlaf, 1988), 115–33.

First, it is acknowledged that those religious leaders who were selected for this study all lived at a time during which Scripture was fluid and no Bible had yet existed. Perhaps, it may be thought that this very factor discounts the entire argument. For example, Skarsaune reports that ". . . from Justin on, there is a gradual wearing down of the distinct characteristics of the testimony tradition (its deviant, combined, interpolated etc. quotations). This holds true for the Greek Fathers, and for the Latin Fathers treated below." He continues:

> In this way, early Christian interpretation of the Old Testament may be said to rest on a Jewish foundation with regard to canon and with regard to the way of handling the biblical text. But during the second century, the "targumic" freedom in handling and interpreting the Greek Old Testament gradually gave way to a different attitude. The Greek text was now increasingly regarded as the *Grundtext*, to be quoted *verbatim*.[74]

These factors were openly admitted above, but in the eyes of the present author, it simply is not the case that the New Testament itself evinces an exegetical approach that differs substantially from that of Hillel, Irenaeus or Justin. Schneider writes:

> In respect of this comparison with the New Testament we may with some confidence quote Stanton; albeit what he says is in reference to the Apostolic Fathers in general, it is particularly relevant to the Dialogue. There is far more artificiality; the fancifulness to be found already in full bloom at the time of the apostles, in the writings of Philo, and no doubt also among the Rabbis, has now far more largely invaded the circle of Christian Thought. New kinds of interpretations have come into vogue; even where an application, in principle the same, is made in the New Testament, it is worked out more elaborately, and much more stress is laid upon it.[75]

---

[74] Oskar Skarsaune, "The Question of Old Testament Canon and Text in the Early Greek Church" in *Hebrew Bible/Old Testament: The History of Its Interpretation. Volume 1 From the Beginnings to the Middle Ages (Until 1300).* (ed. Magne Saebo; Göttingen: Vandenhoeck and Ruprecht, 1996), 441–450, 449, 450. See also Swete's comments in *Introduction*, 406–432, esp. 414 on Irenaeus and 417 on Justin. See also Story, "The Idea of Truth," xx–xxi. For more on the Fathers individually, see Skarsaune, "The Development of Scriptural Interpretation in the Second and Third Centuries—except Clement and Origen" in *Hebrew Bible/Old Testament*. (ed. Saebo), 373–442.

[75] "Some Reflections," 69, quoting G. N. Stanton, but no citation is given. R. P. C. Hanson, on the other hand, sees a degree of restraint on the part of many of the Fathers, including Justin and Irenaeus. See his "Biblical Exegesis in the Early Church" in *The Cambridge History of the Bible: From the Beginnings to Jerome.* Vol. 1 (ed. P. R. Ackroyd and

Schneider goes on to

> agree with Mr. W. Maurice Pryke that it is impossible to prove
> from the Old Testament that Jesus was the Messiah and that origi-
> nally it was not thus that the disciples recognized Him as such.
> Rather did they first of all recognize Jesus by the force of who He
> was to be the Messiah and then bolstered this conviction by evi-
> dences from the Old Testament.[76]

The author has hit the nail on the head here. Ancient exegetes knew nothing of grammatical-historical exegesis and were not burdened with modern objectivity or a post-modern self-consciousness that purposively seeks
out the "violence" that is done by every reading of a text. They occupied
an entirely foreign world wherein such searching of a text in light of a
perceived "oracularity" of the text was understandable and expected.[77] In
response to the objection that the present study examines a special period
in church history, we suggest that the closing of the canon could not have
accomplished what it is commonly thought to have accomplished. This
brings us to our second and final point.

Canonical development, establishment and maintenance involve a
dynamic process that is best described by "entelechy." Entelechy "entails
that an earlier phase contains the potential that is actualized in the suc-
ceeding phase, etc."[78] In other words, a model for the "canonical process"
should be one that, in the end and in a very important sense, does not
admit of closure but rather sustains a perpetual dialectic. Within such a
model, "[w]ith the completed formation of the canon we encounter for
the first time the phenomenon of dialectic . . ."[79] This dialectic, it was
suggested, is analogous to Giaquinta's evangelization problem. In other
words, a closing of a canon does not eliminate dialectic, but much rather,
increases its force. If it is not clear how this can be, consider for a moment
the evangelical view of Scripture that emphasizes Scripture as the foundation of all denominational and ecumenical discussion. In light of the foregoing discussions, it seems more realistic to insist that Scripture is indeed

---

C. F. Evans; New York: Cambridge University Press, 1970), 412–453. Perhaps, it should
be mentioned that Schneider is after Justin for his anti-Semitic legacy.

[76] "Some Reflections," 71.

[77] Even after a "substructure" had been identified. See C. H. Dodd, *According to the
Scriptures*.

[78] Rein Fernhout, *Canonical Texts: Bearers of Absolute Authority: Bible, Koran, Veda,
Tipitaka: A Phenomenological Study.* (trans. Henry Jansen and Lucy Jansen-Hofland;
Atlanta: Rodopi, 1994), 9.

[79] Fernhout, *Canonical Texts*, 75.

a very important facet of denominational and ecumenical discussion but it is not necessarily the foundation. If an evangelical were to insist otherwise, we might suggest with Folkert that this "Protestant view of the Bible is significantly restricted to only certain dimensions of the phenomenon represented by the several names applied to it . . ."[80] As pointed out above, evangelicals commonly employ what Folkert calls "would-be synonyms" to refer to their Bibles, but, in light of the foregoing, it is not clear that "the phenomenon of Scripture" should be practically limited to the Bible. In order to facilitate discussion, let us follow Folkert's paradigm and suggest that a distinction be made between "Canon I" and "Canon II" where neither is necessarily exclusive to the other since both could obtain in a tradition at any time. We shall now attempt to solidify the vaguer notions of open and closed canons into the following two definitions:

> Canon I denotes normative texts, oral or written, that are present in a tradition principally by the force of a vector or vectors. Canon II refers to normative texts that are more independently and distinctively present within a tradition, that is, as pieces of literature more or less as such are currently thought of, and which themselves often function as vectors.

Those who have forgotten their linear algebra or physics may be somewhat confused by Folkert's seemingly obscure choice of terms.[81] He explains, "By 'vector' is meant the means or mode by which something is carried; thus Canon I's place in a tradition is largely due to its 'being carried' by some other form of religious activity . . . The same meaning applies to vector where Canon II may function as a 'carrier' of religious activity."[82] In other words, a Canon I is "carried" by something else (liturgy, etc.); a Canon II can "carry" something else (liturgy, etc.). Now if a Canon II carries the liturgy that carries Canon I, does not Canon II prove the ultimate foundation? So which is Canon II? Some evangelicals may be tempted to identify this very question as *the* question that needs to be ask, but these last two chapters suggest that it is the *wrong* question to ask.

---

[80] Kendall W. Folkert, "The 'Canons' of 'Scripture'" in *Rethinking Scripture: Essays from a Comparative Perspective.* (ed. Miriam Levering; Albany, NY: State University of New York Press, 1989), 170–179, 172–173.

[81] Indeed, Folkert himself writes: "[T]he preceding paragraphs may strike one as the sort of terminological obfuscation better left to small groups at conventions." See Folkert,"The 'Canons' of 'Scripture,'" 174.

[82] Both quotations are from Folkert, "The 'Canons' of 'Scripture,'" 173.

Perhaps it may help the reader to substitute "the New Testament" for Canon I and "Church tradition" for Canon II or vice versa.[83] Or vice versa? Yes, and that's precisely the point! It should not be too difficult to see that within this dialectical complex a Canon can both carry and be carried by some other "vector" within the religio-social system. Take the denominational dispute over the episcopacy as an example. Do the Scriptures carry the episcopacy or does the episcopacy carry the Scriptures? Which is the Canon I and is carried and which is the Canon II and does the carrying? On account of the dialectic, we discovered that both the Scriptures and the episcopacy can legitimately be identified with Canon I or Canon II *at the same time*. These two categories, Canon I and Canon II, it might be noted, correspond in very real ways to the open and closed canons that were loosely described above. An open canon can obviously carry and be carried by other religio-social factors. A closed canon, however, *can also carry or be carried*, and that at the same time.

Canon is often thought of as a final arbiter of disputes (i.e., Canon II). The several examples that were given throughout these two chapters involved Canon I scenarios, but were selected nonetheless in order to more clearly demonstrate the carry-abilities of the various religious leaders that were covered. In order that readers might more easily understand what is being suggested here, Canon I examples were used with hopes that extrapolations to Canon II situations could more readily be envisioned. But before suggesting what issues need to be addressed, we will mention a grave fear that tends to prevent further exploration of the idea proffered here.

The security of canon means to many the obtainment of certainty. Without the security of Canon II, a closed canon, the prospect of certainty is lost and the church (or better yet, individual Christians) is forced to search out alternatives. The alternative to utter certainty, for whatever reason, seems invariably and historically to have been some sort of religio-social anarchy. Michael S. Berger comments on how such a shift "is genuinely problematic only if the subject-object distinction is maintained, the two seen as independent entities situated in an adversarial relationship, where one exerts control over the other."[84] Since one must inevitably control the other, evangelicals will often be attracted to a Canon II-at-all-costs mentality in order to fend off the looming anarchic pulls. Berger recommends another way of looking at the whole interpretive enterprise: "In Wittgenstein's view, the problem of meaning that philosophy has analyzed

[83] For the "minimalist," theological factors might be Canon I; sociological factors Canon II. The other way around for "maximalists."

[84] *Rabbinic Authority.* (New York: Oxford University Press, 1998), 133.

for so long is a false one, rooted in a picture of the world that separates meaning from a person's perception of it."[85] If we can adapt his program for our own purposes, one might access a vantage from which she can say that the Church has been cleaving to a false picture of the relation between Canon II and the rest of the religio-social existential domain. God's people have themselves always been in the thick of the canonical process and necessarily enjoin a canonical dialectic.

When reflecting upon the meaning and relation of canon, Scripture and tradition, it will prove most helpful to constantly remind ourselves that temporal and logical priorities are inherently leveled in the dialectic. Geiselmann observes that "[t]he principle of the Canon did not mean the end of tradition in the Church, but its confirmation . . . The theology of tradition continues uninterrupted from Irenaeus to Augustine despite the canon."[86] Returning to Schmidt's argument, too, we are in a better position to appreciate his delineation of divine, apostolic and ecclesiastical traditions. For reasons that are primarily historical, we can admit that the divine and apostolic traditions have somehow merged.[87] That a very interesting parallel has also been observed by Venema for the "derived authority" of the Old Testament lends credence to the fact that the present study is almost certainly heading in the right direction.[88] The gradual subsumption of the apostolic into the divine is precisely what is responsible for the development of Armstrong's single absolutely authoritative tradition within the life of the Christian Church. That said, the divine-apostolic tradition, nevertheless, maintains a powerful dialectic with the ecclesiastical tradition such that "the secondary or dependent character of ecclesiastical tradition has to be asserted in terms which mean more than a mere chronological posteriority to apostolic tradition, terms which also reflect more than just every Christian's utter dependence on God's grace."[89]

The purpose of these two chapters in a nutshell is to lend historical nuance to the growing inter-denominational consensus that states: "In the course of centuries the church's life and structure became more elaborate. Traditions extend the original meaning of Scripture by theological inter-

---

[85] *Rabbinic Authority*, 134.

[86] Josef Rupert Geiselmann, *The Meaning of Tradition* (London: Burns and Oates, 1966), 26.

[87] See Martin Anton Schimdt, "Tradition, Apostolic and Ecclesiastical". *Reconsiderations: Roman Catholic/Presbyterian and Reformed Theological Conversations 1966–1967.* (New York: World Horizons, 1967), 26–29.

[88] See G. J. Venema, *Reading Scripture in the Old Testament: Deuteronomy 9–10; 31; 2 Kings 22–23; Jeremiah 36; Nehemiah 8.* (Leiden: Brill, 2004).

[89] Schmidt, "Tradition, Apostolic and Ecclesiastical," 29–30.

pretation, reformulation, and reconceptualization, often under the influence of other religions and current philosophical thinking." Ecclesial discussions are now also admitting that "[a]n earlier tradition, furthermore, could be discerned at different stages of growth, for instance as witnessed to in the New Testament, or in the writings of the church fathers . . . "[90] However, both of these canons (Canon I and Canon II) obtained (and continually obtain) concurrently throughout the history of the churches. That this was inherently the case *even from the beginning* we endeavored to illustrate by the representative examples adduced. Emphasis was placed upon a dialectic, one that is often only tacitly acknowledged in discussions of canon and Scripture. More attention must be given to this dialectic if more adequate historical and religious understandings of canons, Scriptures and traditions are to be had in the future.

---

[90] Both quotes are from *Scripture and Tradition: Lutherans and Catholics in Dialogue IX*. (ed. Harold C. Skillrud, J. Francis Stafford; Daniel F. Martensen; Minneapolis: Augsburg, 1995), 26.

Conclusion

I HAVE TRIED in this book to illustrate representative discoveries that are made by younger evangelicals during their time of spiritual formation. My main point is that many young conservatives come to the realization that those who attempt to establish a literally inerrant Bible have to fudge the details a bit. There exists a host of philosophical, theological and historical details that appear to render an inerrant Bible approach to the Christian faith untenable. Of course, not all will be persuaded by these recognitions and there will always be those who will not even concede them as recognitions. Some might respond that one can never overturn inerrancy by merely amassing difficulties.[1] Others might respond that these recognitions, as interesting as they are, are simply not enough to overturn inerrancy.[2] Nonetheless, they are marshaled here for those who are interested in being shown possible ways that academic study can pose serious problems for younger evangelicals with very "high" views of Scripture. The book was written especially for those who feel spiritually responsible for the formation of younger evangelicals and who are interested in investigating how they might best prepare younger evangelicals for these and other recognitions.

During the course of my theological and biblical training, I underwent at least six recognitions that stifled my spiritual formation to the extent that I had all but abandoned the faith. Evangelical leaders and teachers should not unwittingly allow their own students to suffer in this or similar ways. Spiritual hardships and plights are meant to mature us, but

---

[1] Some might argue, for example, that if an argument for inerrancy is formulated deductively, it cannot be refuted inductively. Compare Paul Helm, *The Divine Revelation: The Basic Issues*. (Vancouver: Regent College Publishing, 1982), 80–83; B. B. Warfield, "The Real Problem of Inspiration" in *The Inspiration and Authority of the Bible*. (Phillipsburg, NJ: Presbyterian and Reformed Publishing Co.), 1948, 169–226. Geisler's version of a deductive argument was discussed above in chapter 3.

[2] For example, Douglas Blount, "The Authority of Scripture" in *Reason for the Hope Within*. (ed. M. J. Murray; Grand Rapids: Eerdmans, 1999), 399–422. Compare D. A. Carson who responds in both of these ways: "Recent Developments in the Doctrine of Scripture" in *Hermeneutics, Authority and Canon*. (ed. D. A. Carson and J. D. Woodbridge; Grand Rapids: Zondervan, 1986), 5–48, 23–25.

it is simply irresponsible for elders and mentors not to guide the young through them if they know that they will eventually encounter them.

I, for my part, was all but devastated during this scholastic phase of my spiritual journey. If the existential brunt of the educational experience can be attenuated for younger evangelicals, does it not fall upon evangelical teachers and leaders to do what they can to attenuate it? In my case, I found a defective inerrancy dogma to be the root. Others may interpret their situations differently. Nevertheless, in a ministerial effort to reach countless other younger evangelicals, both directly and indirectly, I have presented a case against teaching that the ETS/EPS variety of inerrancy is the only acceptably orthodox way of thinking about the Bible: so taught, students will not be able to withstand certain critical recognitions that take place during the course of their theological training. I have not primarily written to the younger evangelicals themselves; I am not interested in attempting some sort of student mutiny. I believe that the lasting changes I envisage in this area of spiritual formation must largely come from the top down. Evangelical leaders and teachers must—even if they themselves decide to cling to the ETS/EPS belief—instruct younger evangelicals in such a way that they do not conjoin a belief in an inerrant Bible with that transcendent hope that we are encouraged to have within us.

I know that I am not alone in what I experienced in school. I have witnessed consistent patterns of change in attitude and disposition amongst classmates, colleagues and even professors in at least three evangelical schools—toward the Christian faith broadly and the Holy Scriptures specifically. The transition involves the nagging effect of unanswered questions about the character and integrity of the faith, especially when these are taught to be based upon the undisputed veracity of the Bible. Shifts away from foundationalism among younger evangelicals and the culture more broadly may or may not be relevant here.[3] For example, Paloutzian surmises that "[q]uestions about specific doctrines are probably not the critical issues for most adolescents, but the general mode of knowing—how one knows what is true or false—probably is. It is really the whole underlying process of knowing, and one's own ability to know, that is in

---

[3] See Robert E. Webber, *The Younger Evangelicals: Facing the Challenges of the New World.* (Grand Rapids: Baker, 2002), 96–105. Nancey Murphy observes an express link between inerrancy and the desire to secure indubitable foundations for theology. Nicholas Wolterstorff goes further and argues that the Bible cannot save foundationalism. See Murphy, *Beyond Liberalism and Fundamentalism: How Modern and Postmodern Philosophy Set the Theological Agenda.* (Harrisburg, PA: Trinity Press International, 1996), 16–17; Wolterstorff, *Reason within the Bounds of Religion.* 2nd ed. (Grand Rapids: Eerdmans, 1984), 58–62.

question."[4] I suspect, too, that economic and sociological factors also play causative roles that have yet to be duly acknowledged.[5]

Nevertheless, many young evangelicals have helplessly watched their views shift from the evangelical inerrantist position to a more nebulous, I-know-that-it-has-*some*-kind-of-authority position that becomes less and less defined and more and more obscure over time. The move is from a position that trusted the Bible as an authority in every single detail to one that posits "Yes, the Bible is still authoritative *but* an authority that must be qualified once detail #1, detail #2, detail #3 and so on are taken into consideration."[6] The propensity for qualification is a healthy one since it evinces an attention to details, but above I claimed not only that the attention given to details is superficial but that qualifications have not the versatility to accommodate these and other recognitions. As I remarked in the introductory chapter, citing Noll: "Evangelical scholars . . . need to take more pains, not less, in showing the relation of their research to larger issues of belief."[7] After all, qualifications are very much like harmonizations: they follow a law of diminishing returns. A soup kitchen will run more efficiently if there are more (rather than less) workers to work the stoves, prep the produce, hand out servings, etc. Eventually, though, there comes a point where there are *too many* workers in the soup kitchen and productivity begins to decrease. It seems that there is also a law of diminishing returns for the ETS/EPS dogma of inerrancy and it has long since been reached. The number of qualifications that have to be made in response to intra-biblical interpretation and the earliest use of the canon conjoined with other philosophical and theological issues (to say nothing of issues that have to do with natural science, ancient historiography, redaction and textual criticism and so on) have rendered inerrancy overwhelmingly unfruitful for many young conservatives. The problem is that

---

[4] Raymond F. Paloutzian, *Invitation to the Psychology of Religion*. 2nd ed. (Boston: Allyn and Bacon: 1996), 111.

[5] See Richard Quebedeaux, *By What Authority: The Rise of Personality Cults in American Christianity*. (New York: Harper & Row Publishers, 1982), 103–137.

[6] To readers who are concerned that younger evangelicals will lose their faith without inerrancy, I respond that this sort of scenario only presents a problem *when inerrancy is the default bibliological position*.

[7] Again, this was written over fifteen years ago! See Mark A. Noll, *Between Faith and Criticism: Evangelicals, Scholarship, and the Bible in America*. 2nd ed. (Grand Rapids: Baker, 1991), 170. Compare John J. Brogan's complaints in "Can I Have Your Autographs? Uses and Abuses of Textual Criticism in Formulating an Evangelical Doctrine of Scripture" in *Evangelicals and Scripture: Tradition, Authority and Hermeneutics*. (ed. V. Bacote, L. C. Miguelez, and D. L. Okholm; Downers Grove, IL: InterVarsity, 2004), 93–111.

many ETS/EPS-styled evangelical leaders and teachers have not left students with an acceptably orthodox alternative where they might continue to work out their faiths in due fear and trembling.

It has been my experience that younger evangelicals feel the tension most when they are left with an authoritative Bible whose authority has been practically all but voided by philosophical and exegetical details that regularly keep popping up. What ends up being authoritative in the end is *the evangelical tradition* and this tradition *has to be taken on faith* to the effect that it best represents what is "in" the Bible. But here we see the dialectic that I proposed in the last two chapters on canon.[8] This indeed is a far cry from what younger evangelicals understand by "without error in the originals."

The purpose of the entire book is to inform those evangelical teachers and leaders who communicate, implicitly or otherwise, that inerrancy is a watershed issue that they may be inadvertently obstructing their pupils' spiritual formation. A younger evangelical will need to read but a tiny sampling of the pertinent literature to see that many of today's evangelical scholars believe precisely what those "unbelieving" liberals believed eighty years ago with respect to the authority of the Bible.[9] One question that comes up is: Why was it so bad to believe then what so many evangelicals believe now?[10] In other words, why the controversy in the first place? And with a little reflection comes not a little distrust: If they were so wrong in their judgments, why in the world should I trust you?

For many younger evangelicals are taught that the manner in which the inerrancy tradition can be derived from the Bible is something that was accomplished some time in the past when the biblical details that were presented in the earlier chapters of this book, for example, were not attended

---

[8] Compare the fifth chapter of Kevin J. Vanhoozer, *The Drama of Scripture: A Canonical Linguistic Approach to Christian Theology*. (Louisville, KY: Westminster John Knox Press, 2005). Vanhoozer, for his part, insists upon the theological primacy of Scripture; I, for my part, have tried to illustrate how, practically speaking, this primacy is effectively relativized. Also see Theodore G. Stylianopoulos, *The New Testament: An Orthodox Perspective. Volume One, Scripture, Tradition, Hermeneutics*. (Brookline, MA: Holy Cross Orthodox Press, 1977), 45–61 and David Brown, "Did Revelation Cease?" in *Reason and the Christian Religion: Essays in Honour of Richard Swinburne*. (ed. A. G. Padgett; New York: Oxford University Press, 1994), 121–141.

[9] Which helps explain why "postconservatives" and "postliberals" are now so fruitfully in dialogue.

[10] A candid, "We may have been wrong" would go along way, for example, as opposed to sentiments that mirror those of J. I. Packer's *"Fundamentalism" and the Word of God* (Grand Rapids: Eerdmans, 1958), 37.

to in the way that they are today by evangelicals themselves. Guided critical study of the Bible itself, historically sensitive surveys of church history and historical theology in conjunction with scholarly forays into other related disciplines can easily convince young conservatives that the evangelical inerrancy tradition is arbitrary and historically contingent. The once divinely imbued authority of Scripture is altogether muddled for younger evangelicals, but this is flagrantly contrary to the straightforwardness with which inerrancy is commonly taught in conservative evangelical schools (not to mention churches). In conversations over the last ten years, I have heard evangelical professors and students alike comment upon how many evangelical adults never surpass the understanding of the faith acquired from Sunday school, referring, I believe, to examples of Fowler's classification of a "conversional change that blocks or helps one avoid the pain of faith stage changes."[11] But some eventually advance. Whereas before attending high school, university, and/or graduate school, these younger evangelicals were wont to speak boldly of the trustworthiness of the Bible in all areas upon which it touches (even science!), these same believers after maturing in their educational pursuits grow reluctant to speak of any Bible at all.

I have observed firsthand how those who are preparing for the pastorate have been most severely affected. In the eyes of some with whom I had gone to school, the Bible simply no longer evinces the power to comfort the grieved or to provide a tangible hope to the hurting (or worse, to communicate the gospel). Furthermore, it seemed to them dishonest to preach authoritatively to a congregation once they realized how preaching invariably turns on some arbitrary personal preference for a certain reading of a text whose authority has become so questionable to begin with.[12] These soon-to-be ministers began to express very serious doubts whether the Bible even supported some of the major doctrinal tenets that have traditionally been used to identify these young evangelicals (presumed to represent "orthodox Christianity") over against "the liberal unbelievers." To wit, they have come to wonder why it mattered at all that the Bible supported any doctrine whatever: it simply is not the book that their evangelical lead-

---

[11] See James W. Fowler, *Stages of Faith: The Psychology of Human Development and the Quest for Meaning.* (New York: HarperCollins, 1985), 286.

[12] See, for example, Charles H. Cosgrove, "Toward a Postmodern *Hermeneutica Sacra*: Guiding considerations in Chossing between Competing Plausible Interpretations of Scripture" in *The Meanings We Choose: Hermeneutical Ethics, Indeterminacy and the Conflict of Interpretations.* JSOTSupp 411. (ed. C. H. Cosgrove; New York: T & T Clark International, 2004), 39–61.

ers and teachers or their ordination panels insisted it was. Disillusionment and worse set in; indeed very bitter ways to spiritually form younger evangelicals. My proposal is that conservative evangelical teachers and leaders set out to teach their dogmas of Scripture more responsibly, allowing their students some breathing room to approvingly spiritually furlough in the theological company of committed non-inerrantist Christians.

Retrospectively, I reckon that I never stood a spiritual chance while in school. Prospectively, my opinion is that younger evangelicals will stand even less of a chance to complete their education with an ETS/EPS-like faith in tact. Mention was not made here of problems brought on by recent advances in Ancient Near Eastern studies, textual criticism, postmodern hermeneutics, anthropology and psychology of religion and the natural sciences for the ETS/EPS understanding of the Bible. If these are added to the mix, the cumulative case against an ETS/EPS type dogma becomes insuperably stronger in the eyes of many younger evangelicals. Accordingly, evangelical teachers and leaders should give the nagging details their due. They should wrestle through a new doctrine of Scripture with those under their spiritual umbrella, candidly admit that the inerrancy of the past may actually have been wrong or is, at the very least, not for everyone today. Another suggestion is that they own up to past mistakes of the evangelical churches of a previous generation—for their students' sakes—and admit that the churches do not have all the answers. Conservative evangelical leaders and teachers should be sure not to continue in their spiritual neglect for younger evangelicals by forsaking these basic ministerial responsibilities to them.

If evangelical leaders and teachers really care about the spiritual formation of young believers who struggle with inerrancy, they will try harder not to play down contrary details, try harder to situate findings into the broader scheme of doctrinal beliefs, and more approvingly commend bibliological alternatives to inerrancy as appropriately orthodox. If leaders do not presently care enough about their students to begin doing this, or are not spiritually mature enough, then they should consider doing all within their power to bring themselves to be able to care in this fashion, for the future of evangelicalism may depend upon it.

Afterword

Perhaps the reader is himself or herself a younger evangelical (or any other evangelical for that matter) who has been personally wrestling with inerrancy and maybe has even begun having serious doubts regarding its viability in light of what evangelical scholars themselves have admitted with respect to the Bible. My own experience has been that these doubts can immediately spread to almost every aspect of faith, pushing with great force toward the brink of outright unbelief. The question I find myself asking time and again is: If I want to remain a Christian, where can I possibly go from here? Well, for starters, I would strongly counsel that it is a great mistake to believe that one can willfully try to make oneself believe in inerrancy again by merely sweeping these and similar recognitions under the rug (by simply blaming prior commitments to methodological naturalism, for example). Besides the fact that that would perpetuate the systemic response that this book was written to help curb, it is almost always the case that once a believer travels down the hermeneutical spiral there is simply no way for him to turn back.

The best thing to do, I suggest, is what Gary Habermas advises in one of his books on doubt: take theological inventory. He helpfully distinguishes between "beliefs that are absolutely indispensable and those that invite further research."[1] He observes:

> Crucial doctrines that are foundational to Christianity have at least four characteristics: (1) they are clearly taught in Scripture; (2) they are identified as being centrally important; (3) there are strong evidences for each; and (4) they occur prominently in classic statements of faith through the ages.[2]

Habermas and others have observed that doubt can sometimes have very positive effects.[3] I should note that I only have space here to address those

---

[1] Gary R. Habermas, *The Thomas Factor: Using Doubts to Draw Closer to God.* (Nashville: Broadman and Holman Publishers, 1999), 117.

[2] Habermas, *The Thomas Factor*, 118.

[3] Compare Raymond F. Paloutzian, *Invitation to the Psychology of Religion.* 2nd ed. (Boston: Allyn and Bacon: 1996), 111, 124–127. See also William Lane Craig, *No Easy Answers: Finding Hope in Doubt, Failure, and Unanswered Prayer.* (Chicago: Moody Press, 1990),

younger evangelicals who find deep down that after doubting inerrancy, they are still willing to continue their spiritual journeys as Christians. (I expect these to constitute the majority.) I suggest that such younger evangelicals should heed Habermas' advice of taking theological inventory even if they are persuaded in the end to go in a different theological direction than he does in his book. Although they may feel very connected to one or more evangelical communities, younger evangelicals intuitively understand that they are ultimately responsible to their own spiritual consciences (Rom 14.23). That said, it may be helpful to explicitly state that an inventory of this kind is still desirable even if (1) and (2) above are precisely those that have come under suspicion.

To begin we should remind ourselves that becoming convinced that inerrancy misses the mark as a description of the authority of the Bible does not at all imply that the Bible is now by default good for nothing. In other words, admitting that the Bible is not inerrant is not the same as believing that "the Bible contains only errors" or "mostly errors" or even "a lot of errors." The Bible has been historically recognized as invaluable to the Christian churches for their understanding of faith. God is somehow found in Scripture in a way that he is not to be found in other books. In the Bible the Spirit reveals the gospel of Jesus Christ. Younger evangelicals might well *begin*, then, with Peter Berger's minimal affirmation: "To have faith in Christ means to say that, if there is any meaning at all, it is here that one must find it."[4]

Younger evangelicals can note that Scripture has always played a fundamental role in the construction and development of Christian thought and practice. I suggest that this will continue to be the main selling point for Scripture's authority. Robert Webber presents Chad Allen's attitude toward Scripture as typical of younger evangelicals today:

> I'm moving away from the idea that Scripture is authoritative because so-and-so told me it's "God's infallible, inerrant Word" to the idea that Scripture is authoritative because God's faithful people have taken it to be authoritative throughout history. This is our book! For centuries we the church have chosen the Bible to be the book that calls our lives into question. When you read the

29–41. In fact, the popular, categorical suggestion that doubt is Satan's "device" seems to me to do younger evangelicals more harm than good. See, for example, Joyce Meyer, *Battlefield of the Mind for Kids.* (New York: Warner Faith), 102–116, and *Battlefield of the Mind for Teens: Winning the Battle in Your Mind.* (New York: Warner Faith), 80–87.

[4] *The Precarious Vision: A Sociologist Looks at Social Fictions and Christian Faith.* (Garden City, NY: Doubleday & Company, Inc., 1961), 190.

Bible, you are stepping into a long line of saints—past, present, and future—who look to the Bible to learn about God, humanity, and the relationship between the two.[5]

Younger evangelicals long to be part of a tradition with pedigree. Accordingly, their soul-searching question is not whether the Bible has any errors, but rather, Is this the book that so many before me have used to help them know and love God and what he has done for my redemption? The Bible remains authoritative not because errors have never been found in it but because it is a main component of the great tradition called historic Christianity. To acknowledge this is to realize that if a biblical author happens to be right about a historical matter, it does not seem that we need inerrancy to thank for it. If the author, however, is right about the fact that humans are sinners and that Christ somehow came to save sinners, then it would appear that we do have the guidance that resulted from the author's inspiration to thank for it. God wants us to know what Christ has done and why, but it seems safe to say that he could not care less whether readers of the Bible believe that Balaam's ass could strike up conversations, as the old example used to put it.[6]

How to hold on to the crucial doctrines in an ultra- (or post-) modern age without the apologetic motivation that comes with inerrancy is what younger evangelicals need to satisfactorily work out for themselves. Every generation deals with apologetic concerns in its own way and by doing so today's younger evangelicals will provide a great service for the church-at-large.[7] Although I have no definitive arguments or solutions to proffer here, I might banally point out that admitting the "problem" of an

---

[5] Webber, *Younger Evangelicals*, 168; Webber describes Allen as an editor for Baker Book House.

[6] It does not seem to me that distinguishing history from matters of faith and practice is any more difficult than (or even all that different from) determining what an author's claim is. One major difference, though, is that if some historical claim should prove wrong there will be no subsequent need to try to convince that this apparent historical claim was not *really* what the author was claiming. On the construal of inerrancy as a "post-hermeneutical concern," see the relevant sections of chapter six of Douglas Farrow's *The Word of Truth and Disputes about Words*. (Winona Lake, IN: Carpenter Books, 1987).

[7] Compare with the closing observations made in J. P. Moreland and Garrett DeWeese, "The Premature Report of Foundationalism's Demise" in *Reclaiming the Center: Confronting Evangelical Accommodation in Postmodern Times*. (ed., M. J. Erickson, P. K. Helseth, and J. Taylor; Wheaton, IL: Crossway Books, 2004), 81–107, 107, and remarks made by Nicholas Wolterstorff in "Living within a Text" in *Faith and Narrative*. (ed. K. Yandell; New York: Oxford University Press, 2001), 202–213, 212.

errant Bible in the first place will go a long way toward existentially equipping oneself for finally being able to come to terms with it.

Not all will agree, of course, with the opinion that inerrancy is dispensable,[8] or that it is associated with any hardships at all, but younger evangelical students may already be secretly (and not so secretly) asking David Clines' poignant questions:

> Why is the church being kept in ignorance of what is known in the Academy about the Bible? How can church leaders possibly think it profits the Christian community to be kept out of the picture, even about elementary facts about the Bible?[9]

In the area of biblical theology, John J. Collins has observed how "[m]any Christians of conservative leanings have welcomed the category 'story' as a means of evading the possibility of disconfirmation to which history is subject." Craig Batholomew and Michael Goheen's *The Drama of Scripture: Finding Our Place in the Biblical Story* (Grand Rapids: Baker, 2004) and other works like it come immediately to mind. Collins shrewdly points out that "[t]he freedom from disconfirmation . . . is bought at a price, since it necessarily excludes the possibility of confirmation, too."[10] My advice is that younger evangelicals who wrestle with inerrancy not ignore the conclusions of historical criticism and other relevant fields, persuading themselves that these types of confirmatory questions are irrelevant because they hopelessly evince inordinately modern preoccupations. In fact, some may even pride themselves on their development of specific spiritual strategies that help them to refuse to occupy themselves with confirmatory questions. Fair enough. But this does not negate the fact that critical questions of "truth" have been asked by the churches for at least the last two hundred years and that *some* serviceable answers have been found by those who have unrelentingly asked them. Younger evangelicals do well, I suggest, by understanding themselves as moving beyond these types of

---

[8] See, for example, Dawson McAllister, *Saving the Millennial Generation: New Ways to Reach the Kids You Care About in These Uncertain Times.* (Nashville: Thomas Nelson Publishers, 1999), 114–117.

[9] David J. A. Clines, *The Bible and the Modern World.* The Biblical Seminar 51. (Sheffield: Sheffield Academic Press, 1997), 88–89.

[10] *Encounters with Biblical Theology.* (Minneapolis: Fortress Press, 2005), 21. N. T. Wright puts an interesting spin on the Bible as authoritative story in his lecture, "How Can the Bible Be Authoritative?" Source: http://www.ntwrightpage.com/Wright_Bible_Authoritative.htm. On the increasing multidisciplinary interest in telling and buying into stories, see Stephen Prickett, *Narrative, Religion and Science: Fundamentalism versus Irony, 1700-1999.* (New York: Cambridge University Press, 2002).

questions, but, whatever they do, *they should never go about their religious business as if these questions had never been asked.*

Rather younger evangelicals might take some time to reflect upon the prospect of a believing criticism based upon their own observations that they have made from within conservative Christianity. One helpful thing to realize is that a doubting evangelical is certainly not the only, or the first, student of Scripture who is wrestling with this existentially confounding situation. Other conservative scholars (and others from other traditions) have written remarkably candidly of the enduring tension that has attended their work as scholars and believers. For example, Dennis E. Johnson writes:

> This distinction between God's Word and my understanding of God's Word is hardest to recognize in ourselves, and it is perhaps the riskiest distinction to admit out loud. Simply acknowledging that there may be a difference between what Scripture says so plainly to my group and what Scripture itself actually says raises suspicions that the clarity, if not the authority, of Scripture is about to be compromised.[11]

Johnson proposes, for his part, that conservatives can cope more effectively with what he sees as the modern-postmodern dilemma by trying to learn from both. His strategy is one where conservatives are to give the Bible "primacy" while giving general revelation (i.e., among other things, scholarship) "priority." His is an "all truth is God's truth" approach that acknowledges that all truth is from God and is revealed through his Son, but that human understanding is finite and always only partial. One can discern in Johnson's strategy a tactic of deferment: Things aren't meshing now, but they will on the last day.[12]

Readers would not be wrong, it seems to me, if they interpreted Johnson as implicitly appealing to mystery. The majority of believing scholars (of any tradition) would surely agree that there must always be a place for such an appeal when dealing with things religious; however, various members of different communities will appeal to mystery differently. I, for my part, was driven to the uncomfortable, but relatively firm, conclusion that faith and scholarship are mutually inimical for the study of religious literature because, among other things, I thought it inappro-

---

[11] Dennis E. Johnson, "Between Two Wor(l)ds: Worldview And Observation In The Use Of General Revelation To Interpret Scripture, And Vice Versa." *JETS* 41 (1998): 82.

[12] For a different take, see James K. A. Smith, *The Fall of Interpretation: Philosophical Foundations for a Creational Hermeneutic.* (Downers Grove, IL: InterVarsity, 2000).

priate to invoke an appeal to mystery at this particular juncture of my own Christian thinking.[13] As I continue to reflect upon my personal experience and hear or read those related by others, I suggest that a question that younger evangelicals should entertain more fervently is: When is it acceptable for a believing member of a scholarly community to legitimately appeal to mystery?[14] The willingness of a younger evangelical to appeal to mystery may determine *for her* a personal capacity for a believing criticism. However, believing academic communities will likely not be able to settle upon parameters for appeals to mystery, and, if this turns out to be the case, the burden will fall upon individual believing scholars to create their own niches within which they might conduct their critical scholarship.[15] This is a heavy burden indeed, but the whole point of this book is that younger evangelicals need not bear it alone.

In the absence of consensus parameters for the invocation of mystery, might I suggest a working perspective that might assist believing academics in their respective religious studies. I speak as a wavering evangelical, but others should be able to translate my proposal into their own religious and scholastic predicaments. The proposal is as follows: The feature of a religious enterprise that should most concern younger evangelicals as they involve themselves in their research and spiritual lives is its practicality. In an attempt to convey what I mean by "practicality" I cautiously and critically commend Helmut Koester's description of the formation of the Christian canon mentioned in chapter six as a temporary methodological starting point: "Whatever attested the events of salvation and told the shared story and whatever proved useful for the building of communities was acceptable."[16] Koester maintains that in the early church, writings

---

[13] Some may at this point (if they have not already) reflexively level the hackneyed charge of adhering to methodological naturalism. I, for my part, have no qualms with Michael J. Murray's "Natural Providence (Or Design Trouble)" *Faith and Philosophy* 20 (2003): 307–327.

[14] The most candid discussion that I have found is Davis Young's *The Biblical Flood: A Case Study of the Church's Response to Extrabiblical Evidence.* (Grand Rapids: Eerdmans, 1995).

[15] Halivni's reflections of comparable matters have led him to contrast "traditional" study with "critical" study of Scripture. For his part, he has noticed that he was typically drawn to traditional study of Scripture whenever he sought to recapture his childhood "assurance of security." He claims that he has since been able to fully embrace his own critical approach to Scripture while maintaining a vigorous devotion to Torah. It is interesting to note that he laments the fact that, as happened to Mendolsohn, his students have proven unable to follow in his footsteps in this regard (*The Book and the Sword*, 123–126, 149–151.)

[16] "Writings and the Spirit: Authority and Politics in Ancient Christianity." *HTR* 84 (1991): 353–372, 370.

themselves never constituted the gospel; rather, the gospel consisted of "the saving message that created and sustained Christian faith."[17] In other words, whatever proved practical, serviceable, and suitable for the faith and life of the early church was seized upon by the church for the perpetuation of believing communities and the establishment of new ones. Lee M. McDonald observes similarly with regard to the Pseudipigrapha that "[i]f a particular writing fit theologically with that which was acceptable to a particular Christian community, then it was acceptable even though it may have been written by someone other that the author listed."[18]

Perhaps the oft-quoted 2 Tim 3.15–17 lends not a little support to such a pragmatic biblical venture. According to Brian S. Rosner, "Christians, Paul says, are to do two things with Scripture: believe it, for it testifies to the gospel, and obey it, for it instructs them concerning proper conduct."[19] In 2 Tim 3.15–17, Rosner sees that Paul is claiming that the Scriptures point to the gospel and are useful for ethical instruction.[20] The fact that Scripture is "God-breathed" perhaps should not be immediately plumbed for its implications of ultimate authority as so many often do, but rather for its implications regarding God's ongoing love for his people, especially in light of the gospel of Jesus Christ, such that the Scriptures will ever be *useful* for the edification of the church and the furthering of the kingdom.[21]

Now usefulness is a property that depends upon the user just as much as it depends on what it is that is being used. The critical conclusions presented above, for example, might be taken as evidence that much of

---

[17] "Writings," 366.

[18] *The Formation of the Christian Biblical Canon*. Rev. ed. (Peabody, MA: Hendrickson, 1995), 289.

[19] "'Written for Us': Paul's View of Scripture" in *A Pathway into the Holy Scripture* (ed. Philip E. Satterthwaite and David F. Wright; Grand Rapids: Eerdmans, 1994), 81–106, 100. Perhaps I should explicitly mention that Rosner's stress on the divine origin of Scripture is not disputed here. The realization that our understanding and appropriation of Scripture's authority operate within a substantially different social, cultural, and hermeneutical context has prompted the present author to question whether inerrancy really has a helpful perspective on the nature of Scripture.

[20] "Written," 104; compare William J. Abraham, *Canon and Criterion in Christian Theology: From the Fathers to Feminism*. (Oxford: Oxford University Press, 1998).

[21] James A. Sanders has famously taken a similar course in thought. Among his many works, see his seminal article, "Adaptable for Life: The Nature and Function of Canon." In *Magnalia Dei: The Mighty Acts of God*. (ed. F. M. Cross, W. E. Lemke, and P. D. Miller, Jr.; Garden City, New York: Doubleday & Company, Inc., 1976), 531–560. But see now David L. Dungan, *Constantine's Bible: Politics and the Making of the New Testament*. (Minneapolis: Fortress Press, 2007).

Scripture's "authority" actually lay in its practicality. In other words, the early church's various hermeneutical approaches were so integral to the ancient understanding of Scripture that biblical writers could write "midrash on midrash" in order to further the gospel. But it is crucial that one remembers that this gospel message has been given a historical linearity.[22] This may be a main reason why Christians have traditionally opted for a "Christocentric" hermeneutic, a hermeneutic that deliberately sets out to relate every part of the Bible to Jesus Christ in some manner.[23] This approach may belie a latent acknowledgement that the authority of Scripture is somehow derived by way of specific hermeneutical approaches to Scripture—the kingdom-furthering uses to which it can be put. There, of course, lurk all kinds of dangers in such unabashedly, goal-oriented hermeneutical commitments, but the risk may be presently worth taking for young conservatives if they become persuaded that their inerrantist faith-commitments ineluctably predispose them toward tendentious, one-sided understandings of the Christian religion generally and the Christian Bible specifically, especially given the contemporary climate of conservative academic settings.[24] This will not satisfy for long, though; it is only a suggested starting point.

I hope in the near future to be able to follow up *Inerrancy and the Spiritual Formation of Younger Evangelicals* with a more constructive, theoretical work that will give more specific suggestions as to what positive options younger evangelicals may have once they have distanced themselves from inerrancy. For now, though, a particularly urgent concern is that younger evangelicals not "[take] on prematurely the patterns of adult faith modeled in [their] church. [For] in such cases the growing boy or girl goes through no adolescent crisis. And short of an extraordinarily disruptive young adult 'breaking out' of those cast-iron images of identity and faith formed in childhood, the person remains in that stage for life."[25] There

---

[22] For this fundamental hermeneutical principle, see Richard A. Muller, "The Study of Theology Revisited: A Response to Frame" *WTJ* 56 (1994): 409–417.

[23] See Maurice Casey, "Christology and the Legitimating Use of the Old Testament in the New Testament" in *The Old Testament in the New Testament: Essay in Honour of J. L. North.* (Sheffield: Sheffield Academic Press, 2000), 42–64. See, for example, John J. O'Keefe and R. R. Reno, *Sanctified Vision: An Introduction to Early Christian Interpretation of the Bible.* (Baltimore: Johns Hopkins University Press, 2005).

[24] See Anthony C. Thiselton, "Hermeneutics: Some Proposals for a More Creative Agenda" in *A Pathway into the Holy Scripture* (ed. Philip E. Satterthwaite and David F. Wright; Grand Rapids: Eerdmans, 1994), 107–142.

[25] James W. Fowler, *Stages of Faith: The Psychology of Human Development and the Quest for Meaning.* (New York: HarperCollins, 1985), 286.

is a high propensity for this when the Bible comes precariously near to being a second Christ.[26] For the sake of their own spiritual development and for the sake of evangelicalism itself, irrespective of what position they ultimately adopt, younger evangelicals should do all that they can to keep inerrancy from becoming a test of orthodoxy amongst themselves. Keep inerrancy from becoming—to use Session's phrase—*the* "tolerable first approximation to a person's faith."[27] Surely younger evangelicals will be better off spiritually for it.

---

[26] Markus Barth, *Conversation with the Bible*. (New York: Holt, Rinehart and Winston, 1964), 155. Witness what happened, for example, to Bart Ehrman according to his "Introduction" in *Misquoting Jesus: The Story Behind the Who Changed the Bible and Why*. (San Francisco: HarperSanFranciso, 2005), 1–15.

[27] William A. Session's description of a belief centered faith in *The Concept of Faith: A Philosophical Investigation*. (Ithaca, NY: Cornell University Press, 1994), 52.

Appendix

On Behalf of Pragmatic Arguments

A FEW EVANGELICAL philosophers have remarked to me that, generally speaking, evangelical leaders and teachers are taught to be suspicious of pragmatic arguments and that, as a result, the preceding extended argument will prove minimally persuasive. The observation that inerrancy brings unbearable existential tensions to a good number of younger evangelicals will not be accepted as an argument against inerrancy, they say. At most, it will only suggest to teachers and leaders that in some cases it may prove beneficial to reconsider how inerrancy is presented to their students. If some readers of *Inerrancy and the Spiritual Formation of Younger Evangelicals* are led to reconsider the way they teach inerrancy to students, then this book will have accomplished its primary goal. On the other hand, I could always protest that evangelical teachers and leaders tend to underestimate the legitimate role that pragmatic considerations play in religious decision-making. Either way, if pragmatic considerations *should* not play a major role in theological decision-making that does not mean that they do not frequently do so. In this appendix, I offer a preliminary word on the role of pragmatic arguments in deciding what one should or should not believe.

"My God, Richard Dawkins must be right after all!" exclaims Niles Eldredge in the introduction to his *The Pattern of Evolution* where he describes his initial reaction to observations he had made while vacationing in Puerto Rico.[1] To his relief, he was eventually able to explain why his initial despair had been premature and how Dawkins is *not* right after all in his assertion that evolution can be explained solely in terms of competition amongst genes. When I read Eldredge's account of the mini-crisis that he experienced that summer in the Caribbean, I began to wonder what it would take for an evangelical to have a "My God, Dawkins is right!" experience during the course of making up her mind with respect to what religious doctrines to believe. Sustained reflection upon the matter has caused

---

[1] (New York: W. H. Freeman, 2000), 1.

me to reluctantly acknowledge the import of pragmatic considerations in theological decision-making. What I have learned is that religious decisions are often made internally—and not externally, "internally" in the sense that the existential context of the believer is what is really relevant to such decisions: theological and philosophical arguments are often beside the point.[2]

Eric J. Lott, for example, in his study on the relation between religion and theology, identifies six dimensions of religion to which investigators must attend whenever studying any religion. He writes:

> In the analysis of any particular dimension of a religion we have continually to bear in mind its interconnection and interaction with other aspects of the total structure. No phenomenon in a tradition can properly be understood in isolation from other phenomena, for each functions in interaction with others, thus forming an integrated whole.[3]

According to Lott, two dimensions of religion that are especially closely related are the mythical and doctrinal.[4] In order for an interlocutor to be successful in reconfiguring another person's doctrinal formulations or to be successful in getting an another person to forswear one religion for another, the interlocutor must be able to both de-mythologize and re-mythologize that person's understanding of the world. Lott explains:

> However irritating such a claim may be to some philosophers of religion, and however much even theologians may search for other validating means to religious knowledge, the believer in the end bases life upon the certitude of faith, or the self-authenticating force with which religious vision presents itself . . .
> . . . Theologians may sometimes have attempted, in an apologetic role, to base the validity of their tradition's faith on its social and psychological benefits, or upon its rationality; but this will hardly be the basis of faith as the believer perceives it.[5]

---

[2] For more on this, see Sami Pihlström, "Pragmatic and Transcendental Arguments for Theism: a Critical Examination" *International Journal for Philosophy of Religion* 51(2002): 195–213.

[3] *Vision, Tradition, Interpretation: Theology, Religion, and the Study of Religion.* (New York: Mouton de Gruyter, 1988), 30–31.

[4] Lott, *Vision, Tradition, Interpretation*, 20–24.

[5] Lott, *Vision, Tradition, Interpretation*, 52. See also Stephen R. L. Clark, *God, Religion and Reality.* (London: SPCK, 1998), 123–134. MacIntyre remarks that the "matter of a general cynicism in our culture about the power or even the relevance of rational argument to matters [is] sufficiently fundamental." See Alasdair MacIntyre, *Whose Justice? Which*

It goes without saying that evangelicals are not exempt from this pattern. In fact, a number of evangelical writers explicitly confess it. For example, William Lane Craig candidly admits something along these lines in his book *No Easy Answers*:

> How do I know that my faith is true? Do I know it on the basis of reason? Or do I know its truth by faith itself? Or is my faith founded on authority, or perhaps on mystical experience? How do I know that my Christian faith is true? . . . the answer is that we know our faith is true by the self-authenticating witness of the Holy Spirit within us.[6]

Justification for a Christian's faith, according to Craig, boils down to a spiritual testimony such that an individual's existential context warrants that the Christian faith be true. J. I. Packer, another evangelical writer, recognizes and even expects this self-authenticating quality to sustain Christians in his *"Fundamentalism" and the Word of God*:

> Against each of these [liberal] positions sensitive Christian consciences sense at once that they are false, even before it is clear what in detail is wrong with them. John spoke of the Christian's God-given capacity to discern denials of the gospel for what they are when he wrote: "Ye have an unction from the Holy One, and ye know all things" (1 Jn. ii. 20; cf. verses 26, 27). God's Spirit will not witness to a repudiation of God's Word or a perversion of Christ's gospel . . . A sound spiritual instinct guided them, and we should thank God for the tenacity with which they held their ground.[7]

Many Christians admit that they rely upon the Holy Spirit for the maintenance and calibration of their beliefs. Potential philosophical and religious interlocutors, then, have the challenge of finding a way to get parishioners to somehow suspend what they perceive as a set of self-attesting beliefs if they are going to go about the business of changing people's minds. A provisional suspension of beliefs is ultimately desirable when engaging in real dialogue with a disagreeing believer (or even nonbeliever), especially

---

Rationality? (Notre Dame: University of Notre Dame, 1988), 5.

[6] *No Easy Answers: Finding Hope in Doubt, Failure, and Unanswered Prayer*. (Chicago: Moody, 1990), 32. Compare Craig's contribution to *Five Views on Apologetics*. (ed. Steven B. Cowan; Grand Rapids: Zondervan, 2000), 25–55.

[7] (Grand Rapids: Eerdmans, 1958), 37.

when that believer senses that her existential welfare is being threatened.[8] Pragmatic arguments can prove an excellent way to accomplish this.

A persuasive pragmatic argument requires that one re-conceptualize religious webs of belief in such a way that they are fundamentally retained on the basis of basic pragmatic considerations, perhaps even ones that Jeffrey Jordan describes as "truth-independent." A truth-independent argument is "one which recommends believing some proposition *p* because of the benefits gained simply by believing that *p*, whether or not *p* should turn out true."[9] In order to win a religionist over in religious debate, I suggest that one must eventually convince that religionist that the benefits gained by believing one thing exceed, or at the very least, do not discount, those gained by believing another.

Jordan observes, regarding William Clifford's famous lecture, that "[e]ndorsing [the] evidentialist imperative, many philosophers have held that pragmatic reasons for belief-formation are illegitimate since such reasons do not themselves provide adequate evidence for the truth of the belief."[10] Peter van Inwagen, however, observes that it is indeed curious that the "evidentialist imperative" (to use Jordan's terminology) is employed almost exclusively in invectives against religious beliefs, especially when it could equally be applied to political and philosophical positions.[11] In response to those evangelical thinkers who may take this book less seriously than they might otherwise simply because it is an extended pragmatic argument, I propose to follow van Inwagen's suggestion and grant that an individual's existential, even if incommunicable, insight into a given question or problem can be legitimately permitted as evidence *for that*

---

[8] Compare the "Wittgensteinian" observation that "those who hold religious doctrines do not treat those commitments in the way they would treat an empirical claim." See Stephen Mulhall, "Wittgenstein and the Philosophy of Religion" in *Philosophy of Religion in the 21st Century*. (ed. D. Z. Phillips and T. Tessin; New York: Palgrave, 2001), 95–118, 97. A similar observation is made in John Wisdom, "Gods" in *Logic and Language*. (ed. A. Flew; Garden City, NY: Doubleday, 1965), 194–214.

[9] "Pragmatic Arguments" in *A Companion to Philosophy of Religion*. (Balden, MA: Blackwell, 1999), 352–359, 352. Jordan also classifies "truth-dependent" pragmatic arguments, but we will occupy ourselves with truth-independent arguments since they are clearly more difficult to overturn.

[10] "Pragmatic Arguments," 358. Jordan is referring here to William Clifford's famous dictum that van Inwagen used as the title of his essay below.

[11] Peter van Inwagen, "It is Wrong, Everywhere, Always, and for Anyone, to Believe Anything upon Insufficient Evidence" in *Philosophy of Religion: The Big Questions*. (ed. Eleonore Stump and Michael J. Murray; Malden, MA: Blackwell, 1999), 273–284. That he has mentioned some of what follows in his essay, of course, does not mean to imply that van Inwagen would agree with what we are attempting here.

person for a given belief. [12] The inexpressible insight in mind is one that is obtained by life experience, professional schooling or training, natural intelligence, personality traits, emotional composition and so on and seems to be that upon which many religious believers heavily rely whenever adjudicating competing claims. Under this rubric, one might even include "the influence of the Holy Spirit" in an attempt to incorporate the evangelical expectations given by Craig and Packer above.

If such personal insight is accepted as evidence for belief in a given doctrine, then it would not necessarily be the case that pragmatic arguments wholly obviate evidential concerns. On the contrary, pragmatic arguments might provide a very important form of personal evidence if they were contrived carefully and deliberately with the result that they pass evidential muster before a religionist's intuitive bar—their insight court of appeal, as it were, during the course of persuasive negotiations. At a later point, follow-up arguments are introduced in order to more closely examine whether the pragmatic dimension of a given belief can be rationally substantiated.

Of course, the proposed pragmatic approach does not imply that pragmatic arguments are always to be preferred over other types of argument. Nor does it intimate that evangelicals are fickle in their beliefs, believing whatever they please. It is simply an attempt to do justice to the fact that when a person decides what to believe it seems—at least initially—that the question of whether it is rational for a person to hold a belief is a more paramount concern than whether the belief itself is rational—to use Nozick's way of putting it. [13] Or to paraphrase Feyerabend:

> Even the most puritanical rationalist will then be forced to leave argument and to use, say, *pragmatic considerations* not because some of his arguments have ceased to be *valid*, but because the *psy-*

---

[12] Or we could, following Polanyi, reject the evidential requirement outright and simply appeal with candor to the "operations of the tacit coefficient of knowing," pointing out "how everywhere the mind follows its own self-set standards." See Michael Polanyi, *Personal Knowledge: Towards a Post-Critical Philosophy.* (Chicago: University of Chicago, 1962), 268.

[13] Jordan, "Pragmatic Arguments," 358, citing Robert Nozick, *The Nature of Rationality.* (Princeton: Princeton, 1993), 64–93—where Nozick presents reason as instrumentality and proposes a set of rules for rationality. James T. Kloppenberg, for his part, calls instrumental rationality a "toxin," especially in the context of religion, in his "Knowledge and Belief in American Public Life" in *Knowledge and Belief in America: Enlightenment Traditions and Modern Religious Thought.* (ed. William M. Shea and Peter A. Huff; New York: Woodrow Wilson Center and Cambridge University Presses, 1995), 27–51.

chological conditions which enable him to effectively argue in this manner and thereby to influence others have disappeared.[14]

It should suffice to clarify that when existentially threatening alternatives are being proposed (i.e., that inerrancy is not a spiritually helpful doctrine) and when the express purpose of dialogue is kept in mind (i.e., to merely gain a hearing from a religionist), it might prove prudent to critically defer to Rorty and concede that "we cannot regard truth as a goal of inquiry. The purpose of inquiry is to achieve agreement among human beings about what to do, to bring about consensus on the ends to be achieved and the means to be used to achieve those ends."[15] There is no reason to believe that if one were to accept Rorty's approach provisionally on a local level that she would need to follow him where his neo-pragmatism ultimately leads him with regard to religion, but for the matter at hand, those interested in changing minds of religionists are sometimes well-advised to indeed "see luck where [their] critics insist on seeing destiny."[16] The debate over inerrancy, I believe, happens to be one of those times.

It is not incidental that Rorty's glib reference to a cosmic myth of providence (a belief that everything happens for a reason) happens to refer to a fundamental component of the most widespread religious grand-narratives. This ground level belief—namely, the personal expectations that come with a notion of providential care—can prove a significant obstacle to critical reflection and, hence, genuine religious debate, for a potential interlocutor has to be hypothetically prepared to deconstruct the myth of providence *with the promise of reconstruction* if the interlocutor is actually going to engage the religionist. Thus setting piety against rationality will not go a long way toward eliciting a "Dawkins is right!" response, but pragmatic considerations can nevertheless give the initial, dialogical nudge required to engender a sustained discussion. Pragmatic arguments are never antipathetic to existential concerns; they rather coordinate with them and on occasion even enmesh with them. One might go so far as to think of pragmatic arguments and their variations as "arguments from personality" since the plausibility of these arguments will almost always

[14] To be sure, nay-sayers will be happy to know that where I have "pragmatic arguments," Feyerabend has "propaganda." See Paul Feyerabend, "Consolations for the Specialist" in *Criticism and the Growth of Knowledge: Proceedings of the International Colloquium in the Philosophy of Science, London, 1965, Volume 4.* (ed. Imre Lakatos and Alan Musgrave; New York: Cambridge, 1970), 217.

[15] Richard Rorty, *Philosophy and Social Hope.* (New York: Penguin, 1999), xxv.

[16] *Philosophy and Social Hope*, xxxii.

depend upon what is existentially salient to an individual at any given moment.[17]

To help gain a better perspective on this, one can pause to reflect upon how personally interested evangelicals can become in what we believe. Consider for a moment a vignette where an acquaintance relates the following story to a friend of yours:

> On a frigid December night many years ago, a friend dragged me out of my warm apartment, where I planned to spend the evening in my bathrobe nursing a cold. I had to come with her to the movies, she said, because she had made plans with a pal from her office, and he was bringing a friend for me to meet. Translation: I was expected to show up for a last-minute blind date. For some reason, I agreed to go, knocking back a decongestant as I left home. We arrived at the theater to find that the friend who was supposed to be my "date" had canceled, but not to worry, another friend had been corralled as a replacement. The replacement and I both fell asleep in the movie . . . but four months later we were engaged, and we have been married for nearly 15 years.

A writer claims that this is actually how she met her husband;[18] but let us imagine that the friend is a very religious person. What would her response be? "God planned the whole thing out. It was his plan from the beginning of time!" And if it actually *happened* to a religious person—no one could possibly convince her otherwise!

It is a meaningful thing that the author experienced—she meets a man and eventually marries him—but I would not say that her depth of meaning would have the same intensity for everyone. For example, I might be able to step back and try to see how an acquaintance might find what happened to the author especially meaningful by relating her story to how I met my wife and compare the woman's wonder with my own personal sense of providence at the time[19]—but that's just it! When will it make sense to say that an experience, an event or some philosophical consideration is meaningful in an unqualified sense? Is it not true that to what one person attaches a great deal of meaning another might hardly attach

---

[17] Kenneth Miller's term. See Miller, *Finding Darwin's God: A Scientist's Search for Common Ground Between God and Evolution.* (New York: HarperCollins, 1999), 248–253.

[18] The extended quote is from Lisa Belkin, "Coincidence in an Age of Conspiracy" *The New York Times Magazine* (August 11, 2002): 37.

[19] Carl Jung used "synchronicity" to describe "meaningful coincidences." See C. G. Jung, *Synchronicity: An Acausal Connecting Principle.* (trans. R. F. C. Hull; Princeton: Princeton University Press, 1969).

any? This is where I think we must confess what the statistician Ruma Falk flippantly calls "the stupid power of personal involvement."[20]

Falk's "power of personal involvement" frequently determines whether a pragmatic argument, or what might presently be called, an "argument from meaning." will take. First-person involvement in a series of coincidences is the key to the uncanny sense of wonder that a third party observer often fails to appreciate. A disinterested person is much less likely to be impressed by accounts of coincidences than a participant or otherwise interested party would be.[21] When these coincidences transpire, therefore, the circle of meaning will seem more intense to those who are actually involved and, among these, *to those who are especially open to the possibility that there is meaning to be found.* Unfortunately, in an increasingly nihilistic age, many evangelicals are finding themselves so spiritually debilitated that they believe whatever religious beliefs they believe because they have been taken in by what Hibbs calls "the intermediate, complacent all-American God"[22]—or in other words they believe that those things that are meaningful to them are religiously significant *precisely because* they are meaningful to them.[23] And it is precisely here that pragmatic arguments prove their timely serviceability, not only because they speak to the soul in ways that other arguments do not, but also because they have the potential to implicitly and internally raise the cognizance of fallibility or even fickleness that can result from the religionist's "will to believe." Once this internal consciousness is critically awoken, *then* (and occasionally only then), if one is so inclined, might one fruitfully begin working his way up from a ground and existentially pregnant level of discourse toward a more traditionally "rational" level of discourse that involves arguments, counter-examples, and the like.

---

[20] In an interview with Belkin, in Belkin, "Coincidence in an Age of Conspiracy," 46. Ludwig Feuerbach complained about the logic of personal involvement: "Providence has relation essentially to man," and again, "Providence is a privilege of man . . . Providence is the conviction of man of the infinite value of his existence." *The Essence of Christianity* (trans. G. Eliot; Amherst, NY: Prometheus, 1989), 104, 105.

[21] See, for example, the description of Falk's experiment involving the comparison of responses to the coincidence of students' birthdays by students whose birthdays were coincidental and those whose weren't.

[22] *Shows About Nothing.* (Dallas: Spence Publishing, 1999), 166.

[23] Compare Feuerbach, *The Essence of Christianity*, 105: "God concerns himself about me; he has in view my happiness, my salvation, he will that I shall be blest; but that is my will also: thus, my interest is God's interest, my own will is God's will, my own aim is God's aim,—God's love for me nothing else than my self-love deified."

Suffice it to say that insofar as religionists are personally involved in their religious living, one can always find a role for pragmatic arguments to play. In the context of philosophical and theological dialogue—especially when existentially foundational religious beliefs are at stake—it will often prove advisable not to put all eggs in the basket of direct argumentation, whether informal or otherwise. By becoming more sensitive to the place of pragmatic arguments in the development of religious convictions, one might grow into a better position from which to suggest to someone that she might benefit from provisionally distancing herself from her faith for pragmatic reasons. It may then prove a bit easier for the discussion to eventuate in a full-scale reappraisal of a treasured religious perspective. Though once impossible, dialogue may become a possibility. Indeed, perhaps an active conversation partner will be gained with whom one can *in due course* unleash other more tightly-woven philosophical and theological arguments.[24] Yet a preliminary role for pragmatic arguments may prove a decisive factor early on, one that determines whether a particular position will be entertained at all. In short, I reckon that a primary reason evangelicals believe in an inerrant set of Scriptures is the protection it seems to offer against the ultra- (or post-) modern hermeneutical predicament, a reason I set out to appraise above by means of a cumulative pragmatic argument.

---

[24] Especially when the arguments for and against a position are judged to be equally strong. It may then fall upon pragmatic considerations to bring about a final judgment. Compare the cases of John Stackhouse, Jr. (regarding his embrace of evangelical feminism) and John Loftus (regarding his disaffection from evangelical Christianity). See John Stackhouse, Jr, *Finally Feminist: A Pragmatic Christian Understanding of Gender.* (Grand Rapids: Baker, 2005); and John Loftus, *Why I Rejected Christianity: A Former Apologist Explains.* (Victoria, British Columbia: Trafford Publishing, 2006).

Evangelicals and Scripture
Graham

Noll, Between Faith &
Criticism

Swinburn, Revelation from
metaphor to
Analogy